Last Call at Coogan's

Also by Jon Michaud

When Tito Loved Clara

Last Call at Coogan's

The Life and Death
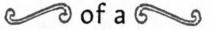 of a
Neighborhood Bar

JON MICHAUD

ST. MARTIN'S PRESS
NEW YORK

Portions of this book were originally published in a substantially different form at NewYorker.com.

LAST CALL AT COOGAN'S. Copyright © 2023 by Jon Michaud. All rights reserved. Printed in the United States of America. For information, address St. Martin's Publishing Group, 120 Broadway, New York, NY 10271.

www.stmartins.com

Designed by Meryl Sussman Levavi

Maps by Jeffrey L. Ward

Library of Congress Cataloging-in-Publication Data

Names: Michaud, Jon, author.
Title: Last call at Coogan's : the life and death of a neighborhood bar / Jon Michaud.
Description: First edition. | New York : St. Martin's Press, 2023. | Includes index. |
Identifiers: LCCN 2022060142 | ISBN 9781250221780 (hardcover) | ISBN 9781250221797 (ebook)
Subjects: LCSH: Coogan's Bar and Restaurant (New York, N.Y.)—History. | Restaurants—New York (State)—New York—History. | New York (N.Y.)—Social life and customs. | Interviews—New York (State)—New York.
Classification: LCC TX945.5.C665 M53 2023 | DDC 647.95747/1—dc23/eng/20221221
LC record available at https://lccn.loc.gov/2022060142

Our books may be purchased in bulk for promotional, educational, or business use. Please contact your local bookseller or the Macmillan Corporate and Premium Sales Department at 1-800-221-7945, extension 5442, or by email at MacmillanSpecialMarkets@macmillan.com.

First Edition: 2023

10 9 8 7 6 5 4 3 2 1

To
Zoraida,
Marcus,
Thomas,
and all the Uptown kids

NORTHERN MANHATTAN

NEW JERSEY

Hudson River

INWOOD

NEW YORK

THE CLOISTERS

FORT TRYON PARK

MANHATTAN

BROADWAY

Harlem River

DYCKMAN ST.

GEORGE WASHINGTON HIGH SCHOOL

34TH PRECINCT

WADSWORTH AVE.

AUDUBON AVE.

GEORGE WASHINGTON BRIDGE

YESHIVA UNIVERSITY

181ST ST.

THE BRONX

175TH ST.

THE ARMORY

HAVEN AVE.

FORT WASHINGTON AVE.

COOGAN'S

NEW YORK-PRESBYTERIAN HOSPITAL

168TH ST.

HIGHBRIDGE PARK

33RD PRECINCT

AUDUBON BALLROOM

AMSTERDAM AVE.

ST. NICHOLAS AVE.

EDGECOMBE AVE.

155TH ST.

COOGAN'S BLUFF

YANKEE STADIUM

SUGAR HILL

BROADWAY

NEW YORK CITY

0 Miles   0.5   1

0 Kilometers   1

© 2023 Jeffrey L. Ward

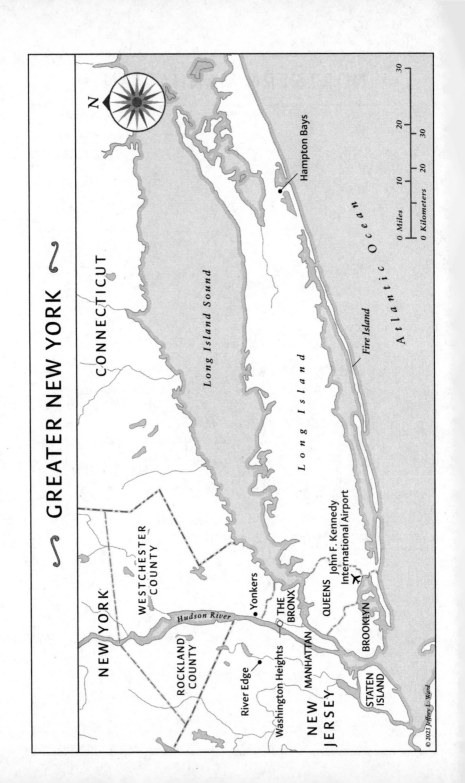

GREATER NEW YORK

N

CONNECTICUT

NEW YORK

WESTCHESTER COUNTY

Long Island Sound

Hudson River

ROCKLAND COUNTY

Yonkers

River Edge

Washington Heights

THE BRONX

MANHATTAN

QUEENS

Long Island

NEW JERSEY

BROOKLYN

STATEN ISLAND

John F. Kennedy International Airport

Fire Island

Atlantic Ocean

Hampton Bays

0 Miles   10   20   30

0 Kilometers   20   30

© 2023 Jeffrey L. Ward

"Washington Heights is a state of mind, not a state of being."

—HERMAN (DENNY) FARRELL JR.

Contents

Part Three: A Moral Pub

Part Four: Homecoming

Prologue

On a sweltering day in July of 1974, an electrician named Joey McFadden lost his footing and fell from the scoreboard that stood beyond the right center field fence at Shea Stadium in Queens, New York City. Eighty-six feet high and 175 feet wide, the board was a signature feature of the Mets' home field, which had opened to the public a decade earlier. Joey, in his mid-thirties, was paid to maintain the board. He fell twenty feet, fracturing his leg in multiple places, and lay there screaming in agony for fifteen minutes until Mets relief pitcher Tug McGraw, who was warming up in the bullpen, heard him and summoned help. It took another two hours for the grounds crew and paramedics to rig a pulley system to lift Joey out from under the scoreboard and get him into an ambulance.

The following spring, Joey sued the Mets and Rheingold Beer—which had donated the scoreboard to the stadium—for $1.5 million, and his wife sued both parties for an additional half million dollars. The settlement from those lawsuits would help fund two legendary New York City saloons. The first, Ryan McFadden's (later just McFadden's) on Second Avenue and 42nd Street, was opened in 1979 by Joey, his brother, Steve "Pally" McFadden, and a friend, Danny Ryan. Steve and Joey were a study in contrasts. Steve, quiet and focused with a sly wit, was good at managing bars; Joey, the rambunctious life of the party, was good at hanging out in them. The dichotomy between the McFadden brothers was emblematic of the conflict at the heart of every drinking establishment: saloons are places for fun, but they are also places of business. Successful bars find a happy balance between these two impulses.

After a falling-out with his brother, Joey left the partnership, selling his stake. This would not prove to be his wisest decision. McFadden's, which was situated across the street from the offices of the *Daily News*, prospered, drawing actors, sportsmen, and journalists as well as the Emerald Society and the Ancient Order of Hibernians, which hosted an annual St. Patrick's Day breakfast at the bar ahead of the parade up Fifth Avenue. In 2001, McFadden's became a franchise, expanding to a dozen locations across the country—including one at Citi Field, the ballpark the Mets opened in 2009 to replace Shea Stadium.

The second saloon that Joey helped open with his payout was Coogan's in Washington Heights. As was the case with McFadden's, Joey's involvement was short-lived, but, after a difficult gestation, Coogan's also prospered, transcending its origins as a traditional Irish saloon to become the neighborhood bar for one of the most complex neighborhoods in New York City, a neighborhood that would undergo dramatic change in the decades immediately before and after the turn of the twenty-first century.

That's the story this book will tell: how an Irish bar in Washington Heights became a beloved community hub so essential that it was sometimes called Uptown City Hall. Coogan's fostered connection and interaction among people from different backgrounds within the neighborhood and beyond. It helped strengthen the neighborhood during a time of crisis, and later, when Coogan's faced a crisis of its own, the neighborhood responded, saving the saloon from going out of business.

It's a story that touches on many of the most serious issues facing the country in recent years: race relations, policing, gentrification, the fate of our urban neighborhoods, and the COVID-19 pandemic. But it's also a story about one small business, the people who worked there, the customers they served, and the community they all called home.

Part One

IN BUSINESS

CHAPTER ONE

⸻ఌ⸻

Why Are We Going to
Open a Place up There?

Joey McFadden was what the Irish call "a chancer": a risk-taker, someone who pushes their luck. He loved practical jokes. Once, he'd gone into a bar dressed as a priest and bought a round for the gobsmacked patrons. When he was not working or at home in River Edge, New Jersey, with his family, Joey could be found hanging out across the Hudson River in one of the saloons in Inwood—the Irish neighborhood located above Washington Heights, at the northern tip of Manhattan. The McFadden brothers had grown up in Inwood, where their older cousin George McFadden owned the Inwood Lounge, a neighborhood drinking spot that closed in the 1970s. Though he'd moved to New Jersey to raise his family, Joey, like many of the Inwood Irish, was constantly drawn back to the comforts and familiarity of the old neighborhood. Especially its bars.

One day in 1983, Joey was drinking at one of those Inwood hangouts, Garryowens, and fell into a conversation with the owner, Billy Wall. Billy told Joey about one of his customers, John Kennedy, who worked in the real estate department at Presbyterian Hospital in Washington

Heights. Kennedy had been charged with finding someone to open up a restaurant near the hospital. Apparently, some of the Presbyterian brass had worn out their
welcome at the Columbia Faculty Club by regularly getting drunk and unruly. They wanted an Irish bar and grill
with white tablecloths—not a deli or an old-man joint or
a little Spanish spot, which is what the blocks around the
hospital currently offered. Kennedy had already talked
to dozens of New York bar and restaurant owners, but
they had turned him down because of the neighborhood.
Nobody wanted to open a place like that in Washington
Heights in 1983. Too dangerous. Too many drugs. Too
much crime. Kennedy had pitched the idea to Billy, and
Billy was intrigued, but he didn't have enough cash on
hand to fund a new place. Billy thought of Joey. Everyone
in Inwood knew Joey had money from that settlement.

Joey was taken with the idea. He'd talk to Kennedy.
But first he called up his old friend Sean Cannon. Sean
had run Tiana Beach Club in the Hamptons with Joey's
brother, Steve. Joey knew Sean had been looking to open
another place ever since Tiana closed. But Sean was skeptical. "Washington Heights? Forget about it. It's loaded
with drugs. Nobody speaks English. Why are we going to
open a place up there?"

Joey wouldn't let it go. He knew that Sean was sometimes guilty of overthinking things, of believing that he
was smarter than everyone else. A week later, Joey called
Sean again. This time, he didn't dismiss the idea out of
hand. "Tell you what," he said. "I'll go take a look and let
you know what I think."

So it was that on a spring afternoon in 1983, Sean Cannon
stood on a corner in Washington Heights, taking pictures

of a row of shops on the far side of Broadway. Sean was tall and lean with a long face and a thin mustache, which angled down over his lip like the wings of a plane. He spoke with a deep, cigarette-roughened voice, choosing his words carefully. He was equally careful about his appearance, dressing in a neat, unfussy way: pressed trousers, collared shirt.

The crossroads where he stood was a busy one, Broadway intersecting with St. Nicholas Avenue and 169th Street. By some measure, you could say that it was the heart of the neighborhood, buses and cars circulating in every direction, a major subway station rumbling under his feet. One block south was the beige brick citadel of Presbyterian Hospital. A little farther down Broadway was the Audubon Ballroom where Malcolm X was assassinated. Half a dozen blocks north, the George Washington Bridge conveyed motorists to and from New Jersey and New England.

Looking closer, Sean noticed details that confirmed his initial concerns. Nearby buildings were covered in graffiti, and people hanging out on the street corners appeared to be scanning traffic for potential customers. On the other hand, there wasn't much competition. The nearest bars were the Rose of Killarney, on St. Nicholas, and the Reynolds Bar, six blocks uptown. Neither served much food. In fact, there weren't many places of any kind to get a good sit-down meal. Over there was a McDonald's. Across the street was a tiny corner spot, the Reme lunch counter. A block south there was a so-so Italian restaurant. And, of course, for carryout food, there was a handful of bodegas and delis scattered here and there. But that was pretty much it for this section of the Heights. Sean took it all in, turning now and then to keep an eye on a drug deal taking place farther east on 169th Street. A car with sky-blue Jersey plates pulled up. The guy on the corner approached, leaning over to speak into the rolled-down window.

Sean turned his gaze west, back across Broadway, and snapped a picture. The shops filled the ground floor of a six-story apartment building that took up half the block. An old Greek diner, the Gold Medal, occupied the corner slot. Next door, as you went south, there was a haberdashery; then a pharmacy; and lastly, a Chinese takeout, La Muralla China—the Great Wall of China. If they weren't already, those unlucky enterprises would soon be out of business. Their long-term leases had expired, and their landlord, Presbyterian Hospital, had them on month-to-month extensions until they could find a new tenant—a tenant willing to open up a bar and restaurant. That was the brutal and capricious nature of the real estate business in New York. A landlord could snuff out years of your work seemingly on a whim.

Sean was no stranger to the area. He'd been born there, in 1942, back when it was part of the Hibernian Archipelago, a group of Irish enclaves that had formed around the Catholic churches of Upper Manhattan. Sean entered the world at a small hospital on Edgecombe Avenue by Coogan's Bluff—an escarpment that overlooked the Harlem River. His father owned a bar called Paddy Kennon's way downtown. It was near the Hudson and was favored by dockworkers. During the Second World War, the family moved to Brooklyn and then north, to Yonkers. Sean worked at his father's bar as a teenager, passing through the Heights each day. Over the previous two decades, he'd seen the slow transformation of the neighborhood. As the city's economy had declined in the 1970s and violent crime had risen, white residents—mostly Irish and

Jewish—fled to the suburbs, and the Dominicans moved in, the shop signs changing from English to Spanish. Some people he knew called it an invasion, but Sean was not as territorial. The city was always in flux; you had to be adaptable.

While at Manhattan College, Sean got a job as a bus-boy at George McFadden's Inwood Lounge. George was renowned in the neighborhood for his communitarian spirit. If you were short on cash, George would extend you credit until you got paid; if you needed a job, George would connect you with someone who was hiring; if you needed a place to live, George knew all the supers on the block. Irish Inwood, with its dozens of bars, became the center of Sean's social life. Often, he and his coworkers would stay at the lounge long after it had closed, drinking and bull-shitting, sometimes going directly to early morning classes from these sessions, sleepless and still drunk.

Though he loved to drink, Sean had no intention of following in his father's footsteps as a saloon owner. He was pursuing a business degree and imagined a future for himself as "a businessman." What that meant exactly, he wasn't sure, but it didn't involve pouring pints. Yet even as he looked toward that vague career path, Sean was being inculcated into the close-knit world of New York's Irish barmen—a multigenerational network of publicans and bartenders who would later help him find work, open businesses, and solve problems. In the end, the connections Sean forged in the saloons of Inwood would prove far more valuable than those he made in the classrooms of Manhattan College.

In August 1964, Congress passed the Tonkin Gulf Res-olution, pushing the United States closer to all-out war in Vietnam. To avoid being drafted into the army, Sean enlisted in the naval reserve. He was selected for pilot training and spent the next five years flying transports around naval bases on the East Coast. At the end of his military service, Sean abandoned his pursuit of a business career when Pan Am offered him a job as a pilot, but 1969 brought a recession, and the offer was rescinded. He wound up back in New York City, bartending. He worked at Jimmy Byrnes's saloon on Second Avenue with Steve McFadden. He did shifts at Gladstone, Plushbottom and Co. on Third Avenue. He was finally coming around to the idea of opening a saloon of his own, maybe with one of the McFaddens. He and Steve were living together in a bachelor apartment on Lexington Avenue and 95th Street. When they weren't working, they liked to hang out at a local pub called Pudding's. One of the bartenders there was a funny, quick-witted guy from Yorkville, a poet and storyteller named Peter Walsh. He was another potential business partner.

In 1975, Sean and Steve leased Tiana Beach Club in Hampton Bays. That spring they dug out the buildings on the plot, clearing the flotsam and jetsam left from the winter storms, repairing anything that had broken, and repainting the exterior in time for the opening. Tiana was in action from Memorial Day to Labor Day. The music and partying started at 11:00 a.m. and went into the night. Tiana and its neighbors, the Boardy Barn and Cat Ballou's, catered to the same patron base: sunburned working-class weekenders and day-trippers from the "Celt Belt" of Northern Manhattan, the Bronx, and Queens, with a scattering of outer-borough Italians, and a handful of Long Island locals thrown in.

Larry Kirwan, who would later front the band Black 47, performed on that circuit as part of a progressive-rock duo called Turner and Kirwan of Wexford. "It was the paradise of the proletariat," he recalled. "People would come up in droves from the beach. The price of beer was incredibly cheap. The idea was to get them in there and get them soused and then raise the prices around eight o'clock." According to Kirwan, drug use was widespread at those beachside bars, and included "liquid speed," which patrons added to drinks with an eyedropper. "Speed makes you drink more," Kirwan recalled. "So, the whole place, including us, would be speeding our butts off. It was just a wild scene."

When the season ended, Sean and Steve worked at saloons and restaurants around Manhattan. By this time, they'd moved into a large apartment on Park Avenue. From one of its windows, you could see the planes taking off and landing at LaGuardia Airport, a vision of Sean's lost career. A little later, Peter Walsh of Pudding's moved in with them. The apartment became the setting for impromptu parties. The front door was left unlocked so that members of the building staff could come up and join the fun during their breaks. Sometimes they were late getting back to work, causing other residents to wait impatiently for an elevator or a doorman to summon a cab.

The good times continued for four years, until the property owner Sean and Steve leased Tiana from failed to pay his real estate taxes. The plot was sold at auction. Sean and Steve put together an investment group and tried to purchase the land, but they were outbid. However, now that he'd had a taste of success in the bar business, Sean was eager to do it again. Steve had opened a new place on 42nd Street; maybe this spot in Washington Heights would be Sean's chance to hit it big.

Sean crossed Broadway and walked around the 169th Street side of the Gold Medal diner. He took a picture of the red metal kitchen door, which was locked, then went back to the corner and walked south toward the hospital. The sidewalks were full of people—doctors, nurses, medical students, discharged patients, and families who'd come to visit ailing relatives. Where were all of these people going to eat lunch? he wondered. Surely some of them needed a drink too. He crossed 168th Street and entered the main hospital building. Again, crowds of people. He wandered around looking at the medical suites and the doctors' offices. It was a bustling little city within the city. In here it was easy to forget the drug deals and other crimes taking place outside. He noticed a barbershop. Barbers were like cabdrivers and bartenders. They knew the secret lives of their neighborhoods. Sean waited, reading the paper. When his turn came, he got in the chair and started talking to the barber, saying he was thinking of opening a restaurant on Broadway, a block north of the hospital. "What can you tell me about the area?" he asked. The barber said he'd never set foot on Broadway. "I live in Jersey. I've worked here thirty years. I drive over the bridge in the morning, park my car in the garage downstairs, come up here, cut hair all day, go back down to the garage, get in my car, and drive home. What do I need to go out to Broadway for?"

But Sean thought differently. Newly shorn, he went home and called up Joey. "I'm in."

❧

CHAPTER TWO

In over Their Heads

Sean and Joey incorporated themselves as 600 W. 169th Street Restaurant Inc., got a verbal commitment from Kennedy and Presbyterian, and went to work. As an inducement, Presbyterian would collect no rent until the place was open. To further save money, Sean and Joey, who were equal partners in this venture, would do as much of the demolition themselves as they could. They began in the space that had once been La Muralla China. The first sledgehammer blow released a horde of cockroaches. It was a bad omen for the months ahead.

To negotiate the lease, Sean had hired an expensive attorney referred to him through connections at the New York State Liquor Authority. He knew from his experience with Tiana Beach Club, where a simple nondisturbance agreement would have allowed him and Steve to retain their lease, that having a good lawyer was essential. For that reason, he and Joey were willing to pay extra for top-notch representation. But, all appearances to the contrary, Sean quickly realized they'd hired a dud. In a meeting at the offices of the hospital's attorneys, it became apparent that the man negotiating on their behalf—the man wearing the $600 pair of shoes—hadn't even read the proposed lease. Every time Sean raised a concern, the attorney would reassure him, "Don't worry, we'll work it out." They fired him on the spot.

In desperate need of new legal representation, Sean and Joey turned to a reliable source—the Inwood Lounge. Through a former coworker, Sean got the name of Saul Victor, whose practice specialized in commercial real estate—especially restaurants and hotels. Sean called up Victor and explained the situation, but Victor made it clear he wasn't taking on any new clients. Sean kept him on the line, talking about Washington Heights and the Bronx. Victor had been born in the South Bronx and went to night school at City College in Upper Manhattan. He still had a soft spot for those areas. Like a bartender with a flush customer, Sean schmoozed and parlayed Victor until he finally agreed. Victor negotiated a twenty-one-year lease, which was signed on September 23, 1983.

In the meantime, the Gold Medal, the haberdashery, and the pharmacy all closed and vacated the premises. Sean and Joey came up with a plan for how they wanted to lay out the space. There would be three main rooms: a bar, a dining room, and a function room, plus the capacious basement where the liquor safe, walk-in freezers, beer barrels, and prep kitchen would go, along with a low-ceilinged office that was as cramped as the captain's quarters in a submarine. It was going to be a big restaurant, 4,200 square feet and able to seat 250 people. They hired an architect to put their vision on paper and a contractor to make it a reality, but soon they realized that they were in over their heads—financially and otherwise. Sean was astounded at how quickly the fifty grand he'd saved up disappeared. And Joey seemed to have gone through his settlement money by then too. But George McFadden, who believed in Sean and Joey's venture, came to the rescue, opening a home-equity line of credit on his primary residence to help finance the construction. Sean also took out a $210,000 mortgage on the business.

That kept the wolf from the door for a while, but Sean continued to look for investors. He asked his roommate, Peter Walsh, if he wanted to come in for 20 percent of the business—taking 10 percent each from his and Joey's shares. Peter, who'd recently sold his stake in Pudding's, loved the idea that Coogan's was close to the medical center. Being near a hospital or a funeral home was a virtual guarantee of success for a bar, he believed. Peter thought highly of Sean, but he had concerns about Joey. Sure, he was great fun to drink and tell stories with, but was he too wild and unpredictable to be a reliable business partner? Steve was the McFadden you wanted to be in business with. In the end, Peter invested a small amount of cash with Sean and received no ownership share or decision-making authority. If the business was profitable, there would be dividends down the road.

With the influx of money, the place started coming together. Sean found a lumber dealer in the Bronx who had enough mahogany to shape the large rectangular bar top he'd designed. They began thinking about the menu. It was going to be simple: burgers, steak and potatoes, French dip sandwiches. They'd also come up with a name. At first, they had considered calling the place Maxwell Hall after the nurse's residence at Columbia, but some alumni from the School of Nursing had voiced their disapproval, and Sean settled instead on Coogan's, named after Coogan's Bluff, near where he'd been born.

One afternoon, as the restaurant was taking shape,

there was a knock at the door. Outside on the sidewalk Sean saw a man dressed in an elegantly tailored suit. Local state assemblyman Denny Farrell was, in some respects, an embodiment of Upper Manhattan's heterogeneous population. Born of African American and Irish parents, he'd worked his way up from an early career as a garage attendant and cab driver to become a member of the "Harlem Clubhouse," an informal political organization that also included Congressman Charlie Rangel and future New York City mayor David Dinkins. Farrell himself was then preparing to run for mayor against Ed Koch. Tall, charismatic, and urbane, Farrell was skilled at power politics. He introduced himself to Sean. "So, what's going on in here?" he asked. Sean told him that he was planning to open up a bar and restaurant. "Need some help?" Farrell inquired. At first, Sean wasn't sure what Farrell meant by "help," but the assemblyman clarified: "I may have some people who need work." Sean said, "OK," and gave Farrell his phone number.

As construction continued, Sean began to have his own misgivings about Joey. Somehow it seemed that Joey always got to the mail before Sean did. Money disappeared unexpectedly from the business account. One afternoon when he was paying the bills, Sean saw that there were checks missing from the back of the checkbook. He knew that Joey had taken them—likely to pay for drugs or to pay off gambling debts.

He was dismayed more than he was angry. The McFaddens were like family to him. And this place had been Joey's idea, after all. He wanted it to succeed for both of them. But he understood now that Peter had been right: there was no way Coogan's was going to prosper with Joey as a partner. The next time Joey came in, Sean confronted him. "You gotta get out of this, or it's going to end up bloody, Joey," he said. "You gotta sell your stake." Joey, downcast, agreed to sell his share of the business. Things would not be the same between Sean and the McFaddens after that.

It was a decision that solved one problem but created others. If Joey went, Sean would have to repay George as well. How, though? His savings were gone, and the mortgage funds were dwindling fast. One option was just to sell the whole damn thing to someone else—his stake as well as the McFaddens'. But he felt in his gut that Coogan's was going to succeed. All he had to do was hang on, get it opened, and the money would start flowing in. The only other option was to take on new partners. But who would want to come in at this point? Peter had already turned him down, save for that small investment. It seemed like every barman in Inwood had passed on the location. That left only the hospital. He contacted John Kennedy at Presbyterian, who put together a small group of investors who would be able to buy 60 percent of the business—the 50 percent owned by the McFaddens plus 10 percent of Sean's stake. That got Joey out. It would take a couple more years to pay off George, whose money was tied to the mortgage Sean had taken out. But now Sean suddenly found himself a minority owner of his bar and restaurant.

Sean's new partners were Peter Kennedy, Kevin Kiernan, and Larry Schwartz (KKS). All three worked in hospital administration in the city, but like many men, they'd long dreamed of owning a bar. The new owners knew little about the saloon trade, which left Sean still very much in charge of getting Coogan's up and running and managing its daily operations.

Financially secure again, Sean focused on getting the

doors open. The plywood fencing came down, revealing the white walls and black doors of the bar's exterior. A grid of small square windows flanked each door. The name of the bar was painted in white cursive over the doors, "Coogan's," surrounded by a lasso that emanated from the "g." Above the main entrance, there was a long awning that projected across the sidewalk, inviting entry. "Daily Specials | Restaurant | Tap Room | Party Room" announced the exterior signage. Inside, the décor was simple and unpretentious: exposed brick, wood paneling, and wood floors. Banked black leather seats around the edge of the dining room, with wooden tables and chairs in the middle. Green tablecloths. The bar felt like a pub, and the high-ceilinged, light-filled dining room resembled a homespun Viennese café.

Early in the fall of 1985, they put the final touches in place. Ice machines and other appliances were installed. The interior walls were painted white and green. Lamps with curved and conical shades were suspended from the high ceiling. Sean hired staff: an Irish chef; Dominican kitchen workers and porters (two of them referred by Farrell); Irish waitresses from his many bar connections; and a manager named John Armstrong who'd worked at Tiana. The beer and the liquor arrived, and the bar was stocked.

All this activity had drawn the attention of local pedestrians. Apparently, the neighborhood needed a place like Coogan's as much as Sean had hoped. Every day he was asked the same question multiple times: "When are you going to open?" "Soon," he said. "Very soon."

There was one problem, though: Con Edison had not connected the gas. Sean called again and again, spoke to customer service representatives, left messages. Nobody called him back. Desperate for income, he decided that

Exterior of Coogan's in the early years.

they were going to open anyway. A date was selected: Thursday, October 31, 1985. Halloween.

Without gas, Sean had to figure out what he was going to do about food. He turned to his network of Irish barmen, asking his friend Jimmy Flynn, who owned a place up in the Bronx, if he could use his kitchen. At 4:00 a.m. on Halloween, Sean arrived with trays of beef. By 8:00 he loaded the cooked meat into his car and drove south to Washington Heights. He delivered the trays through the kitchen door to be sliced and put into sandwiches. Fortunately, the Board of Health inspectors did not visit that day.

Sean checked in with Armstrong and the rest of the staff. Everything was ready. They'd gone over the plan a million times. Coogan's would officially open at 11:00 a.m. Tired and smelling like roast beef, he drove back home to his apartment on Park Avenue. He wanted to get a haircut, take a shower, and then maybe sleep a little. He felt calm and unhurried. Armstrong was young, but he was capable. It would all be fine. As Sean showered, he tried to think of the many things that could go wrong. But they'd anticipated everything, he was sure of it. He lay down to close his eyes for a few minutes and woke to find it was one o'clock in the afternoon.

By the time he found parking uptown, it was nearly two. The place was alive. Drinkers surrounded the bar like spectators at a boxing match. Waitresses and busboys rushed around. The echoing sound of construction, which had filled Sean's ears for months, was now replaced with music, ringing cash registers, and laughter. It was exactly as he and Joey had imagined it. Their dream had become reality.

Armstrong appeared, his face red with stress and anger. "Jesus, where the hell have you been?"

Sean smiled at him. "It's OK," he said. "We're in business!"

❧

CHAPTER THREE

Uptown

Ownership of Washington Heights has been contested at least since Henry Hudson sailed past Upper Manhattan in 1609. The indigenous Munsee people had a long-established encampment site called Shorokapok (sometimes rendered as "Shorakkopoch") on the eastern edge of what is now Inwood Hill Park. The forced displacement of the Munsee has been reduced to a folk tale in which Peter Minuit, in 1626, "purchased" Manhattan island for sixty guilders. In actuality, by the eighteenth century, Dutch and English settlers had steadily dispossessed the native peoples of their lands through violence and negotiation. Disease also took a heavy toll. A turnover in population would become a pattern for the area—in the words of the historian Robert W. Snyder, it would "not be the last time comfortable residents of Northern Manhattan found their world turned upside down by the arrival of new people."

During the Revolutionary War, the invading British forces drove General George Washington and the Continental Army out of Brooklyn into Manhattan. The Americans had constructed a fortification near Manhattan's highest point, in what is now Washington Heights. Named Fort Washington, it stood on a rocky cliff some 230 feet above the Hudson River. British soldiers and Hessian mercenaries took the fort, killing nearly 60 and capturing some 2,800 Americans, but not before Washington had escaped across the Hudson to New Jersey. Though he lost the battles for New York, Washington went on to win the war, and his name became omnipresent in Upper Manhattan. A high school, two bridges, a road, and a bus station are all dubbed in his honor.

Following independence, Upper Manhattan remained largely rural farmland. By the late nineteenth century, though, much of the land in Washington Heights and Inwood had been gathered into country estates owned by wealthy New Yorkers who were drawn there by its bucolic landscape, beautiful vistas, and proximity to the city. Their names still adorn street signs and green spaces in the area: the artist and ornithologist John James Audubon; James Gordon Bennett Sr., the founder and publisher of the New York *Herald*; C. K. G. Billings, the president of a Chicago power utility; the financier James Hood Wright; and the richest of them all, John D. Rockefeller Jr.

Another prominent landowner in the area was James Jay Coogan, who made a name for himself building and selling furniture on the Lower East Side. Coogan had political ambitions. He married Harriet Gardiner Lynch, the great-granddaughter of John Lyon Gardiner, who had been granted extensive lands in New York by King George I, including a large chunk of Northern Manhattan. When Harriet's father, William, passed away, that real estate came under Coogan's control. After failed attempts to become mayor, Coogan cultivated the favor of Tammany Hall leader Richard Croker and was elected the second Manhattan Borough president in 1899. His name was preserved in the moniker for the escarpment over the Harlem River and the hollow below.

The metropolis to the south finally began to encroach on Upper Manhattan at the turn of the twentieth century. Massive civil engineering and infrastructure projects primed the uptown neighborhoods for development. In 1904, the subway reached 157th Street. The following year, service was extended into the Bronx. In 1931, the George Washington Bridge opened, connecting Washington Heights and New Jersey. A year later, the IND line (the A train) reached its terminus at 207th Street in Inwood. George Washington High School moved to its current building in 1925, and Yeshiva University opened its campus in the Heights in 1929. In 1935, Rockefeller donated to the city the land that became Fort Tryon Park, where the Metropolitan Museum of Art built the Cloisters to house its collection of medieval and Byzantine art.

Many of the art deco apartments that now characterize the northwestern part of the neighborhood were constructed during these decades: block after block of five- and six-story buildings with steam heat, large rooms, and wooden floors. Other areas uptown offered cheaper housing. The building that would later become home to Coogan's, 4015 Broadway, was erected in 1915 by the James Livingston Construction Company, which built half a dozen other apartment buildings. These buildings were inhabited by Irish, Jewish, Greek, and Cuban immigrants, some of whom arrived directly from their homelands. For others, though, the Heights provided an escape from the cramped and unsanitary ghettos of lower Manhattan. Ethnic groups began claiming sections of the neighborhood. In the 1930s, a huge influx of German Jewish refugees, fleeing the rise of Hitler, turned the western Heights into "Frankfurt on the Hudson." The Greek enclave was centered around Wadsworth Avenue. By the 1950s, Puerto Ricans began moving to the Heights. Just south of the neighborhood, a middleclass African American community flourished in Sugar Hill. Many of them had come to New York during the Great Migration, having escaped the Jim Crow South. Relations among these various ethnic and racial groups were not particularly harmonious. In the years leading up to and during the Second World War, Jewish youths were beaten up, and synagogues were defaced by Irish gangs. And Black residents from Harlem were harassed if they strayed too far from their home turf.

Baseball also played an important role in the neighborhood's development. Early in the twentieth century, Washington Heights was home to two of the city's three major league franchises. In 1891, the New York Giants relocated from just north of Central Park to Coogan's Bluff. In 1911, the owner, John T. Brush, built the Polo Grounds, a U-shaped concrete stadium—"an absurd and lovely thing," as Roger Angell once described it (p. 159)—in the hollow at the base of the cliff after the prior structure there had burned down. The team would go on to win ten National League pennants over the next quarter century, drawing thousands to their games. Less than a dozen blocks northwest of the Polo Grounds was Hilltop Park, home to the New York Highlanders—later known as the Yankees—who, from 1913 to 1923, shared the Polo Grounds with the Giants before moving to a permanent home in the Bronx. (It was during their time in Washington

Heights that the Yankees acquired a pitcher named Babe Ruth from the Boston Red Sox.)

In 1922, the land on which the Highlanders had played their home games was purchased by Edward S. Harkness, a philanthropist whose father was an early and major investor in Standard Oil. Harkness, who was on the board of Presbyterian Hospital, donated the twenty-two acres, along with a million dollars, to facilitate a union between Presbyterian and Columbia University's College of Physicians and Surgeons. When it opened in 1928, Columbia-Presbyterian was one of the first academic medical centers in the world to combine a major hospital, a medical school, and a research facility. In the ensuing decades, Columbia-Presbyterian grew rapidly, adding disciplines and facilities, acquiring property, merging with New York Hospital to become the largest hospital in the city and one of the largest landowners and employers in Upper Manhattan. (The hospital had purchased 4015 Broadway in 1968.)

An early promotional pamphlet referred to the medical center as "the Fortress on the Heights," evoking the area's Revolutionary War past and likening the institution to "an arsenal in the battle against human disease." It was a telling metaphor. Even as Columbia-Presbyterian provided some jobs and stability to the economy of Washington Heights, it often seemed walled off from the neighborhood around it and aloof from the concerns of local residents.

By the middle of the twentieth century, the population of Washington Heights and Inwood had grown to more than two hundred thousand. It was a thriving neighborhood with good transportation, abundant parkland, theaters, swimming pools, movie houses, and homes for a community of immigrant strivers. Maria Callas, Henry

Kissinger, and Harry Belafonte had all spent some of their formative years there. But, in the second half of the twentieth century, the neighborhood would be transformed once again, as many of its longtime white residents relocated to the suburbs and a wave of immigrants from the Dominican Republic moved in.

❧

CHAPTER FOUR

The Dividing Line

One of those immigrants was my mother-in-law, Grecia
Solano. Grecia grew up on a farm in the small town of
La Isabela, on the outskirts of Santo Domingo. Her family
raised chickens, cows, and pigs, plucked mangoes from
the trees. During her teenage years, her father made her
hide whenever men sent by the country's dictator, General
Rafael Leónidas Trujillo, combed through the area looking for girls to take back to the presidential palace. While
out riding her bike one day, she encountered a young man
named Salvador Matos and took a liking to him. Before
long they were married with a daughter, Zoraida, who'd
one day become my wife. A son followed. When the children were still toddlers, Grecia and Salvador, in their early
twenties, went separately to the United States looking for
work and a better life, leaving the children behind with
their grandparents. Trujillo was dead by then, and the
country was in turmoil, and a new American immigration
law made it easier for migrants from the developing world
to arrive and settle in the United States.

Grecia went first to Queens, New York, and then to
Lynn, Massachusetts, but eventually, like so many other

Dominicans, she found her way to Upper Manhattan and rented an apartment on Haven Avenue. In Washington Heights, most people spoke Spanish, and there were Dominican shops, restaurants, and hair salons. It made the dislocation and the cold winters easier to bear. Grecia worked a variety of menial jobs before landing a union position as a cleaning lady at Columbia-Presbyterian. She and Salvador had divorced, and Grecia remarried, giving birth to twins. Her second husband died soon after, killed in a car crash. She kept working, living frugally, sending what she could back to the DR to support her extended family and build a home there for retirement. Because she was on the night shift and because she feared the streets of Washington Heights, she didn't go out much. Her life revolved around the handful of blocks between her building and the hospital. Socializing meant eating, drinking, and dancing in the nearby apartments of friends and coworkers. Like so many Dominican Americans of her generation, Grecia was caught somewhere between the two countries, no longer living in her homeland but not yet fully at home in America.

Grecia arrived in Washington Heights in the mid-1970s, a watershed moment for the neighborhood and for New York. The city was undergoing a painful transformation from an industrial economy to one based on service and information. Well-paid manufacturing jobs that had sustained the working class during the postwar years were disappearing. Urban renewal and "slum clearance" programs transformed neighborhoods across New York. With the city on the verge of bankruptcy, the municipal government laid off workers and implemented a policy of planned shrinkage, hastening the reduction of the population in lower-income neighborhoods by cutting back on essential services such as firefighting. In the face of such economic decline and rising crime, many white residents of middle- and working-class neighborhoods fled to the suburbs. In Washington Heights, it was the Irish, the Jews, and the Greeks who steadily moved out, relocating to Long Island, Westchester County, and New Jersey. Helped by federally subsidized mortgage financing that was generally denied to people of color, many whites left the city in search of newer housing, safer streets, and communities where they could live amid a more homogeneous population. With its substantive Irish population, River Edge, New Jersey, where the McFaddens moved, was but one example.

Between 1950 and 1980, the population of Washington Heights and Inwood dropped from 214,000 to 190,000. By 1980, the proportion of whites in Washington Heights had fallen by half, to 39 percent, and the number of Hispanics, (likely undercounted), had increased to the same. Newly arriving Dominicans moved into the apartments vacated by working-class white families. More than 250,000 Do- minicans immigrated legally to the United States between 1960 and 1980 (as did an unknown number of undocu- mented migrants). The majority settled in New York City, which, for a while, became the second-largest Dominican community in the world, after Santo Domingo.

The mass migration of so many Dominicans was in large part a direct result of more than half a century of Ameri- can meddling in Dominican political and economic affairs. In the name of preserving influence in the Caribbean and ensuring American business and trade interests, the United States invaded the Dominican Republic in 1916 and oc- cupied the country for the next eight years. The dictator, Trujillo, who had trained with the occupying U.S. Marines, seized power in 1930. For three decades, he ruled by creating fear in the populace, assassinating those who opposed him, and crushing the free press. On Trujillo's orders, his forces massacred fifteen thousand migrants from neighboring Haiti as they crossed the border, slaying many of them with machetes. Trujillo's 1961 assassination, carried out with the backing of the CIA, triggered a new period of unrest. His democratically elected successor, Juan Bosch, was overthrown after only seven months in power by a coalition of conservative forces: the military, the industrialists and landowners, and the Catholic Church. In 1965, as a populist Left-leaning movement tried to reinstate Bosch, the United States invaded again, seeking to prevent the Dominican Republic from becoming what Lyndon Johnson called "a second Cuba." The following year, Joaquín Balaguer, who had served under Trujillo and who was the preferred candidate of the Dominican establishment and the Americans, defeated Bosch in elections marred by violence and intimidation. Balaguer, who remained in power for twelve years, began restructuring the economy in a manner that led to increased unemployment among lower-skilled workers. His government tacitly encouraged emigration of the excess labor by readily issuing passports. The U.S. Immigration and Nationality Act of 1965 had done away with longstanding national-origin quotas that favored immigrants from northern and western European countries and opened the United States to arrivals from the developing world. A number of leftist Dominicans who had supported Bosch took the opportunity to go into exile. Plenty of others simply fled poverty and the lack of opportunity.

Many Dominicans made their home in Washington Heights, concentrating most densely in the southern and eastern parts of the neighborhood, where rents were the cheapest. Often, like Grecia, they had uprooted themselves from small, rural communities. They brought that village perspective to their new lives, which were centered around the building they lived in and the block it was on. People in Washington Heights identified themselves as being "on the 3rd" or "on the 4th," meaning 183rd or 184th Streets (or 163rd or 164th). Their frame of reference was so geographically limited that the first two digits of the street number were redundant. To stray four or five blocks from home was to find yourself somewhere unfamiliar.

Thus, Washington Heights was made up of an array of small urban villages. Broadway, which bisected the neighborhood at a northwest-to-south diagonal, was seen as a dividing line. West and north tended to be wealthier, whiter, middle class, and "safer" than the south and east, with better housing stock and lower crime. Life in the Castle Village co-op development near the Cloisters, or along the more prosperous reaches of upper Fort Washington Avenue in the 180s, was markedly different from life in the lower 160s near Amsterdam and Edgecombe. Broadway was neutral territory, lined with essential services and businesses used by all: banks, pharmacies, bodegas, laundromats, subway stations, clothing stores, travel agencies, places where you could wire money overseas, and, of course, the hospital. In time, Coogan's would become another of those essential places. Its location on 169th and Broadway was both near the center of the neighborhood and on the dividing line. That location, and its proximity to the hospital and the subway, would be crucial in helping it draw people from all quadrants of the Heights.

Coach Dave Crenshaw, who would become a regular at Coogan's, grew up in southeastern Washington Heights on the border with Sugar Hill. Crenshaw's parents, both African Americans, were entrenched in the community. His mother, Gwen, was on the school board, and his father, Richard, was active in local Democratic politics. Crenshaw was raised with the expectation that he would also be involved. His passion was sports, and even before he turned twenty, he was looking for ways to combine athletics and activism. The section of the Heights where he lived—sometimes known as 6 Block City—had become a hub for drug sales, but it was also home to families. With its overcrowded, underresourced schools and its dangerous streets, there were virtually no safe venues for organized sports or outdoor activities. In the mid-1980s, Crenshaw began taking groups of school-age children from the neighborhood to experience the outdoors across the Hudson in New Jersey and Pennsylvania. A few years later, he started chaperoning squads of girls to the Carmine Street recreation center in Greenwich Village to participate in weekend basketball tournaments organized by a coach there, Ray Pagan. "My community was at war. We had to get out of the block. It was the only way we were going to show the kids we were going to do something different and *be* something different," Crenshaw recalled. "We were no longer allowed to play in the streets. Everyplace was a drug spot. We just had to get out. We weren't going to grow by staying in the neighborhood."

In the Village, Crenshaw's kids competed against teams from all over the city. Crenshaw said that the experience showed the youngsters that "all people who don't look like us ain't against us." He named his program "Uptown Dreamers." With help from Pagan, educator and activist Al Kurland, and Blanca Battino, the principal of PS 128, Crenshaw began running youth athletic programs on weekends—and eventually after school—in Washington Heights. He brought together African American, Dominican, and Puerto Rican kids from different sections of the neighborhood. Teens mentored the younger children. Volunteering and community public service were expected to get playing time on Crenshaw's teams. The Dreamers plucked litter off the streets and cleaned the playground and ball courts at Edgecombe Park. Over time, Crenshaw would form partnerships with the Mailman School of Public Health at Columbia and nonprofits such as the Community League of the Heights and the Police Athletic League. And he would also become close with the owners of Coogan's. Stocky, broad-shouldered, loud, and quick to laugh, Crenshaw seemed to be everywhere uptown. "I'm a Black man in a Latino neighborhood, and they trusted me with their sons and their daughters. I'm very proud of that," said Crenshaw.

A mainstay of Crenshaw's youth was Wilson's Bakery and Restaurant on Amsterdam Avenue and 158th Street, which had opened in 1947. "It was a community place. Wilson's was our Sylvia's," Crenshaw recalled, referring to the famous soul food restaurant some thirty blocks south in Harlem. It was a place you went for celebrations. "When you dined there, you wore your Sunday best." Like all good neighborhood spots, Wilson's had a diverse clientele: young and old, white and Black, wealthy and poor. The restaurant was known for hiring local teens so they could learn about the hospitality business. Crenshaw fondly remembered going into Wilson's in the morning to get a cinnamon bun for breakfast. The buns were so large that he split them with friends.

Even as crime rose in the neighborhood, Wilson's remained a favorite spot—until the summer of 1985, when the restaurant's sixty-five-year-old proprietor, Thomas Wilson, was gunned down in front of his Bronx home. He had complained to police about a gang who was selling drugs outside his restaurant. Writing in the *Daily News*, Earl Caldwell noted, "In the city, there are not many places anymore that get the mix that Wilson's had. . . . The place was special. But special doesn't come overnight. It takes building."

The restaurant closed in the wake of Wilson's murder, and drugs continued to be sold on the sidewalk. With Wilson's shuttered, Crenshaw said, there was nowhere in the neighborhood where you could get a first-class sit-down meal. "We had no *family* place."

CHAPTER FIVE

Special Doesn't Come Overnight

Thomas Wilson was killed three months before Coogan's opened. It was a time of crisis uptown. Leo Fuentes, a child of Dominican immigrants who would become a regular at the saloon, recalled how crack became "the air we breathed" in Northern Manhattan. In middle school, Fuentes sometimes hung out on the promenade of a small neighborhood park, talking to his friend Wilbur as Wilbur sold crack. Neighbors arriving to buy a vial interrupted the teen boys' exchange of banter. One spring night a woman who had no money asked Wilbur for a short. When Wilbur refused, the woman said, "It's Mother's Day. Can't I get a short?" The discrepancy between the wholesome celebration of motherhood and the woman's desperate addiction opened Fuentes's eyes to the mundane ways that the drug had altered everyday life in Washington Heights. "Crack corrupted everything it touched," Fuentes later reflected.

It also produced waves of violent crime. The newspapers detailed the brutality that accompanied it: John Chase Wood, a young Columbia-Presbyterian doctor was shot dead on Riverside Drive after refusing to surrender his wallet to two muggers; Linda Green, a nursing supervisor at the hospital, was beaten to death by an assailant while sitting in her car next to her apartment building on Bennett Avenue; three Yeshiva University students were injured in a sniper attack on a dairy restaurant near the campus, part of a spree of anti-Semitic assaults; and the month before Coogan's opened, there was a shootout between rival drug gangs just a few blocks north of the bar, with no fatalities but many shaken nerves. The situation had gotten so perilous that the Columbia-Presbyterian Medical Center seriously considered relocating to another part of the city.

The violence, the flourishing drug trade, and the rapid demographic changes stoked mistrust among the ethnic populations in Washington Heights. Many whites who had opted to stay in Northern Manhattan were made uneasy by the rapid increase in the Dominican population. A 1984 editorial in the biweekly *Uptown Press* titled "Racial Tensions Rising; Lets Communicate" called for "a mini-summit" of neighborhood leaders and institutional representatives from all parts of the community. "Many of us, for example, do not understand the Dominicans, their recent history, their hopes, dreams and goals. How, for example, do they differ from the other waves of immigrants who have made Washington Heights and Inwood their entry point to New York City?"

Some were not so mystified. For Monsignor Thomas Leonard, the bilingual pastor of the Church of the Incarnation, the Dominicans and Irish were "so alike, it's uncanny." Both were from majority Catholic nations on partitioned, impoverished islands with agrarian societies. Both had been invaded and colonized by imperial powers. There was a shared history of emigration under duress

Sean Cannon

and a love of music, drinking, dancing, and storytelling. But those similarities did not resonate for everyone.

Sean was too focused on his bar's lack of a functioning kitchen to waste time worrying about clashing ethnic resentments. Getting up at 4:00 a.m. to cook roast beef in the Bronx was not a sustainable way to run a restaurant—or a life. He'd have to figure out a way to provoke a response from Con Edison. He hired an unscrupulous local handyman to connect the kitchen at Coogan's to the gas supply, bypassing the Con Edison meter. He then called up the utility and told them what he had done. "If you want to get paid for the gas I'm using, you need to send someone out here to fix this." The issue was resolved within a week.

By that time, Coogan's was already on its way to being a hit with its intended primary audience—the staff, patients, and families of the Columbia-Presbyterian medical center. Very quickly, they were serving 250 lunches a day; on Thursdays and Fridays, there was a line to get in. Municipal employees, especially police officers, many from the 34th Precinct and the Manhattan North Narcotics Bureau, also adopted Coogan's as a hangout. Off-duty cops from other precincts, who had been in the habit of drinking in Queens, the Bronx, and upstate New York, began stopping in en route to their homes in Rockland and Orange Counties. For those who dined at Coogan's, the regular presence of so many law enforcement officers helped make it feel like a refuge from the dangerous streets outside. According to Dave Crenshaw, it also earned the restaurant an early reputation for being a police hangout, especially at night. "At first, it was a cop bar. Cops and hospital. It wasn't a community bar in the beginning."

Washington Heights in the 1980s was a working-class, liberal-Democratic, majority Dominican neighborhood, but its elected officials still reflected the demographics and machine politics of the previous generation. None of the major elected officials were Dominicans: The local Congressmen, Ted Weiss, was Jewish. The state assemblymen for Upper Manhattan were Denny Farrell, who was Black and Irish, and Brian Murtaugh, who was Irish American. State senator Franz Leichter and city councilman Stan Michels were Jewish. In the 1970s, Dominicans had begun entering races for seats on school boards; in the following decades, they rose to power slowly, challenging and ultimately displacing the Irish, Jewish, and African American incumbents. Coogan's would be one of the venues at the center of that change.

Leading the way was a trio of Dominican politicians: Guillermo Linares, Adriano Espaillat, and Maria Luna. They emerged from the policy areas most directly affecting the lives of Dominican immigrants: education, criminal justice, and housing. The cerebral Linares had immigrated to the United States as a teenager and put himself through college driving a cab and working in a bodega. He began his political career advocating for better schools in the neighborhood. Espaillat, who arrived in the United States as an undocumented immigrant in 1964, worked for the New York City Criminal Justice Agency and served on the 34th Precinct Community Council. Luna, who had moved to New York from the Dominican Republic in the early 1960s, worked for a housing-rights group called the Riverside Edgecombe Association. Luna came up through the Audubon Reform Democratic Club, which had been founded by anti–Vietnam War activists in 1966. (Coach Dave's father, Richard Crenshaw, was an active member.) The club's leader, Alfred Blumberg, who felt that it was part of his job to bring Dominicans and other immigrants into the Democratic fold, helped foster Luna's career. Luna was elected a Democratic district leader in 1983 and later became a member of the Democratic National Committee. All three of these young, ambitious Dominicans served on the community board.

Denny Farrell, however, was the key figure in establishing the saloon's popularity with the neighborhood's political class. The bar was located close to his offices, and he went there often after work with members of his staff. One junior aide, Al Taylor, fondly recalled Farrell taking him to Coogan's for dinner after Taylor was accepted to law school. There was simply no place like Coogan's between Harlem and Inwood. It was large enough to hold fundraising events, and it had a function room for private gatherings. Farrell was the chairman of the county Democratic Party and would go on to be the state Democratic chairman and head of the Assembly's Ways and Means Committee. That would make him the third most powerful person in New York state politics after the governor and the Speaker. Linares recalled that Farrell's early adoption of the saloon was pivotal in making it central to uptown politics. Espaillat agreed: "If you wanted to see Denny, you went to Coogan's. He would hold court there on Saturdays."

As Earl Caldwell wrote of Wilson's, "Special doesn't come overnight." Not everyone in Washington Heights felt welcome at Coogan's in those early years. Dania Zapata, who would later work there as general manager, remembers thinking that the bar, with its black-painted doors, looked like a funeral home. One of Grecia Solano's sons, who grew up a few blocks away, recalled that it seemed "too fancy" for Washington Heights. And, as Coach Dave observed, some saw it simply as a cop bar.

While business was good, rifts began to appear in the complicated partnership that owned Coogan's. To Sean's surprise, Kevin Kiernan announced that he wanted to leave his hospital job and take up a full-time position at the restaurant. Sean had issues with this idea, the most significant being that Kiernan didn't have any experience working in a saloon. Not only that, but Kiernan announced that he didn't want to tend bar. What he had in mind was an office job with a nine-to-five weekday schedule. Sean had the same schedule in mind for himself. After two decades of weekends and late nights in saloons owned by other people, he finally had his own place, and he wanted to reap the rewards. He was in his mid-forties, married, and planning to start a family. It wasn't merely that Kiernan had no relevant experience; it was also that he hadn't paid his dues. Sean didn't like the entitlement, but he was no longer calling all the shots, so he complied with the request, carving out an office job for Kiernan, cobbling together various administrative responsibilities for him. It wasn't quite a sinecure, but Kiernan's performance suggested that he believed a good part of his duties consisted of pulling up a chair at the bar and drinking with the hospital workers.

A second source of friction was money, specifically profit sharing. Sean dubbed himself "the bean counter." He controlled the bar's finances, and he abhorred the idea of anyone—a partner, a patron, or a vendor—having the upper hand on him. Most bars in those days kept two sets of books, an external set for accounting and tax purposes, and an internal set for profit sharing. Cash income that was included in the internal books might not always find its way into the "official" external ledgers. At that time—before the use of credit and cards became widespread—Coogan's was a 90 percent cash business, so the differences between the two sets of books could be substantial. Every saloon had its own procedures for handling this bifurcated accounting. In the case of Coogan's, the internal books were kept largely in Sean's head, as was the formula for calculating the profits that were shared among the owners. Those profits—i.e., the monies left over after all the payroll, bills, and debt payments had been made—were delivered periodically in envelopes. By paying himself a high salary, Sean effectively reduced the bar's profit. Reducing the profit cut the size of the envelopes. Though he owned only 40 percent of the business, he was the one who'd created Coogan's, and he was the one running the place every day, and those were two large variables in his formula for calculating his own salary. Sean thought it only fair that this extra work and his seniority should be reflected in his pay. Keeping the apparent profits low was also part of a longer-term strategy to reduce the cost if he ever wanted to buy out his partners, something he hoped one day to do.

A third source of conflict was Sean's drug use. He favored cocaine. In his own estimation, the white powder made him a "crazier drinker." He would disappear from the restaurant, leaving John Armstrong, the floor manager, in charge. Sean would embark on coke-fueled sprees that lasted days, taking him from one watering hole to another all over the city, tearing it up with old friends from the lounge and Tiana and Jimmy Byrne's. He tried to hide his habit when at work, but his absences riled his fellow owners. Even as Coogan's grew as a business, it began to fall apart as a partnership. Convinced that KKS were plotting to buy *him* out, Sean pushed toward a confrontation with them. He wanted to resolve the tensions that had been building. But before that collision and resolution happened, John Armstrong announced that he was leaving to open his own place, a brewpub, on the Upper East Side. That vacancy would have to be filled, and once again, Sean turned to Inwood for a solution.

∾

CHAPTER SIX

Exactly Who You'd Hope to Find Behind the Bar

"There's this idea that if you're a member of a certain ethnic group, you can walk into that ethnic group's bar and be at home," observed the journalist Jim Dwyer, a longtime resident of Washington Heights, who adopted Coogan's as his local. "I've never found that to be true. I'm as Irish as anyone around New York and I don't feel comfortable in every Irish bar."

Irish saloons are such a familiar part of New York City's streetscape that it's easy to think of them as interchangeable, as if they were all minted from the same template, featuring a lacquered wooden bar top, black-and-white tile floors, frosted glass lampshades, neon signs in the windows, and a jukebox full of Thin Lizzy and the Chieftains. And, indeed, today there are design firms that sell prefabricated Irish bar kits (a pub in a box, as some call it) delivered all over the world. But, to Dwyer's point, there has long been a wide range of Irish saloons in New York, serving a varied clientele.

In her memoir, *Drinking with Men*, Rosie Schaap conjured "a taxonomy of bars," ruminating on the differences between dive bars and old-man bars, corner bars and neighborhood bars, and the many iterations of the sports bar. I found myself wondering what a subset of that taxonomy devoted to Irish saloons would look like. The list would have to include the tribal neighborhood drinking dens like Ned's in Yorkville and McKenna's on Hudson Street, where heads would turn if a stranger entered; the boisterous party palaces of Murray Hill and the Upper East Side, like Dorian's, that served as hangout and hookup spots for the young and single; the big Midtown taverns like Neary's and Rosie O'Grady's that catered to theatergoers, tourists, and office parties; the basketball and hockey bars near Madison Square Garden, like McHale's, that were packed with Knicks and Rangers fans in the hours before and after a game but were empty in between; the steam-table joints like the Blarney Stone with their sweating smorgasbords of soft vegetables and brined meats; the storied museum pieces like McSorley's and the Old Town, where you could drink up a different era; the raffish hangouts for writers, musicians, and actors like the Lion's Head or the White Horse; and, of course, many other subcategories scattered all over the five boroughs, some that would welcome you and some that would not.

Where Coogan's would fall within that taxonomy was an open question. One of the people who would ultimately have a say in answering that question was a Greenwich Village bartender named Dave Hunt. Dave, who held court at Jimmy Day's off Sheridan Square, believed that his primary responsibility was not to pour drinks but to make people feel comfortable, whether they were Irish or not. Jimmy Day's, which opened in 1972, was the kind of spot where people congregated after other bars and restaurants had closed for the night, and it was frequented by the sort of motley crowd you might expect from a Greenwich Village watering hole of that era: celebrities, gangsters, longshoremen, nurses from St. Vincent's Hospital, and bridge-and-tunnelers out for a night in Manhattan. Dustin Hoffman, William Hurt, Norman Mailer, and Billy Idol all drank there. So did the cast of *Saturday Night Live*. It was near enough to the courts and 1 Police Plaza that an ambitious young Dominican community activist from Washington Heights, Adriano Espaillat, would drop in for a burger when his shift at the Criminal Justice Agency ended at 11:00 p.m.

Dave was pale, freckled, and jowly, with light ginger hair, round gold-framed glasses, and a gravelly, nasal New York voice. "He's exactly who you'd hope to find behind the bar of an Irish saloon," said one former regular, retired NYPD detective Bill Cannon. "Friendly and welcoming, with a quick wit." Dave had been at Jimmy Day's since 1973 and developed a loyal following. "He seemed to come with the place," remembered Cannon.

Before becoming a bartender, Dave had taken sociology classes at Fordham. Observant and analytical, he enjoyed watching the interactions among the eclectic groups of patrons across the bar. Saloon work was sometimes a party, and the parties were sometimes work, but there were few other businesses in the world where it was acceptable to call out sick saying, "I got shitfaced last night, I can't come in."

When not on duty, Dave was an active member of what he called "the Irish American saloon society," a loose confederation of New York barmen, waitresses, and their friends who bounced around the city—and out to Hampton Bays in the summer—buying rounds, chatting each other up, and chasing good times. The McFaddens were part of that society, as were Sean Cannon and his wife, Maureen Mullarkey, who waited tables at Jimmy Day's. It was Maureen who first suggested that Dave should go to work at Coogan's. "Sean needs a manager, and I think it'd be a good fit for you," she said to him one afternoon in the spring of 1987.

Though he loved the boisterous fun at Jimmy Day's, Dave was by this time in his late thirties, with young children and a newly purchased home in River Edge, New Jersey. He'd also recently given up drinking. Afraid that booze was going to wreck his marriage, he'd checked into an Alcoholics Anonymous facility in Connecticut for a two-week detox. His newfound sobriety, along with his burgeoning domestic responsibilities, made the prospect of a daytime management job appealing. "It was a maturity thing," he recalled.

Managing a saloon was also a necessary step toward his dream of owning one.

Like the McFaddens, Dave had grown up in Inwood, during a time when it was the last fully Irish neighborhood in Manhattan. At the center of Dave's childhood—and at the center of Inwood itself—was one of the islands in the Hibernian Archipelago: the Church of the Good Shepherd, on the corner of Broadway and Isham Street. In the 1960s, the church held as many as fourteen Masses on a typical Sunday, split between the church itself and the Good Shepherd School auditorium. One priest estimated that as many as twenty thousand people attended Mass at Good Shepherd each Sunday. Among those attending was Dave; he was also a pupil at the Good Shepherd School. Sporting activities, often sponsored by the church or the school, filled his weekend and after-school hours. Basketball was a particular passion, whether it was a three-on-three game in Inwood Hill Park or the more formal full-squad contests sanctioned by the local Catholic Youth Organization.

Dave got to know another basketball-playing resident of the neighborhood, Jim Carroll, who went on to renown as a poet, musician, and, most famously, the author of *The Basketball Diaries*. Dave remembers him as a husky kid with game—until he started using heroin. Carroll's family had relocated to Inwood from downtown; his memoir is full of scathing comments about the neighborhood. Riding the A train uptown was like "taking a trip to Albany." It was full of "old biddy penguins" and "Catholic school bullcrap."

Saloons were central to life in Inwood. Walter Winchell is said to have called the area "Ginwood," and locals joked that if you sent a kid out for a pint of milk, he'd pass two bars before he got to a store with a dairy case. Dave started drinking in those establishments when he was a teenager. One of his favorites was George McFadden's Inwood Lounge. McFadden's cousin Barbara and Dave's aunt Bea had come over from Ireland on the same ship in the 1920s. Such were the deep connections in the neighborhood—ties that went back across the Atlantic and back through generations.

Dave's childhood friend Patricia Conlan remembers him as someone who moved easily between different and sometimes adversarial groups. Inwood was a working-class "love it or leave it" neighborhood. Yet, despite being known as a "pinko" for his liberal political views—he was in favor of the civil rights movement and against the Vietnam War—Dave was welcomed in saloons such as Garryowens where there were regular sendoffs for Inwood boys who went willingly to fight in Southeast Asia and intermittent wakes for those who didn't come back alive.

Both of Dave's parents were Irish immigrants. His

mother was a housewife who later worked at the concession stand at 30 Rockefeller Center—the Top of the Rock. His father was a plumber for Schrafft's, a New York restaurant chain. He was a hard-working, disciplined man, with regular habits, home by 5:30 every night unless there was an emergency. The sense of identity and loyalty that existed between Schrafft's and its employees was a crucial part of Dave's childhood and would later be a model for him when he ran his own restaurant. Schrafft's had succeeded by offering homestyle meals at an affordable price in elegant surroundings. It was one of the first American restaurant chains to cater specifically to women. The owner, Frank Shattuck, hired women to work in his restaurants, not only as waitresses, but also as cooks and managers. He believed that a female staff would be more attentive and respectful to female customers. Though not particularly progressive in his political views, Shattuck was ahead of his time in offering pregnancy leave and profit sharing to his employees.

Dave grew up between these opposing models: the rough-and-tumble, male-dominated Irish saloons of Inwood and the genteel, welcoming dining experience offered by Schrafft's. Under his watch, Coogan's would become a hybrid of those influences: an Irish bar that was hospitable to women and children and also a refuge for the working people in the neighborhood—a new category for the taxonomy. As to whether his father's connection to Schrafft's influenced his decision to pursue a career in the hospitality business, Dave scoffed. It was drinking and partying that had drawn him to bars, simple as that.

When he finished his freshman year at Fordham, Dave took twelve months off to work for Volunteers in Service to America (VISTA), a forerunner of AmeriCorps. He wound up in Milwaukee, driving a bookmobile and delivering books to the children of migrant laborers who worked in the city's leather-tanning factories. Returning to New York in the summer of 1969—the summer of Woodstock and the Stonewall riots—Dave needed work. On the student placement board at Fordham, he found a position advertised at the rate of $2.50 per hour, nearly a dollar more than the minimum wage. The employer was Your Father's Mustache, a "banjo bistro" in Greenwich Village, part of a chain of kitschy theme restaurants that featured employees in straw boaters, faux Tiffany lamps, and nightly performances by Dixieland jazz bands. Dave was a waiter, a doorman, a roving floorman—an enforcer who kept things in line. He was good at these jobs. By the time the holidays rolled around, he'd earned the trust of the manager, Ed Flint. "I want to take a couple of days off," Flint said to Dave. "Do you think you can handle it?" He'd been on the job three months.

The local alumni of Dayton University had selected that Monday for their annual reunion at Your Father's Mustache. There was a line down the block. The Daytonians were drinking the place dry. Dave didn't want to find out what would happen if they ran out of beer. He went to the office and called Ronnie Sader, the chain's comptroller. "We've got six kegs of beer left. The next scheduled beer delivery isn't until tomorrow. What do I do?" Sader said, "Call up Schlitz and tell them you need an emergency delivery of twenty kegs of beer right now, or all their equipment will be on the street in the morning." Dave got on the horn and made the threat. The beer came and the day was saved. He'd found his calling. There was no way he was going back to college.

One afternoon in the late 1970s, Dave, who was then living in Greenwich Village, went uptown to take his mother out for lunch. After seeing her home, he dropped into Mc-Sherry's, a pocket-sized bar near the subway entrance on Broadway and 207th Street. Joey McFadden was there, with a crowd of friends. He had just received his payout from the lawsuit he'd filed against the Mets and Rheingold, depositing the check that very morning. Joey was ecstatic. He had a roll of bills in his pocket, and he was buying rounds. Dave joined in the celebration. Neither of them knew it yet, but Joey's settlement was going to fund the bar that would one day become Dave's livelihood.

CHAPTER SEVEN

Managing

People in Washington Heights tended to think of Inwood as the northern section of their neighborhood, while people in Inwood tended to regard Washington Heights as a different neighborhood altogether. During Dave's school years, the rivalry between the two was so fierce that, on a bus back from a swim meet downtown, he and his classmates had chanted "Fuck the Heights! Fuck the Heights!" as they passed through the 160s and 170s. Washington Heights may have been familiar to Dave, but it wasn't home turf. And though he'd been to Coogan's a few times as a customer, once he started working there, in June of 1987, he needed time to get his bearings with both the staff and the neighborhood they served.

His assignment was clear. "My job was to make sure that Sean didn't have to be there. If Sean had to be there, I wasn't doing my job." He spent the first few weeks sampling a range of duties. He worked at the service bar, an entry-level position pouring drinks for customers in the dining room (and receiving no tips). He worked at the main bar. He greeted and seated customers at the front of house. He spent time in the basement office with Sean, going over

Dave Hunt in the service bar.

inventory, scheduling, and invoices. Dave also shadowed Armstrong and found his treatment of the saloon's customers to be brusque at best. On the days when there was a line out the door for lunch, people sometimes complained about the wait. Armstrong's response, Dave recalled, was that if they didn't like it, they should go someplace else. It was not a service model Dave would follow.

He got to know the rest of the staff. There were the bartenders, Chris Budos and Eddie O'Neill, and a squad of Irish waitresses: Eileen, Anne, and Paula. The kitchen was run by chef Jimmy Callahan, who was soon to be replaced by Miguel de la Cruz, an indomitable presence on the line. Before coming to Coogan's, de la Cruz had worked as a cook at Sea Fare of the Aegean, one of the city's finest seafood restaurants. The menu at Coogan's expanded over time to showcase his skills with fish and shellfish. There was an Indian service bartender named Davinder, whom Sean had dubbed "Vinny." And there was Frankie Reyes, the Dominican service bartender, a friendly neighborhood kid who seemed to remember everyone's name after meeting them for the first time. (Relegating staff of color to behind-the-scenes roles in the kitchen and the service bar was in keeping with the Irish saloon tradition. That dynamic would change over time at Coogan's.)

Dave quickly realized that managing Coogan's was going to be more arduous and frenetic than bartending at Jimmy Day's. Lunchtimes were especially wild. People flooded into the restaurant from the medical center. The dining room and the function room were thronged. To accommodate the construction crews working on the Milstein Hospital Building, a sandwich station was set up in a DJ booth in a corner of the barroom. Customers got a sandwich and then helped themselves to macaroni salad or potato salad. Glasses of beer were put on the bar for self-service and snatched up as soon as they were filled. No individual orders were taken. The cost for such a lunch was $3.95. It was a high-turnover hospitality model: get them in; get them fed; get them out.

Managing meant having a hand in everything that went on: bussing tables; expediting kitchen orders; taking reservations; running up and down the stairs to fetch supplies; tapping a new keg; filling a staffing shortage. Your Father's Mustache had taught Dave the importance of systems, and sometimes, to keep the systems at Coogan's moving, he threw a strategically timed temper tantrum in front of an indolent waiter or lackadaisical cook. He called it "creative tension." Though now a teetotaler, Dave found that this new job still took a toll on his family life. He was so exhausted by the time he got home from his shifts at Coogan's that he barely had the energy to engage with his wife and children. His young daughter Kate was resentful of his long hours and came to think of Coogan's as being akin to "another woman" in her father's life.

Coogan's, unlike Jimmy Day's, was not a celebrity hangout, but nevertheless certain regulars started to emerge from the crowd of daily customers. In the mornings, as soon as they opened their doors, a crossing guard named Peggy Cain came bustling in from her post on 173rd and Broadway. "Hello, Princess!" she'd say to the female staff as she made her way to the bar, where she sat, in uniform, drinking until the start of her afternoon shift. Peggy the Crossing Guard (as she was known) was a fixture at Coogan's, sometimes returning in the evenings with her elderly father for dinner. When her father passed away, Dave helped her organize the piles of Veterans Affairs paperwork he left behind.

The local councilman, Stanley Michels, came to Coogan's so often that people joked he must be a silent partner in the business. Bearded and bespectacled, Michels was known for championing environmental causes; in December of 1987, he'd sponsored the act that required designated "no smoking" areas in all enclosed public spaces in the city. As frequently as Michels was in Coogan's, his chief of staff, Steve Simon, was there even more often. Simon, a member of the Audubon Democratic Club, had walked into the saloon the first week it was open and taken an immediate liking to the place. Figuratively, he never left. A workaholic bachelor, Simon dined there three or four times a week, exchanging gossip, brokering deals, and generally keeping his finger on the pulse of the neighborhood. A spot like Coogan's, where the day's work could be carried on after hours, was a godsend for lifers in nonprofits and local government like him.

Coach Dave Crenshaw's mother, Gwen, also became a regular. "She would stop in either by herself or with her husband, Richard," Dave Hunt recalled. "She was stern, but you knew right away that this was a community activist who was to be respected and dealt with accordingly."

In the evenings, when the after-work crowd had gone home, cops from the 34th Precinct and the Manhattan North Narcotics Bureau came in at the end of their shifts and set up camp at the bar. One of those officers, John Roe, said, "It was like we'd found a home. There were about eight of us that used to hang out there every night." There were other members of the squad who came less frequently to Coogan's, including an undercover cop named Chris Hoban, who often wore a Hotel California jacket. Roe fondly recalled the service he and his partners received. "They treated us like kings." He took a particular shine to Frankie Reyes, the Dominican service bartender. "He was like our maître d'."

With drug sales rampant in the neighborhood, the narcotics team was busy. The buy-and-bust operations they used to collar drug dealers were dangerous and sometimes violent. Stress from the job often found its release at Coogan's, in laughter and joking and drinking. Some cops felt that they couldn't take workplace traumas home with them. *Your wife's not going to understand. Your kids aren't going to understand. Your friends aren't going to understand. The only people who are going to understand are here at Coogan's.* And so, the bar became an impromptu mental health clinic for some of its regulars. That "therapy" could take the form of intense conversation or goofing off. Roe and another officer, Chris Power, would sometimes do magic tricks with scarves to entertain their fellow cops—and any other customers who happened to be nearby.

Dave admired the work that these officers did. They were also familiar to him. Irish neighborhoods like Inwood produced a bevy of cops as well as bartenders. One night there was a new face among the officers at the bar. Dave introduced himself. "I don't think we've met. I'm Dave Hunt."

"I'm Brian Hunt."

"Really? Hunt isn't a very common Irish name. Where are your people from?"

"Roscommon."

"That's where my family's from!" Dave then began to ask detailed questions about Brian's family and their ties to that county in the center of Ireland. Brian, unable to answer, said, "Hold on, let me call my dad."

He went to the pay phone and dialed his parents at home. His mother answered and summoned Brian's father, a retired cop, who came begrudgingly to the line. "Where are you? Is everything OK?"

"I'm at a bar in Washington Heights."

"Jesus, what are you doing up there after hours?"

"Look, one of the managers here, his name is Hunt. His family's from Roscommon."

"Is that so," his father said, and then began to ask Brian a series of detailed questions about Dave that Brian couldn't answer.

"Why don't I just put the two of you on together," Brian finally said. He went back up to the bar and said to Dave, "My dad's on the phone. Would you mind talking to him?"

Dave grabbed the handset and got into an animated

conversation with Brian's father. After some minutes, he hung up the phone and returned, shouting at the bartender: "Inkeep! A round of drinks for my Irish cousin and his friends."

Another part of Dave's job was supervising large parties. One of the first was a wedding reception in the back room, which had been booked before he started. Looking over the worksheet for the reservation, Dave guessed that Sean and Armstrong had been only too happy to dump this event on him. "They knew it was going to be a shitshow," he said. The reception was for seventy-five people, which exceeded the seating capacity for the room (seventy-two). The bride and groom also wanted space for a DJ and a dance floor. It was a steamy afternoon in late August. The air-conditioning system couldn't keep up, and the overcrowded space turned into a hotbox. By the end of the reception, the bride's makeup was running down her face.

More successful was a party that city councilman Stanley Michels and some neighborhood residents threw for Steve Simon to celebrate Simon's tenth anniversary on Michels's staff. Before Coogan's opened, there had been no comparable space in the neighborhood to hold private gatherings or parties. Local political clubs were forced to convene in apartments or houses of worship.

More than a hundred people were invited to the celebration, filling the main dining room, drawing politicos from down the block and relatives from as far away as Florida. There were toasts and roasts, tributes from Monsignor Thomas Leonard and members of the community board. Michels presented Simon with a desktop nameplate that read MAYOR OF WASHINGTON HEIGHTS. Dave, watching from the corner of the room, saw one of the neighborhood's social and political networks come to life.

They needed a place to connect. Here was an opportunity to expand the bar's mission beyond the hospital and the police. It could become a community space.

CHAPTER EIGHT

∾

One of the Toughest Days

Four months after Dave had joined the staff, a cabdriver named Ray Carroll and his wife, Elizabeth Noback, went to Coogan's for dinner. Carroll was tall and clean-shaven; Noback, diminutive and dark haired. They lived on Haven Avenue, a few blocks away, and dined regularly at the restaurant. They'd gotten to know Sean, who was on duty that night. Another owner, Kevin Kiernan, was also there.

Sean greeted Carroll and Noback warmly and chatted with them while they ate. Near the end of their meal, as they were sipping Irish coffees, Carroll, who suffered from epilepsy, felt the first signs of an oncoming seizure. His body stiffened and his face began to twitch. Sean and Noback helped him into the back room. The twitches came more violently. He took shallow, panting breaths and appeared to lose consciousness. Carroll was having a grand mal seizure—causing him to experience a series of convulsions. As a 911 call was placed, Sean got on top of Carroll to prevent him from harming himself. By the time the paramedics arrived, the worst of the seizure seemed to have subsided, and Carroll had regained consciousness. As is often the case for 911 calls—especially in heavily policed neighborhoods—cops arrived with the medics. Soon after that, all hell broke loose in the back room.

It's difficult to fully reconstruct what transpired that night, but by the end of it, both Carroll and Sean had been arrested: Carroll for assaulting a police officer; Sean for second-degree assault, possession of cocaine, and resisting arrest. A brief article published a day later in the *Daily News* highlighted the police brutality observed by witnesses on the scene, quoting one who said that the cops—ten by his count—ran "right over to the epileptic and the other guy and began beating on them." Carroll told the reporter, "All I wanted to do was finish my seizure and go home, and all the police wanted to do was use me and the other man for a punching bag." According to the article, EMS records noted that Carroll was "violent and abusive," and a police spokesman said that the cops took "appropriate action under the unusual circumstances."

Recalling that night many years later, Sean said that there had been a dispute with the paramedics over whether Carroll should be taken to the hospital. Noback wanted her husband to be examined by a doctor, but EMS, citing his improved condition, refused. That disagreement, according to Sean, escalated into a physical confrontation with the police, at the end of which Sean found himself bleeding from the head. The officers escorted him and Carroll over to the Columbia-Presbyterian emergency room. Once Sean's head was stitched up, they transported him to the 34th Precinct and put him in a holding cell. In the morning, he was taken downtown to the Manhattan Detention Complex. As for Carroll, according to the *Daily News*, police "reversed" his arrest after he'd spent the night handcuffed to a hospital gurney.

Dave was unaware of all of this until the next morning when he arrived at work and read an incident report Kiernan had left for him. He regretted that Kiernan had not called him at home the night before and felt that he might have been able to negotiate a better outcome if he'd gotten to the bar in time. In Dave's mind, the violent response from the officer, even if unjustified, was to be expected. In those days, according to Dave, "if you touched a cop, you were going to get a beating." His immediate concern, however, was that the police might return with a search warrant and toss the place. He told everyone on staff to go to their lockers and get rid of any illegal substances and was surprised by how many of them ran down to the basement.

The police did not come back that morning, but the 34th Precinct wouldn't let go of the incident. The precinct's commander reportedly forbade his officers from patronizing the bar. Not all of them complied with this ban, and Coogan's remained a hangout for plenty of cops from other precincts and commands.

After spending the weekend behind bars, Sean had his day in court and was released on six months' probation. He returned to work with a newfound dislike for the police, which was a problem given how many cops drank there. There were other problems too: Sean's arrest only worsened the growing tensions between him and his fellow owners.

Tensions also remained high out on the streets of Upper Manhattan over the coming year. A little after 7:00 p.m. on the evening of Tuesday, October 18, 1988, two undercover police officers, Chris Hoban (he of the Hotel California jacket) and Michael Jermyn, entered an apartment building in Morningside Heights, a neighborhood just below Harlem. Two men met the officers at the front entrance and led them up to an apartment where a third man waited. Hoban had bought cocaine from these men a week earlier and he was back with a search warrant to purchase more and to apprehend them. An arrest team waited outside. But the transaction hit a snag when Hoban and Jermyn refused—per NYPD protocol—to sample the merchandise. Suspicious, the dealers shouted, "Sniff, sniff! Policia! Policia!" Hoban declined, saying that the coke was for his girlfriend and continued counting out the money to pay them. One of the sellers, Bienvenido Castillo, put a gun to Hoban's head and suggested he reconsider.

Hoban again refused.

The officers were then ordered to put their hands up so they could be searched. The dealers found nothing on Hoban, but when they frisked Jermyn, they found his service revolver in his waistband. Hoban tried to knock Castillo's gun out of his hand. A brawl and a shootout ensued in the close confines of the apartment and Hoban was shot twice, in the head and chest. One of the dealers, Manuel LaRosa, was also shot. The arrest team apprehended the third dealer as he tried to leave the building, but Castillo managed to escape into the streets, prompting an intense manhunt across Northern Manhattan. It would be nine days before the FBI arrested him in Puerto Rico. Both Hoban and LaRosa died on the scene from their gunshot wounds.

Later that same night, as the hunt for Castillo intensified, two uniformed officers, Michael Buczek and Joseph Barbato, responded to a 911 call from a woman on 161st Street near Broadway suffering from stomach pains. In the building's lobby, the cops encountered the arriving EMS technicians. One of them asked Buczek how Chris Hoban was doing. "Not so good," responded Buczek.

Just then, three men came down the stairs, walked past the cops, and hastily exited the lobby. One of them was carrying a bulky black bag. The officers followed the men out onto the street and ordered them to stop. Instead, they fled toward Broadway. The officers pursued. Rounding the corner, they now saw only two men. Buczek caught up with one of them, Pablo Almonte Lluberes, and grabbed his jacket, but he kept running. The second man, Daniel Mirambeaux, turned and fired his gun, hitting Buczek in the chest. Barbato dove to the ground, and shot four times in the direction of the men, before running back to check on his partner. Lluberes and Mirambeaux turned the corner and got into a livery cab commandeered by Jose Fernandez, the third man, who had escaped earlier with the black bag. In the bedlam of it all, the contents of the black bag fell onto the street: three kilos of cocaine that they had just stolen from an apartment in the building on 161st Street. Police broadened the manhunt, stopping traffic on the West Side Highway and the George Washington Bridge and staking out departure terminals at JFK, but all three men managed to escape to the Dominican Republic.

Buczek was taken to Columbia-Presbyterian Hospital, where he died from his wounds.

A few blocks away at Coogan's, Dave heard the sirens and observed the rush of activity around the hospital—news vans, police cars, curious bystanders. Later, the owners of Coogan's developed a "cop-shot protocol," keeping additional workers on call to come in on short notice to deal with the sharp increase in business that these incidents generated. That night, however, they had to scramble as newspaper journalists, television crews, and radio reporters rushed in, along with cops who came to the hospital to give blood and check up on their brethren, and the politicians who arrived with their entourages ready to give statements.

News about Chris Hoban and Michael Buczek filtered into the bar through television and radio reports, chatter among the customers, and a series of urgent phone calls. While Hoban was not a nightly regular, he'd been to Coogan's often enough that his death felt close to home. As the evening wore on, members of Hoban's team, including Roe, gathered at the bar, forming a knot of shock and grief, rehashing the night's events.

Dave welcomed them and gave them their space, telling the staff to keep a respectful distance and approach only when needed. Frankie Reyes, the service bartender on duty that night, came to Dave and said he wanted to go and offer his condolences to the cops. Frankie was their maître d', after all. Dave was hesitant. He loved that Frankie wanted to make this gesture, but he was worried that the police might not be receptive on a night when two of their fellow officers had been killed, possibly by Dominicans.

"I don't know, Frankie. I'm not sure they would welcome it," Dave said.

But Frankie insisted. "I know Chris. I know these guys. I've got to say something." Dave assented and watched as Frankie approached the officers. One by one, the cops accepted Reyes's handshakes and embraces, hugging him back and fighting away tears.

That Tuesday was the first time in a decade that two New York City police officers had been shot and killed on the same day. Adriano Espaillat, who was the president of the

34th Precinct Community Council that year, remembers going to a ribbon cutting for the Salomé Ureña School in Inwood the next day with the news on the front page of every city paper and foremost in everyone's mind. "2 COPS SHOT DEAD 3 MILES & 3 HOURS APART," blared the *Daily News*. "2 Policemen are Shot and Killed in Separate Manhattan Incidents," reported the *Times*. "It was a horrible morning. One of the toughest days in the city of New York," Espaillat later said. Johnny Moynihan, another young police officer who had joined the service six months after Buczek, remembered a sense of grief descending on the precinct, with "a lot of tears shed."

Beyond the loss of life, there was a renewed awareness of the divide that had so concerned Dave the night before: the mutual distrust that existed between the Dominican community in Upper Manhattan and the predominantly white police force that was charged with protecting them. Law enforcement officers were frustrated by the lack of help they received from the public in thwarting the drug dealers and investigating crimes such as the murders of Hoban and Buczek. Many Dominicans on the other hand justifiably felt that the police were prejudiced against them and unnecessarily aggressive when making stops. (Sean's own experience had taught him how excessive police action could be.) Some in Washington Heights also wondered how the lucrative crack cocaine trade could function so openly without a level of corrupt participation from the police. All of this conflict and apprehension was a local manifestation of the national "War on Drugs" that was declared by the Nixon administration and had been intensified under Reagan's presidency. Drug enforcement policies such as "mandatory minimum" sentencing became a tool of oppression used against racial minorities that led to

increasing prison populations and escalating tensions between police and communities of color around the nation
while also largely failing to curtail the sale of illegal drugs.
Washington Heights was but one of many neighborhoods
where this ongoing confrontation was taking place.

The killings of Michael Buczek and Chris Hoban
would reverberate for a long time in Upper Manhattan.
For some, the night the two officers died drove home the
urgent need to bridge the distance between the community
and the cops who served them. The Buczek family decided
to honor their lost son by forming a charitable foundation
in his name. Michael loved sports; Dominicans love baseball. They thought, Why not create a Little League? And,
to help foster trust between the police and the community,
why not have cops from the local precinct coach the kids?

Michael's father, Ted Buczek, or Mr. B as he was known,
was a World War II veteran who worked as an accountant.
In the months after his son's death, he relentlessly lobbied
those who were involved in the investigation of his son's
murder and the creation of the Little League: detectives, politicians, and civic officials. The owners of Coogan's quickly
embraced the effort and connected the Buczek family to
possible allies in the neighborhood, including Stanley Michels, the community board, and the Parks Department.
Johnny Moynihan, who was Buczek's right-hand man,
later became the league's president.

Six months after Hoban's and Buczek's deaths, the league
opened its debut season at a ragged ballfield in Highbridge
Park. Coogan's was one of the first local businesses to sponsor a team—a team that would carry Chris Hoban's name.
In the years to come, the Little League became a source of
pride in the neighborhood and a model for the use of sports
as a unifying force—a model that Coogan's would later em-

ulate. More than forty kids who played in the Little League have gone on to become police officers. Others have become firefighters, teachers, and nurses. Two former players were drafted by big league teams, but as Mr. B, who passed away in 2010, remarked, the goal of the Police Officer Michael Buczek Little League was not to produce ballplayers, it was to build "major league citizens."

The creation of the Little League has added two special days to the community's calendar. The first is Opening Day in the spring, which features a parade up St. Nicholas Avenue, through the heart of the Dominican business community. Traffic comes to a stop, and people emerge from shops to cheer the procession. At the ballfield in Highbridge Park, there are speeches by politicians, police brass, and community leaders followed by a cookout and a baseball game. And every autumn, after the end of the season, a memorial Mass is held at St. Elizabeth's Church on Wadsworth Avenue to remember the slain officers and to reaffirm the desire for peace and cooperation in Washington Heights. After the Mass, families and close friends of the fallen gather in the back room at Coogan's for lunch.

∽

CHAPTER NINE

Reorganization

While the community around them was working toward finding some common ground on the baseball diamond, the bad blood that had been building between Sean and his partners reached a boiling point. Just weeks after the deaths of Hoban and Buczek, KKS again accused Sean of withholding a fair share of the profits. Sean disagreed, saying Coogan's still had a lot of debt (which was true). He continued to argue that the profit shares were based partly on the amount of work each of the owners contributed, and nobody worked harder than he did. Sean's partners were not satisfied with this answer. They raised questions about Sean's absences and his unpredictable schedule. They mentioned his arrest the prior year. Sean took umbrage. "Go fuck yourselves," he said. "You can't run this place without me!" KKS said they were willing to try. Sean angrily left the bar and drove home in the company car. Later that day his partners, who had a second set of keys, went down to Park Avenue, found the vehicle, and drove it back uptown.

Sean's departure left Dave Hunt in a tight spot. He was Sean's guy. The Monday after the Thanksgiving weekend,

Larry Schwartz called Dave and told him that while he liked Dave's management style and would have been happy to keep him on as manager, the other partners wouldn't allow it. It was a moot point: even if he'd been retained, Dave would have resigned out of loyalty to Sean. A few days later, he received a missive on Coogan's letterhead telling him that "due to a management reorganization in the restaurant, we find it necessary to relieve you of your duties" and that he would be kept on the payroll through the end of the year. Dave had given up a long and stable career at Jimmy Day's to come to Coogan's, and now, barely eighteen months later, he'd been fired. He had a wife, a mortgage, children to feed, and no college degree. What was he going to do?

Though he no longer worked at Coogan's, Sean still owned 40 percent of the business. Once he cooled down, he began to see this latest setback as an opportunity. Every day that passed, he knew, the inexperience of his partners would make their jobs managing the restaurant more difficult—especially now that Dave was also gone. If they'd had the sense to keep Dave, they might have been all right. Sean felt his leverage increasing. He heard through his network of locals and employees that Larry Schwartz, the lynchpin of KKS, was getting frustrated with the situation. Like anyone who's been let go from a job, Sean wanted his absence to be painful for his former partners. He wanted to be *right*. But he had bigger plans in mind than just a triumphant return. He wanted to be rid of KKS, to own the place himself. This was his chance. He called Dave. He was going to try to take over Coogan's. Did Dave want to come in with him?

Dave certainly wanted to be in on the deal, but without an ownership stake, he couldn't afford to play Sean's waiting game. While Sean recruited other investors, Dave drew on his connections, tending bar at a number of Irish saloons around town. One of the first people Sean turned to was his former roommate, Peter Walsh, who had run Pudding's, the bar around the corner from Sean's Park Avenue apartment, and had made an earlier investment in Coogan's. Where Sean saw himself as a man of jokes and punchlines, Peter was a true storyteller and performer. Give him a few cocktails and he'd be up on the bar, leading the room in a sing-along. But Peter was also a go-getter, aggressive and charismatic. Sean liked that about him and wanted those qualities for Coogan's.

❧

CHAPTER TEN

A Poet Walks into a Bar

Plenty of poets have gone broke drinking in New York's saloons, and at least one—Dylan Thomas—famously died after downing too much whiskey in a certain Greenwich Village hostelry. Few, however, have gone into a bar in New York City and emerged with an ownership stake in the establishment, but that is just what happened to Peter Walsh. Peter grew up in Yorkville, on Manhattan's Upper East Side. He graduated from Marist College and served two years in the army during the Vietnam War. He was stationed in Okinawa, Japan, where he was part of a psyops team and wrote for the base newspaper. He also led workshops on improving race relations between Black and white GIs. Improbably, he came across a scholarly journal with Yasuko Stucki's article, *Yeats's Drama and the Nō: A Comparative Study in Dramatic Theories,* in one of the camp latrines and pocketed it. On his way back to the United States after completing his tour of duty, he passed through Dublin and, with dreams of James Joyce and Brendan Behan filling his head, he talked his way into a diploma course in Anglo-Irish literature headed up by the poet and novelist Brendan Kennelly at Trinity College.

Peter's knowledge of the Japanese theater's influence on Yeats's plays was especially persuasive.

In 1975, when he was settled once again in New York, Peter edited and published an anthology of poems by expatriate Americans—*12 Passports and a Stowaway*—that included three of his own poems. One of these, "Yesterday's Tomorrow," deals with the trauma of serving in Vietnam:

> *he'll get home to bang walls*
> *shell-shock shoot his wife*
> *why not? He banged strangers*
> *but t t t t tomorrow's battle*
> *will be yours and mine*

When *12 Passports and a Stowaway* was published, Peter orchestrated a launch event—where else?—in a neighborhood bar, Pudding's on Lexington and 90th. Peter was the only contributor in attendance. Opened in 1966 by Buzzy O'Keeffe, the legendary restaurateur who would go on to be the proprietor of the River Café in Brooklyn and the Water Club in Midtown, Pudding's was then under the stewardship of a man named Denis Kenny.

The book launch was a great drunk-up. Showing an early sign of his nose for business and his gift for promotion, Peter insisted to the crowd that he would not sell single copies of the book. "Nobody reads poetry except the people who write it (and their mothers), so you have to buy a box of books. You can use them as coasters or stocking stuffers, but you've got to buy the box." Prompted by inebriation and exuberance, his well-heeled friends bought every last copy.

This was a surprise to the bar owner, Kenny, who had

Right to left: Denis Kenny, Steve McFadden, Sean Cannon, Peter Walsh, and Pudding's bartender Thomas Von Bischoffshausen at Walsh's book launch in 1975.

expected a modest turnout at best. He was stunned to see these friends of Peter's shedding fifty- and hundred-dollar bills at the bar, giving a huge lift to a sleepy weeknight's business. Watching the young poet count his takings, Kenny asked, "How would you like to become my partner?" Peter looked at the wad of bills in his hand and immediately agreed. He bought into a bar with a book of poetry.

Peter grew up in a railroad flat on East 86th Street, in the Yorkville section of the city, then predominantly German, Jewish, and Irish. (The Marx Brothers and Lou Gehrig had ties to Yorkville. So did Jimmy Cagney, whose tough-guy image and stellar career would come to occupy a totemic place in Peter's imagination.) Peter's father, James J. Walsh, was a liquor taster for Seagram's but otherwise rarely touched alcohol. It was Peter's belief that his father's bland Irish diet—salt and pepper were considered strong flavors in the Walsh household—helped keep his palate clean. Peter's mother was a homemaker who worked part-time at Bloomingdale's and in local dress shops. Clothes were important to her. Peter and his siblings were always well dressed, a sartorial habit that stayed with Peter throughout his life. When he was nine, his mother was taken with the idea of lederhosen and dressed her son in them. Ridiculed by the street kids of Yorkville, the youngster learned to stand up for himself and fight. He would later box, a skill that would serve him well as a bar owner.

The idea of a nine-to-five office job never appealed to Peter. He wanted a career in the arts—acting or singing— but bars, drinking, and partying kept getting in his way. The seed was planted early. At the age of eight, he was dispatched from Yorkville to spend part of the summer with his unmarried aunt Florence at her seaside home in Rockaway, Queens. Soon after his arrival, she taught him to make her nightly cocktail, a Manhattan, straight up, calling instructions to him from her chair in the living room. "Pour some from the brown bottle. A little more. Yes. Now the red bottle. Good. Now stir it. Bring it here, my boy." His reward was a maraschino cherry.

A decade later when he was a college student, Peter spent a pair of summers farther out on Long Island, in the Hamptons. By day he worked for a real estate agent named Ben Stoddard. Nights he hustled singing and performing gigs in the local bars and clubs, including a brief stint as a DJ at Tiana Beach Club.

One afternoon while Peter and Stoddard were in Lyons, a saloon in East Hampton, the bartender collapsed from an apparent heart attack. After the ambulance took the stricken man to the hospital, Stoddard offered Peter's services to his friend, Vinny Lyons.

"Have you ever tended bar before?" Lyons asked.

"Sure, I have," Peter proclaimed, though serving his aunt her nightly drink a decade earlier was the bulk of his experience. He stepped into action, feigning confidence. "What can I get for you?" he asked his first customer.

"Manhattan, straight up," said the man.

Peter's career was built on that very mixture of brazenness, charisma, and uncanny good luck. At Marist, he registered for a junior year abroad in London. Someone at Seagram's gave him a letter of introduction to Dr. Terry James, the Welshman who was the principal conductor of the BBC Light Orchestra. James lived in Earl's Court. When Peter showed up at his door, bleary-eyed from his transatlantic flight, James invited him to take up residence there. That night Peter, in a jacket borrowed from his host, accompanied James to a wedding where the conductor's good friend the actor Richard Harris was also in attendance. Peter couldn't believe his good fortune. One day in and this was already the greatest year abroad imaginable. But when James left for a tour of Germany, Peter pushed his luck by renting out rooms in the conductor's flat to three female students from University College. Three weeks later, when James returned earlier than expected from his tour, he found a roaring party full of drunken youngsters taking place in his home. He kicked them all out, including Peter.

The next day, Peter was drinking in the Kings Head in Earl's Court when he looked up from his pint and saw James seated on the other side of the pub. James summoned him. Peter apologized and in short order they were having

a merry time. James decided he would allow Peter to re-
sume living with him. "But no more parties!" the older man
warned. It turned out that James's social life circumvented
the need to throw parties. Before long, the visiting student
from New York was knocking back peach martinis at the
Savoy with James and Harris. Harris's good friend Peter
O'Toole sometimes joined them for a night out. Sitting in
a West End pub, watching O'Toole and Harris sing "I'm a
Rover" to an enraptured roomful of punters, Peter had to
ask himself: Who needed college parties when you could
enjoy this caliber of company? He wanted a career full of
such nights.

❧

CHAPTER ELEVEN

Mutual Admiration

When his friend Sean Cannon walked out on KKS, Peter was himself temporarily out of the bar business—save for his small investment in Coogan's. He and Denis Kenny had bought and later sold the building in which Pudding's was located. Two months after the sale, Kenny was diagnosed with brain cancer. Visiting him in the hospital, Peter asked Kenny how he was feeling. Kenny replied, "I don't know, it's the first time I've ever died."

Peter took some of his proceeds from the sale of Pudding's and went on a spree in Europe, staying in expensive hotels and eating in fancy restaurants. When he returned to New York, he got a job as a booker with Hospital Audiences, Inc. (HAI), an arts nonprofit, but he wanted to use the remaining Pudding's cash to buy into another bar. Coogan's seemed like a good option. Periodically, he went up to Washington Heights to collect his payouts and cast an eye over the place. Though Coogan's did good business, he felt that there was something missing. It seemed to lack a soul, a sense of fun and adventure. What it needed was an impresario, someone with a vision and a willingness to experiment. Someone like himself. Once Sean was fired, the other owners rarely seemed to put in an appearance. *Who was in charge?* he wondered. He suspected that funds might be going missing from the till. From his experience at Pudding's, he'd developed a maxim: nobody ever thinks they're stealing from a bar; they merely believe that they are giving themselves the raise they deserve.

Peter knew and liked Dave Hunt. For years, he'd heard about a legendary Greenwich Village bartender who worked at Jimmy Day's. Their paths finally crossed in 1977 on a night when Dave introduced himself by buying a round for the drinkers at Pudding's and dropping a big tip for Peter. On the surface, Dave and Peter might have seemed a less-than-ideal pairing. Peter was artistic, impulsive, at times scattered. Dave was methodical, thorough, and a creature of habit. But they were bound by the shared experience of growing up in New York during the decade after World War II. They had been raised with the largesse and expectations of the New Deal. Unlike Sean, who was mainly focused on his own prosperity, Dave and Peter shared a belief in the promise of New York as an engine of social cohesion and upward mobility. Left-leaning centrists in their politics, they were, above all, institutionalists. Both embraced the idea that the city's major pillars could—and should—be made to work for the benefit of everyone. They admired loyalty, public service, and sacrifice. Cynics might find it corny, but this communitarian view, in which political affiliations were secondary, allowed them to embrace people of widely differing stances. It would be foundational to the way they'd do business together. They retained an old-fashioned reverence for the American Dream, not least in part because they thought they were living it: the children of immigrants making their fortunes in the free-enterprise system. Coogan's, if they could swing it, would be their slice of the pie.

The main obstacle to their dream of taking over Coogan's was the reality that Peter, Sean, and Dave did not collectively have enough money to assume the bar's debt and buy out the 60 percent of the business owned by Kennedy, Kiernan, and Schwartz. They would need additional partners. Peter's older brother, Vincent, a commercial insurance broker, was willing to be an investor and an owner, but he wanted nothing to do with the day-to-day running of the bar. Dave provided a fifth partner, his accountant and New Jersey neighbor, Garry McAllister. McAllister's condition for joining was that he would assume accounting duties for the bar, a demand that gave the other partners pause. But, in the end, they needed Garry's cash and relented.

Meanwhile, KKS had indeed grown frustrated by the daily hassles of running the bar and restaurant. They were ready to sell. Saul Victor negotiated the deal and, in the late spring of 1990, Sean Cannon, Dave Hunt, Peter Walsh, Vincent Walsh, and Garry McAllister took over Coogan's.

On the day that ownership changed hands, Dave, who was concerned that the handoff might provide an opportunity for mischief—or theft—asked Benny Barrerio, "a legitimate tough guy" he knew from Jimmy Day's, for a favor. While Dave, Sean, Peter, and the rest signed papers in Saul Victor's office, Barrerio sat at the bar in Coogan's waiting for the pay phone to ring. A soon as the papers were signed, Dave called. "It's done." Barrerio hung up the phone and told the bartender that he was off duty. Then Barrerio stepped in and held the fort until the new owners arrived. There would be no funny business during the transfer.

When he got uptown, Peter opened the register, and, in

front of staff and customers, counted the cash in the drawer. The total was meaningless; it was the gesture that was important. Anyone planning to steal from the till was put on notice that the new management was watching. Other changes were coming, too. The owners would be a much stronger presence than their predecessors. In the coming weeks, Sean, Peter, and Dave began weeding the staff, bringing in loyal old hands from their previous establishments, making the place their own.

Part Two

COOGAN'S CASTLE

CHAPTER TWELVE

Passing the Word

One day, Sybil Dodson-Lucas went into Coogan's and introduced herself to the owners. Dodson-Lucas had grown up in Harlem, where her family had deep cultural and political roots. She was a staffer on David Dinkins's mayoral campaign, and once Dinkins took office, she worked on a citywide program to bring women and minorities into the construction trades. She wanted to see the same groups in Coogan's. She offered her services to the owners as a front-of-house greeter. Her pitch was simple: "In order to really know this community and get the kind of clientele you need, you need to know who's coming through your door."

Dodson-Lucas saw the part-time job—four hours after work on weeknights—as an extension of her civic duties. Not that it was entirely selfless; her daughter was taking dance lessons at the Alvin Ailey Theater and she needed the extra income for tuition. If Coogan's thrived, she thought, it could be a benefit to the neighborhood. "I would have people passing the word that this was a place where you could come and have a meal and settle concerns in a welcoming setting,"

Dodson-Lucas said. She wanted Coogan's to become "truly diverse, a true reflection of our community."

As they relaunched Coogan's, Sean, Peter, and Dave were only too happy to have someone with Dodson-Lucas's charm, tact, and connections greeting patrons as they entered. Her knowledge of the city's political class proved invaluable to the owners. Dave recalled her helpful way of making introductions, "Oh, David, look who's here! You remember Judge So-and-So from Queens, don't you?" Having her as the evening face of the restaurant signaled to the neighborhood that Coogan's was changing, opening its doors to people who might not have felt welcomed under earlier management—in particular, women and people of color from the neighborhood.

In addition to her job in the Dinkins administration and her part-time gig at Coogan's, Dodson-Lucas was a member of the local community board. Created in 1977 as part of a reform effort to decentralize city government, community boards were intended to connect city services to New York's neighborhoods. Boards also consulted on questions of land use, zoning, transportation, and recreation in addition to issuing liquor licenses, but their power was limited. Prior to the creation of the 311 hotline, the community board was where New Yorkers went to complain about potholes, noise, or a lack of heat. It's also where a number of aspiring politicians started their careers.

Manhattan is subdivided into a dozen community boards; Community Board 12 serves Washington Heights and Inwood. There are fifty volunteer board members, appointed by the borough president for two-year terms without limits. Like any politically appointed body, a community board is susceptible to cronyism, but members are usually selected because of their active roles in the local community. A district manager administers the board, scheduling meetings, setting agendas, brokering peace, and generally pushing board activities forward. CB 12's meetings, which took place three blocks from Coogan's in offices provided by Columbia-Presbyterian, would regularly adjourn to the saloon.

The longstanding district manager of CB 12, Anne Loftus, had died of a heart attack in September of 1989. Her young assistant, Brenda Rosado, assumed the role of acting district manager. Rosado was twenty-three, making her the youngest district manager in New York. Despite her youth, she was shrewd, opinionated, and caring, qualities that helped her deal with the contentious situations that arose at board meetings and in the board offices. One morning a few days after assuming her new position, Rosado was speaking to a police officer, Sergeant Robert Tracy, of the 34th Precinct, who'd come for a meeting of neighborhood agencies. Still grieving her mentor, Rosado asked him if he'd ever met Loftus. "Yes," he replied. "To be honest, I found her a little stiff." Rosado told the officer his comment was insensitive. "Calm down," Tracy replied. "I was the responding officer the night of her death. That was the first time I ever saw her." It was an early introduction to Tracy's gallows humor.

Rosado, who had an overprotective boyfriend and rarely drank, almost never went out after work. But one evening she was invited to a ribbon cutting for a new location of the Office of Victim Services on Fort Washington Avenue. As the reception wound down, some friends suggested they go to Coogan's for a drink. Her companions were surprised that Rosado wasn't familiar with the saloon.

The whole neighborhood appeared to be inside Coogan's that night. Crowded and lively, it felt safe and comfortable. The women Rosado had come with dispersed, connecting with others at the bar. Everyone seemed to be having a good time; everyone seemed to know each other; and nobody was giving her a second glance. Was this party happening here every night without her? How had she never been to Coogan's before? She felt drawn into the mix. Not being a drinker, she wasn't sure what to order, so she asked for a beer—any beer. It was the first of many she'd have at Coogan's.

One of Rosado's responsibilities as district manager was to preside over a monthly meeting of representatives from all of the major city agencies in the neighborhoods. At the 34th Precinct, the responsibility for attending was distributed among the sergeants, including Robert Tracy, the officer who'd made the morbid joke about Loftus. Tracy had taken a liking to the young district manager. He went back to his commanding officer and said that, in the interests of continuity, he was going to be "a team player" and keep attending these monthly meetings, sparing the other sergeants the drudgery. The news was met with bemused incredulity from Tracy's fellow officers who were more than happy to be relieved of this duty.

Tracy was in charge of the Community Patrol Officer Program (CPOP) for Washington Heights and Inwood, supervising a squad of twelve officers, each of whom was responsible for a sector of the neighborhoods. CPOP officers were charged with developing relationships with the residents of their sectors by attending the meetings of block associations and cultivating other partnerships in order to build communication and trust between the community and the police. Tracy's regular attendance at CB 12 meetings was part of this effort.

After one such meeting, a colleague invited him to Coogan's for a drink. Tracy went back to the station house, changed into civilian clothes, and headed to the saloon. There, to his surprise, he found Rosado at the bar with her friends. He approached her and offered to buy her a drink. Thus began the courtship between the Irish American police sergeant and the Puerto Rican district manager.

By then, Rosado had broken up with her controlling boyfriend and moved into an apartment on Wadsworth Avenue, in the northern part of the Heights, with Ivy Fairchild and another friend, Raquel Cepeda. Fairchild was steeped in the politics of Northern Manhattan. She had worked for numerous local elected officials and had recently become the director of community affairs for Columbia University's medical campus.

She assumed that post at a moment when Dominican politicians—Luna, Espaillat, Linares—were beginning to push their way into positions of power in Upper Manhattan. Appointing a Dominican woman to head community relations showed the university's recognition of the changes that were taking place in the neighborhood. Fairchild called on Columbia to be more attentive and responsive to the needs of the community—to be a better local stakeholder. Fairchild also embraced the role of mentor to a younger generation of neighborhood women. She collaborated with activist Al Kurland to form a not-for-profit girls' empowerment group called the Ivy League. Eva Matos, who grew up in the Heights and worked as Fairchild's assistant, recalled her boss's fearlessness and self-confidence,

Ivy Fairchild dancing at Coogan's.

especially on occasions when she was dealing with a roomful of powerful men. Matos, who'd never had a woman of
color as her boss before, thought, "If Ivy can do that, then
so can I."

Fairchild soon realized that Coogan's was the perfect
conduit between the university and the neighborhood. It
was seen as neutral ground, an easier setting than her office for certain kinds of dealmaking.

For their part, the owners of Coogan's embraced the
subtle power that women such as Dodson-Lucas, Rosado,
and Fairchild wielded in the neighborhood. Here was a
chance to welcome a new section of the community into
their saloon. They cultivated those relationships, which,
over time, became friendships. Before long, if business was
slow at the bar, Dave would call Rosado and Fairchild
at home and say, "It's too quiet here. Why aren't you at
Coogan's?" "We're home in our pajamas, Dave," Fairchild

would reply. "Well, put on some clothes because I'm coming to pick you up!" He'd hop into his car and drive up to their apartment on Wadsworth Avenue to taxi them back to Coogan's so they could liven the place up.

CHAPTER THIRTEEN

こう

Eyes on the Street

While Coogan's was becoming more integrated, the neighborhood outside its doors remained on edge. About six months before the new owners took over the bar, an Immigration and Naturalization Service agent named Joseph Occhipinti launched a task force known as Project Bodega, targeting Dominican-owned delis and grocery stores that he suspected of hiring undocumented immigrants and serving as money-laundering fronts for drug cartels. Occhipinti and his team raided fifty-six bodegas and other businesses, later claiming that their owners were connected to an operation that "cleaned" as much as $500 million annually in proceeds from drug sales. He seized guns, drugs, and stacks of cash and made thirty-nine arrests that resulted in twenty-five convictions and led to forty-three deportations. The aggression of his methods outraged many in the Washington Heights community who experienced Project Bodega as a reign of terror intended to humiliate and intimidate them. Community leaders alleged that the raids aimed to sabotage the 1990 census, resulting in an undercount of the Dominican population, which in turn reduced the funding for essential services in Upper Manhattan.

The controversy over the raids spilled into city, state, and eventually national politics. In April of 1990, the newly elected mayor, David Dinkins, denounced Project Bodega on the steps of City Hall in front of a demonstration organized by the Federation of Dominican Merchants and Industrialists. Dinkins had won 70 percent of the city's Hispanic vote, which had helped him secure a narrow victory over his Republican rival, Rudy Giuliani. The following year, a grand jury in New York indicted Occhipinti on twenty-five counts of conspiracy, civil rights violations, embezzlement, and making false statements. He was found guilty of seventeen of the civil rights counts and sentenced to thirty-seven months in prison. In the end, Occhipinti served only a fraction of that time. President George H. W. Bush commuted his sentence just before leaving the White House in January 1993.

To some residents of Washington Heights, the commutation was proof that law enforcement would never be held fully accountable for its excesses. But in the eyes of those trying to police the neighborhood, the prosecution of Occhipinti by the federal government was seen as a boon to drug dealers and money launderers. If the raids had been intended to reduce violent crime in the neighborhood, they failed. In 1990, the 34th Precinct posted the third highest homicide total in the city—133 murders, and also thousands of burglaries, robberies, and car thefts.

With such turmoil taking place outside their doors, safety became a fundamental concern for the owners of Coogan's. Because there were so few safe public places in the neighborhood, people who found peace and security at their restaurant were likely to return. "Once people feel safe," said Peter Walsh, "they can make room for joy." To provide room for joy, the owners became custodians of safety. All three men subscribed to writer and urbanist Jane Jacobs's notion that shopkeepers and small business owners play an irreplaceable role in keeping the neighborhood peace as "streetwatchers" and "sidewalk guardians." And it didn't take long for Sean, Peter, and Dave to become what Jacobs called "public characters": eyes on the street who were widely recognized as reliable sources of local information connected to a broader network of similar neighborhood figures.

As they assumed control of Coogan's, the owners took a series of steps to ensure their customers would feel safe. Every morning the publicans, or a member of the staff, conducted an inspection of the bar's exterior, looking for crack vials, litter, urine, feces, blood, graffiti, or shattered glass. The bodily fluids were scrubbed away. The glazier was summoned to replace any damaged panes. Before they opened for business, all tags were covered up with a cheap can of paint and brush kept at the ready.

Similarly, the bar's owners rebuffed any attempts by street vendors to set up in front of Coogan's. As the vendors were unfolding their tables and unpacking their wares, Dave would go out and stop them before they could get comfortable. "Sorry, fellas, today's the day we wash the sidewalks." He'd return with a hose and begin spraying the pavement. The vendors soon discovered that *every day* was the day the sidewalks outside Coogan's were hosed down. Eventually the pavements were watered every two hours. The rights of the vendors, who were a part of Washington Heights's distinctive street culture, were the source of ongoing debate in Upper Manhattan, the subject of editorials and community board meetings. Peter saw street vendors as competitors who did not invest in the neighborhood the way that small businesses did. He argued that having vendors in front of their doors disrupted the flow of pedestrians, detracting from the bar's walk-up business. Not everyone agreed. Advocates such as the Street Vendor Project have argued that street vending complements brick-and-mortar establishments, while also providing employment and essential goods to neighborhood residents at affordable prices.

Equal attention was given to safety inside their hostelry. For Dodson-Lucas, it began with establishing clear boundaries around the way people acted. "As long as you behaved yourself, you were welcome," she said. While some other bars in the neighborhood were known as drug spots or gambling dens, the owners of Coogan's actively deterred those activities on their premises. They became adept at weeding out belligerent or troublemaking patrons, developing a kind of sixth sense for an impending eruption of violence. They followed patrons into the bathrooms if they suspected drugs were about to be sold. "One person to a stall!" was the edict. Peter developed a technique for moving potential brawlers out of the bar. He'd place himself in front of the troublesome patron and engage them in conversation, but pretend he couldn't hear what the patron was saying. "I'm sorry, what was that? What did you say?" As he kept this string of questions going, he'd slowly back toward the door until he could shove the frustrated individual out onto the pavement. They also hired a Presbyterian Hospital security sergeant named Joe Belton—Big Joe—to be their evening doorman. The fact that many customers thought Belton bore a striking resemblance to heavyweight champ Evander Holyfield only enhanced his intimidating presence. Some approaching troublemakers, seeing Belton at the door, simply turned around and walked away.

There were other, less obvious ways to create a safe environment. Dave and Sean carefully curated and priced the menu and drink selections to discourage those looking for a cheap night out. "If you've only got $20 to get shitfaced on Saturday, I don't want you in my bar," said Dave Hunt. "Coogan's became the working person's bar," recalled Dave Crenshaw, who himself became a more regular visitor after the change in ownership. "Their prices were a little bit higher, which was good because that meant that working people were coming. It meant that your girl could go to the bathroom, and you didn't have to worry about her. It wasn't like that in the other places [uptown]."

As a result of these efforts on the part of ownership, a mood of de-escalation prevailed among those who came to Coogan's. Police detective John Bourges recalled drinking in plain clothes at the bar one evening with his partner Gil Ortiz. Two men next to them got into a heated argument, exacerbated no doubt by the large amount of alcohol they had consumed. One of the men jumped off his stool and began shouting. "Oh yeah? Fuck you! I'm going to kill you!" He reached into his jacket pocket for a concealed weapon, but the blade—a butterfly knife—had fallen to the floor. Ortiz quietly picked it up, holding the knife out of sight as the argument quelled and the two men went back to drinking. Then he surreptitiously handed the knife to a bartender, who stashed it away safely. "We could have arrested that guy," Bourges said. "But we didn't want to make a scene. Everyone was having a good time."

There were nights at Coogan's when all those who gathered inside its walls conspired to create an alternate universe

Holiday party at Coogan's, 1990s.

to the quotidian and dangerous world out on the streets of Washington Heights. Outside, there was crime, suffering, danger, anxiety, and the cold shoulder of a bigoted country. Inside, there was comradeship, joy, and an atmosphere where you could let your guard down. You came up the stairs from the graffiti-strewn subway; you disembarked from a crowded bus rank with body odor and the smell of a day-old egg salad sandwich someone had forgotten in their briefcase; you hustled up the block from your job at the hospital. You passed through those black doors and left your troubles behind. You entered the sanctified space of warm greetings, inebriation, laughter, music, and storytelling. And you didn't want to leave.

External validation of the owners' efforts to provide a safe environment came with the arrival of a new police commander at the 34th Precinct—Nicholas Estavillo, a former Marine who was born in Puerto Rico and spoke Spanish. Community policing was a priority for Estavillo, who advocated for the hiring of more nonwhite officers. Soon after his arrival in Northern Manhattan, Estavillo began visiting large institutions in the precinct: Yeshiva University, the Nagle Avenue Y, Columbia-Presbyterian, as well as the area's houses of worship. In the course of these orientation meetings, he kept hearing that a particular bar on Broadway was a force for good. Estavillo was skeptical. He knew about the arrest of one of the bar's owners and that the precinct's officers had been discouraged from going there. And yet, hospital administrators, priests, and politicians told him that this bar was vital to the neighborhood. His curiosity was piqued. He began visiting Coogan's after work, changing into civilian clothes and walking from the precinct house on 183rd and Broadway to 169th Street, taking in the street life on his way south. Domino players and vendors. And drug dealing, yes, but what struck him the most was the noise: the shouting, the music that shook the bones in your body, the endless cacophony of car horns.

All of that racket and tumult was left behind once you passed through the doors of Coogan's. He saw immediately that the priests and politicians had been right. The bar was a kind of sanctuary. You felt your blood pressure drop when you came in. The owners were doing something right. He looked into the arrest history and other police data and, aside from the incident with Sean, found little of concern. Not only did he lift the ban on Coogan's, but he introduced himself to the owners. And soon after that, he began holding regular meetings with his lieutenants in the back room. He'd been looking for someplace away from the precinct house to meet with them, a place where they could get comfortable and speak freely, without fear of being overheard. Coogan's was such a place, safe and welcoming. The bar's owners were delighted to have Estavillo's business and thrilled to see the ban on their establishment finally removed.

❦

CHAPTER FOURTEEN

Artsy-Fartsy

As part of his role as a neighborhood public character and streetwatcher, Peter liked to stand in the doorway of Coogan's and take in the scene, greeting passersby, exchanging jokes, keeping an eye on their stretch of Broadway. One afternoon, he noticed a man walking by with a large portfolio under his arm. "Hey, show me your work!" Peter called out to him. The man, who was in his forties, with short-cropped hair, stopped and approached the saloonkeeper, opening the portfolio to reveal a cache of drawings and paintings. The style was lushly realistic and skillfully drawn—somewhere between Norman Rockwell and Edward Hopper. Among the sheaf of drawings and paintings were scenes of city life: people hanging out in front of bodegas, kids running in the street and splashing in the streams of a fire hydrant. They vibrated with color and joie de vivre. Peter introduced himself. "How would you like to do an exhibition in the new Coogan's Art Gallery of Washington Heights?" (He'd made up the name on the spot.)

The artist's name was Samuel Garcia. He was born in

Puerto Rico and grew up on his parents' farm. In 1953, when he was eight, the family relocated to Washington Heights. For Garcia, that was an idyllic time and one that he frequently evoked in his work: stickball games, soap-box derbies, doo-wop singers on the corners, kids on roller skates lining up for the Good Humor truck. Garcia also produced nostalgic landscapes and cityscapes of his native Puerto Rico: markets, beaches, horse-drawn wagons, and tin-roofed shacks. Like Peter, he had served in the army—in his case, in Germany—and, like Peter, he had serious artistic ambitions. When Peter called out to him from Coogan's doorway, Garcia was on his way to a gallery where his work was to be shown. The gallery was a joint project of Columbia-Presbyterian Hospital, Community Board 12, and Arts Interaction, the Washington Heights & Inwood Council for the Arts. Garcia was surprised and delighted by Peter's offer and replied that there were many talented artists in Washington Heights. "Would you be interested in displaying their work as well?"

Peter said he would.

"Then you should speak to my wife, Carmen," said Garcia. "She works at Presbyterian Hospital and is a board member of Arts Interaction. And you should also talk to Joe Hintersteiner. He's the gallery's curator and an artist himself." Hintersteiner, a watercolorist, had emigrated from Austria to New York in 1937, part of the wave of German-speaking Jews fleeing the rise of Hitler. For decades, he had been active in promoting the arts in Upper Manhattan.

In short order, Carmen Garcia came to Coogan's and met with Peter. They agreed that each month a different lo-cal artist would display their work in the back room, which quickly became known as the Gallery Room. Hintersteiner selected and organized the shows, hanging the paintings himself. A frail, slender man in his mid-seventies, he drew a concerned crowd of Coogan's waitstaff every time he ascended a ladder to mount a work of art.

The collaboration between Coogan's and Arts Interaction led to an influx of artists to the bar—exactly what Peter had hoped for. Every Friday a group of them convened at what they called "the Artsy-Fartsy Table" to commiserate and exchange ideas. Among the regulars were the Garcias, Hintersteiner and his wife, Marguerite, Leo Glueckselig (another refugee from the Nazis), and a younger artist named Matthew Spatz. The artists collaborated on seasonal works for the bar, including a series of "Monster Panels" for Halloween, which depicted habitués of Coogan's as characters from classic horror movies. For Christmas, they created murals of a wintry Washington Heights streetscape: snowball fights, carolers, Christmas tree sellers, and Santa's sled parked on Broadway in front of Coogan's. This jovial depiction of the neighborhood ran counter to what the rest of the city and the world were seeing on the news. Garcia and his collaborators sought to capture the essence if not the documentary reality of the Heights; the state of mind, if not the state of being.

Over time, Garcia became the de facto artist-in-residence at Coogan's. Some of his paintings were added to the ever-growing collection of art and photography on the walls. The owners commissioned him to create illustrations that they turned into promotional posters and flyers. For a number of years, the cover of the Coogan's menu featured one of Sam Garcia's works: a hunky white chef modeled after Peter and a lissome, brown-skinned waitress modeled after Brenda Rosado, both wearing green Coogan's aprons, standing on either side of a groaning board of produce and roasted meats. Behind them soared the George Washington Bridge and the Highbridge Water Tower.

Garcia's light-filled, joyous depictions of a diverse urban life conveyed exactly the spirit that Coogan's owners wanted the bar to embody. Coogan's gave Garcia a place to show his work, and Garcia gave Coogan's a distinctive visual identity. It was the kind of mutually beneficial partnership that would become the bar's hallmark.

Another aspiring artist who found a home at Coogan's during this time was Bryan Dotson. Dotson had grown up in a coal-mining family in eastern Kentucky, but he knew early on that he wasn't cut out for that line of work. He found his calling in a community college production of Neil Simon's *California Suite*, and in 1987 he moved to New York to pursue a life on the stage. The flight to LaGuardia was his first trip on an airplane.

He had a short-term sublet in Hell's Kitchen and got a job as a bartender at one of the fifth-floor public terraces at Trump Tower. He'd lied about his bartending experience, which was nil—his hometown was dry. As soon as he was offered the position, he ran to a bookstore and bought a cocktail guide. Some mornings when he arrived for work, he rode up in the elevator with the celebrity tycoon whose name adorned the building. When the elevator stopped at the fifth floor, Trump would smile at Dotson and say, "Have a great day. Bring in lots of money."

By 1990, Dotson had moved to Washington Heights, settling into a one-bedroom apartment. Despite the neighborhood's reputation for crime and violence, it seemed no worse to him than Hell's Kitchen—at least not until one night when the Dominican proprietor of a local bodega told him he should be careful. "Why's that?" asked Dotson, who was tall, broad-shouldered, and blond-haired. "Because people around here might think you're an undercover cop and shoot you in the back of the head."

Looking for a job that would be more conducive to auditioning, Dotson walked into Coogan's and asked if they were hiring. From his Dominican neighbors, he'd heard that it was expensive and fancy. Someone else had suggested that the bar looked like a funeral home. None of this made Dotson eager to venture in, but he was feeling desperate. Dave Hunt interviewed him on the spot. At the end of the interview, Dave asked him if he could start the next day.

It was the summer of 1990. Dave, Peter, and Sean had been in charge only a matter of weeks and they were still cleaning house. When Dotson showed up for work the next day, he was introduced to the waiter who would be training him. Moments later, that waiter walked out the door after being fired. It turned out that he had been adding service charges to checks without telling the diners, in the hopes of getting two tips out of the meal. The owners had warned him but to no avail. He'd done it again moments before Dotson's arrival, and was promptly let go. This left only Dotson and one other waiter to handle the lunchtime rush. The next day, Dotson was entirely on his own, but, unlike previous places where he'd worked, the owners of Coogan's backed him up, bussing and cleaning tables for him, processing payments. His misgivings about the place were quickly forgotten.

Finding time to audition, Dotson was accepted into an off-off-Broadway repertory company named Love Creek Productions. In 1991, he was cast in a show called *Touch Me, Touch Me Not*. Coogan's ownership made copies of the flyer for the show and inserted it in the menu as they seated customers. Peter himself bought seventy-five of the ninety-nine available tickets for one of the nights and resold them to regular customers at the bar. When the curtain went up, Dotson was greeted with thunderous clapping and cheers. The applause continued throughout the performance culminating in a standing ovation at the end. One of his costars turned to him and said, "What did I just experience?"

 ❧

CHAPTER FIFTEEN

Alliances

The sustained effort to make Coogan's into a safe and inclusive neighborhood hangout was good not only for the saloon's standing in the community but also for the bottom line. Business picked up, particularly on weekday evenings, which had been a dead time. Before long, the bar and restaurant, along with its busy catering arm—which served the hospital, the university, and other clients all over Manhattan—were bringing in about $35,000 a week, a significant improvement from earnings under the prior ownership. That increase in income was welcome not least because the new partners had agreed to take on an additional $75,000 in debt when they bought out KKS.

Paying off that debt became a priority for Dave. When Sean had been singularly in charge of Coogan's finances, he'd paid vendors on his schedule, not theirs, which gave him a sense of financial control. By contrast, Dave—and Peter—felt that the best way to build relationships with vendors was through trust; and the best way to generate trust was to pay your bills promptly. In an attempt to get their debt under control, Dave—who was in charge of supplying and provisioning Coogan's—called around to

Sean Cannon, Peter Walsh, and Dave Hunt, circa 1992.
Photograph by Sam Garcia

each vendor offering them a choice: he would either pay off all their outstanding debt and close the account, or he would pay the current invoice cash on delivery as well as the oldest outstanding invoice each month until they were caught up. All but one vendor opted for the latter option. The one vendor who chose full payment and termination later came to Dave to ask him to reopen the account. "Let's let bygones be bygones." Dave declined the entreaty and held on to his bygones.

The difference in approach to bill paying was representative of a larger difference in philosophy among the three on-site owners. Sean owned 40 percent of the business, and each of the other partners held 15 percent, which meant it took at least three of them to outvote him, but many of the day-to-day decisions were made by the trio of Sean, Peter, and Dave. In that subset, Sean outranked his co-owners.

Dave had fretted that whenever there was a conflict, his partners were likely to vote against him as a bloc. Sean and Peter had lived together and done business together before. That alliance seemed natural, but much to Dave's surprise, Sean and Peter didn't gang up on him. Instead, an unspoken alliance began to form between Peter and Dave. More often than not, it was Sean, the largest shareholder, who was isolated.

Their diverging philosophies manifested tellingly in their schedules. Sean worked a nine-to-five day as often as he could and seemed eager to get out of the neighborhood before dark. He continued to feel that his mission was to serve the medical center, and he did that best during daylight hours through the lunchtime business and catering. For Dave and Peter, the fun of Coogan's really started after the sun went down, when Sean had left for the day. That was when the new regulars like Sybil, Ivy, Brenda, and the artists came in. Both men believed that continued neighborhood outreach was the future for Coogan's. They also began to see it as a way for their saloon to become more than just another small business, for it to become part of the community. It would take half a dozen years for the rupture to happen, but the friction caused by their diverging approaches would eventually prove fatal to the partnership with Sean.

Peter and Dave didn't realize it yet, but a more compatible partner was already in their midst, working in the dining room as a service bartender. Her name was Tess O'Connor. She had a wide, expressive face, blue eyes, and blond hair. She had done accounting at Hospital Audiences, Inc., the performing arts agency where Peter worked between

Pudding's and Coogan's. Late in the summer of 1990, when Peter invited his former colleagues to a launch party at the bar he'd bought in Washington Heights, Tess also went along. She'd recently moved to New York from England, and she was looking to meet people and visit new places. Peter was charismatic and fun, and the celebration at Coogan's enjoyable despite the uptown location. Not long after, Tess called Peter up to invite him to a mutual friend's birthday party. Peter blew off the invitation, but cajoled Tess into coming to Coogan's to work part-time. "I know you make no money down there," he said. "Come up here and do some bartending on weekends."

Peter was right: she did need the money. She started at Coogan's in January of 1991 and did not have a propitious beginning. Sean, who was over six feet tall, had designed the bar around his physique. Tess, who was about eight inches shorter, found that many of the glasses racked above the bar were out of her reach. (Female bartenders at Coogan's stood on crates or used rulers to slide glasses off their rails. Some male bartenders wore lifts. Most simply avoided the overhead racks by keeping an array of glasses at hand on their work surface behind the bar.) When Tess was at the service bar, Bryan Dotson, who had once faked his own knowledge of bartending, talked her through the process of mixing cocktails. Peter, Dave, and Sean soon found other work for her. She was good with numbers and didn't get flustered easily. Before long, she was tasked with helping out with the accounting twice a week. Suddenly, she was earning some surplus income. And Coogan's fed her. On one of her designated workdays, the staff meal was chicken potpie in a bread bowl. It became her favorite item on the menu and an extra incentive to start thinking about working full-time at this restaurant in Washington Heights.

Tess grew up in Kingston upon Thames, in southwest London. She was raised to believe that she was Irish, even though her father was born in Scotland. His parents were Irish, so he viewed himself as Irish—or Scottish when he was in Scotland. But growing up in London, Tess and her siblings felt that they were English, and they spoke with English accents. Their world, though, was populated with Irish transplants. Tess's first job was bartending on weekends in the social club of St. Agatha's Church. She was a teenager, still in school. Most of the bar's clientele consisted of elderly Irish men, who would chat and sing and joke with each other, and with Tess. Tess's father would come in after a round of golf with friends and have a pint. It was cozy, familiar, and familial.

Given her ancestry and work experience, it was apt then that Tess ended up going to study hospitality and tourism management at Ulster University in Derry, the famously fractious second-largest city of Northern Ireland. Derry is so divided along religious lines that it has two names: Protestant Unionists, who want Northern Ireland to remain part of the United Kingdom, insist on calling it Londonderry. It is the Jerusalem of the Irish conflict, a walled city claimed by both sides, contested for centuries. Derry was the scene of some of the bitterest sectarian violence during the Troubles, including Bloody Sunday, in 1972, when British soldiers opened fire on a protest march, killing fourteen people.

For Tess, the move was a difficult one, at least initially. She had never been to Ireland, north or south. Her fellow students didn't know what to make of the chasm between her Irish name and her English accent. Tess didn't know what to make of them either. The tribal codes and mores in Northern Ireland can be a challenge to decipher for newcomers, and the province can seem insular and hostile to outsiders. On top of that, there were the bombs. This was the mid-1980s, and Tess heard (and sometimes felt) explosions during her early days in Derry. After six weeks, she went home to London and talked to her parents about her apprehensions. Her mother told her to stay in England; her father told her to go back, believing it would be a good life lesson. "You'll get more education outside of the classroom," he said. After a week, she returned and settled in. "I had the time of my life," she later recalled.

Tess completed her degree and, like many newly minted graduates, wasn't immediately sure what to do with herself. Her college boyfriend had an internship at the United Nations, and he convinced her to accompany him to New York. Her parents were far more concerned about her relocating to the Big Apple than they had been about her going to college in Derry. Tess persisted and convinced them to allow her to go. At the last minute, her boyfriend's visa was denied. He had to settle for an internship at the European Parliament in Brussels. Tess wanted to change her plans too, but her parents—who were not thrilled with the boyfriend—suddenly warmed to the idea of her going to New York. And in the end, that was what she did.

She crashed with the sister of a friend from college, sleeping on the floor in an apartment in Queens. On her second day in New York, they bumped into a woman that Tess's host had once worked for as a babysitter. Her name was Jane, and she was in desperate need of a live-in nanny. This is the encounter that changed Tess's life. On the spur of the moment, Jane invited Tess to move into her Upper West Side apartment and look after her kids. At the end of the summer, when the kids went back to school, Jane brought Tess in to interview for a part-time job in the accounting department at Hospital Audiences, Inc., the nonprofit where she worked. She was hired. When her visa expired, her employer sponsored her for another and offered her a full-time position.

Tess moved out of Jane's apartment and into a share on the East Side. Then Peter invited her to come up and work part-time at Coogan's. Even though she'd lived for three years in the terrorized city of Derry, she still found Washington Heights, in the early 1990s, to be "dicey at best." If she worked late, Peter would often drive her home, singing and telling stories like the men in St. Agatha's social club. The partners liked Tess and wanted to have her work full-time at Coogan's. Peter was already speaking of her as a kind of Mary Poppins—someone who made problems go away and whose calm temperament was well suited to the combustible trio of Irishmen who ran the bar day-to-day. For her part, Tess wasn't sure she wanted to spend the rest of her working life in a saloon, but this would do for now.

CHAPTER SIXTEEN

Uprising

Independence Day celebrations in Washington Heights were traditionally loud and unruly. Fusillades of illegal fireworks were launched from sidewalks and rooftops; celebratory gunshots were fired into the sky; and vehicles kitted out with huge speakers roved the neighborhood, blasting music at volumes that shook windowpanes and made the ground tremble. But during the Fourth of July weekend of 1992—and the days that followed—Northern Manhattan experienced an unprecedented eruption of violence and civil unrest that would further shape relations between the police and uptown residents for years to come. Those daunting events also offered the owners of Coogan's an opportunity to prove the bar's utility to the community during a time of crisis.

On the night of Friday, July 3, three plainclothes officers from the 34th Precinct—Michael O'Keefe, Tommy McPartland, and Matteo Brattesani—drove down St. Nicholas Avenue in an unmarked Chevrolet. All were members of the precinct's anticrime squad, known as Local Motion, after a surfing-equipment decal on their car's tinted rear window. The unit had a reputation in the neighborhood for brutish tactics, with some residents viewing them as the ultimate expression of "us vs. them" policing.

As the cops stopped at the red light at 162nd Street and St. Nicholas Avenue, O'Keefe spotted a young man, seemingly overdressed for the sultry summer weather in a black sports jacket, which he repeatedly pulled across his abdomen. Suspecting that the man was concealing a weapon, O'Keefe hopped out of the car while his partners circled the block. En route, they stopped to collar a man for carrying a .357 Magnum. But before they could arrest him, they heard a frantic distress call from O'Keefe's radio. O'Keefe did not say the address, though, and McPartland and Brattesani were unable to get to him immediately. But two other officers cruising nearby did. When they entered the lobby of 505 West 162nd Street, they saw O'Keefe with his torso covered in blood, standing over the hand-cuffed body of a young man. O'Keefe was holding his police revolver in one hand and a loaded .38 Smith and Wesson in the other.

The man on the floor was José—or Kiko, as he was known—Garcia. He was a twenty-three-year-old Domini-can who lived in an apartment a few blocks away. He had been shot twice and was declared dead half an hour later at Columbia-Presbyterian Hospital.

What exactly transpired in that lobby on the night of July 3 remained uncertain for some time, causing rumors to spread around the neighborhood and in the media cov-erage that ensued. The NYPD asserted that O'Keefe had behaved properly and had killed Garcia in self-defense after Garcia violently resisted arrest; they said that Gar-cia was a drug dealer who was "high on cocaine." First Deputy Commissioner Ray Kelly defended O'Keefe as an "aggressive, active, and good" officer. However, among those who lived in the nearby streets, a different account circulated, one in which O'Keefe had viciously beaten an unarmed Garcia with his police radio before shooting him in the back, even as he pleaded for mercy. The widespread experience of stop-and-frisk policing made this account a credible one to many in the neighborhood. This alternate version of events, which soon made it to the airwaves and the front pages of the city's newspapers, inflamed long-simmering resentment of the police in the neighborhood, and that became manifest on block after block during a week of protests and violent uprising.

Without the viral imagery and instant reach of social media that we have today, the initial dissemination of rumor and anger took time to build. Over the weekend, mourners for Garcia erected a memorial of flowers on the sidewalk outside of 505 W. 162nd Street. White candles were arranged on the pavement to spell out Garcia's name. Inside the lobby, someone dipped their fingers into the bloodstains on the wall to write "KIKO WE LOVE YOU." There were also early signs of the unrest to come. Trash cans were set alight. Bricks and bottles were tossed. Car windows were smashed.

Dave and Peter were in charge of Coogan's that weekend. As was his annual custom, Sean had picked his children up from their last day of school and headed to a house on Fire Island for three weeks of beach. Sean's absence during what turned out to be a pivotal series of days in the neighborhood's history was a fluke of scheduling, but it also ended up revealing the diverging priorities for the trio of owners. And so, as Washington Heights went up in flames, it was left to Dave and Peter to figure out how to respond.

The restaurant was half a dozen blocks northwest of the scene of Garcia's death. With Columbia University out of session and a number of regulars away for the holiday, the Fourth of July was not normally a busy time at the bar. Rain on Sunday also dampened the mood. Soon the owners began hearing some of the rumors that were swirling in the neighborhood regarding the way in which Garcia was killed. Dave and Peter knew O'Keefe but not too well; like many of the officers from the 34th Precinct, the members of Local Motion also drank at Coogan's.

On Sunday night, Jim Dwyer, a writer for *Newsday*, came in and told Dave that he had just interviewed a resident of 505 West 162nd Street who claimed to have seen O'Keefe execute Garcia and that he was about to file an article about it. After interviewing her, Dwyer had positioned himself on the first-floor landing from which she said she had witnessed the shooting. He noted that the lobby where the killing had taken place was only visible from the landing if you were kneeling.

Dwyer knew that tensions mounting on the streets of Washington Heights were about much more than the lone incident between Garcia and O'Keefe. Over the past year, in American cities, there had been a succession of violent protests prompted by longstanding grievances over the unequal and harsh treatment of people of color by law enforcement. The previous summer, three days of rioting shook Crown Heights in Brooklyn after a rabbi's motorcade struck two children of Guyanese immigrants, killing one of them. Black and Hasidic youth clashed on the streets, but Black protestors' anger was mostly directed at the police sent to quell the situation. Eight months later, buildings and businesses in several Los Angeles neighborhoods were burned to the ground after the acquittal of four policemen who had been videotaped savagely beating an African American man named Rodney King. The memories of those confrontations were still fresh in the public consciousness when Garcia was killed.

The morning of Monday, July 6, the accusations of police brutality against O'Keefe hit New York's newspapers and airwaves. HE BEGGED FOR LIFE said the front page of the *Daily News*. NAPALM THE 'HOOD was the headline in the *Post*, a reference to the cop who was overheard on the police frequency saying, "Bring in the napalm; bomb the Three-Four." Trying to manage the escalating crisis, Mayor David Dinkins, the city's first Black mayor, who had been widely criticized for his passive handling of the disturbances in Crown Heights, came uptown late in the afternoon and met with members of Garcia's family. He promised them a thorough investigation. That Dinkins chose not to visit the 34th Precinct station house didn't go unnoticed. Officers were reminded by Ted Buczek that Dinkins, when he was Manhattan borough president, had failed to attend the funeral for his son and Chris Hoban. Many police officers were already pissed off at Dinkins for proposing the establishment of an all-civilian, fully independent Complaint Review Board to investigate charges of police misconduct. That week, instead of the mayor, federal investigators returned to the 34th Precinct to continue looking into accusations of its cops profiteering from the drug trade. Meanwhile, O'Keefe, who had called in sick each day since the fatal confrontation with Garcia, had not yet been interviewed by investigators. He was hiding out in Queens, at his mother's house, which was staked out by reporters and television crews.

Later that afternoon, protesters marched past the apartment building where the mayor had just finished meeting with Garcia's family, chanting in Spanish, "There'll be a riot if there isn't justice!" They headed to the building where Garcia was killed, and they were met there by Guillermo Linares, the forty-year-old city councilman. Linares, the first Dominican to hold elected office in the city, was a loyal ally of Dinkins and served as a conduit between the mayor's office and the people of Washington Heights during this crisis. Councilman Stanley Michels, Manhattan borough president Ruth Messinger, and the city's human rights commissioner Dennis deLeon were also there. Linares convinced some of the protesters to accompany them to a vigil ten blocks north at the Broadway Temple United Methodist Church, but many did not seem interested in such peaceful symbolism. They were all soon joined by another group of marchers from City College in Harlem, swelling their ranks to five hundred. "To the precinct! To the precinct!" they chanted.

Standing in the doorway of Coogan's, Peter and Dave watched the chanting protestors head up the St. Nicholas Avenue side of the intersection with Broadway. Though safety was a high priority for the owners, the restaurant, unlike many businesses in the neighborhood, did not have retractable metal shutters to protect its frontage. As they tracked the marchers north, the owners felt some relief that the protesters hadn't come directly past the bar.

The unrest was already causing strife among some of their regulars. Brenda Rosado had come into the bar earlier in the day on her way up to the precinct house to meet with Nicholas Estavillo. She was wearing an NYPD shirt. Dave worried if it was safe for her to be seen in such attire and Rosado angrily responded, "What, because I'm Hispanic, I can't support the police? I work with these guys. I know they wouldn't do that." This put Rosado at odds with many in the neighborhood, including her roommate, Ivy Fairchild, who had been demonstrating against the police. When Rosado got to Estavillo's office, the precinct commander seconded Dave's concerns, insisting that she change into a softball shirt that he gave her. Rosado had come to tell Estavillo about Linares's planned protest march that evening. Her notice gave Estavillo time to put together a response.

The commander set up a line of dozens of police in riot gear at 181st Street and Broadway to block the protesters from reaching the precinct house. It was early evening when the marchers arrived, the sun going down. Linares, Michels, Messinger, and others linked arms to try to keep the peace between the officers and the marchers. Some of the protestors, frustrated by the blockade, left and moved east toward St. Nicholas and Audubon Avenues, where the situation disintegrated as darkness arrived. Cars were set on fire. Stores were looted. Bottles and stones were thrown at police. Helicopters droned overhead. Bands of protesters ran along the pavements shouting, "Killer cop!" Someone burned O'Keefe in effigy.

At Audubon and 145th Street, police officers pursued bottle throwers into a six-story apartment building, chasing them to the roof. One of the pursued, Dagoberto Pichardo, a twenty-eight-year-old Dominican man, fell from the rooftop and died. Almost immediately rumors spread that one of the officers, Lieutenant Roger Parrino, had pushed him to his death; police, in turn, accused Pichardo of being a drug dealer who first attacked the officer. Dinkins went on Channel 41, a Spanish-language station, late that night to plead for calm. "The destruction and anger is understood," he said, "but it is not the answer." The mayhem continued for hours.

In the dawn light, the uptown streets looked like the images Americans were used to seeing from the world's conflict zones: Beirut and Belfast. That morning, Dave Crenshaw passed through the aftermath on a bus taking Boy Scouts to a camping trip outside the city. He quietly seethed as he listened to others on the bus exclaim about what a terrible neighborhood Washington Heights was.

Early in the evening, Dave and Peter decided they would stay open all night—they feared the bar might be targeted if they closed. Most other restaurants on nearby blocks were shut down. But Dave and Peter figured a variety of people would benefit from Coogan's staying open: doctors and nurses treating the wounded at Columbia-Presbyterian; journalists who needed a base from which to file their stories; police officers and firemen who came in to eat, unwind, and strategize; and political leaders who needed a place to talk to each other and everyone else at Coogan's.

Throughout the night, reports of violence came in from the streets, but the proximity of the hospital and the presence of so many cops inside kept the mayhem from entering the doors. Nevertheless, emotions ran high. Adriano Espaillat recalled having a heated exchange with Estavillo at the bar one of those nights and other cops moving in to surround him. That exchange never escalated beyond shouting and finger-pointing. As business dwindled, Dave and Peter sent their staff home, keeping only a skeleton crew. After midnight, Estavillo convened a meeting of his lieutenants to plan for the next day. In the small hours, when the immediate danger seemed to have passed, Dave got in his car and drove back home to River Edge. Finally, around 4:00 a.m., with the bar and dining room still not empty of customers, Peter Walsh lay down on a bench seat in the Gallery Room, drew a tablecloth over himself, and fell asleep.

The next day, Tuesday, July 7, a public meeting was hastily organized at PS 28 on 155th Street. Mayor Dinkins and Cardinal John O'Connor, along with Linares and Charlie Rangel, addressed the packed auditorium of three hundred young people. Dinkins implored the crowd: "We want justice, but we want peace," Dinkins said. "Justice we will have, but peace I beg you for." O'Connor said that he believed the community should have faith in the integrity of the investigations that had been announced into the deaths of Garcia and Pichardo the previous day by District Attorney Robert Morgenthau. Unconvinced, a teenage girl spoke up, "They shot him like a dog, but worse than a dog. Because Americans, they respect their dogs, but they don't respect their Dominicans."

On St. Nicholas Avenue that morning, shops had reopened, and men played dominos on the sidewalks, but by 1:00 p.m. many businesses had shuttered their doors in anticipation of further chaos. Through the day there were flurries of rock- and bottle-throwing around the neighborhood, and in the afternoon about a hundred protesters attempted to shut down the George Washington Bridge. Linares again led a march along Broadway toward the precinct house. Police had erected a barricade at 181st Street, but the protesters were allowed to pass. Linares, Messinger, and the Reverend Al Sharpton all addressed the crowd that packed the street. "Rally with dignity, but no violence," said Sharpton. "Keep the pressure on." The assembled protesters chanted "Policia, asesinos!" Someone set aflame an effigy of a cop. In some parts of the neighborhood, residents took up positions on the street to guard their blocks from the looting and destruction that had taken place the night before. The NYPD's senior command mobilized three thousand additional police officers from around the city, an overwhelming reinforcement for a precinct that was normally staffed by 130 cops.

By 6:00 p.m. that evening, hundreds had lined up outside the Rivera Funeral Home, where a wake for Garcia was taking place. Dinkins had announced that the city would pay to fly Garcia's body back to the Dominican Republic for burial and had also invited the Garcia family to Gracie Mansion. He was sharply criticized by the police for these decisions, but his actions likely averted a powder keg of a New York City funeral for Garcia. From the funeral home, several hundred people marched south to the apartment building where Garcia was killed, carrying the three wreaths that had been placed on his coffin. They threw bottles and rocks at the police and shouted, "Justice for José Garcia!" and "Arrest Killer Cop O'Keefe." Three hundred officers in riot gear appeared and quickly dispersed them. As a result of the massively increased police presence, and the outreach work done by the mayor's office to calm the situation, the unrest on Tuesday night was of a more limited scale than on Monday night. There were twenty-four arrests and no fatalities. Eighteen people, including ten cops, were treated for minor injuries.

That evening, Nicholas Estavillo, the commander of the 34th Precinct, was eating a meal in the dining room at Coogan's. Peter sat down opposite him to chat for a moment. Just then, a meeting of local elected officials in the Gallery Room broke up. Peter noticed Guillermo Linares exiting the meeting and heading for the door. He suggested to Estavillo that he and Linares should talk. Estavillo declined the offer, but Peter got up from his seat nonetheless and intercepted Linares before he could leave the restaurant. "Come with me," he said, taking the councilman by the arm and leading him to Estavillo's table.

"Do you guys know each other?" Peter asked. From the wary way the police commander and the politician eyed each other, it was clear that they did. Peter pulled out the chair opposite Estavillo and encouraged Linares to sit down. Then he stepped away, allowing the two men to speak in private.

From the beginning of the crisis, there had been bare-bones communication between Estavillo and Linares. On Friday, the night that Garcia was killed, Linares heard the rumors that were coursing through the neighborhood, went to the precinct building, and asked to see Estavillo. He was told that the commander was not there. On Saturday evening, Linares returned home from Independence Day celebrations downtown to find a voice message from Estavillo telling him that there had been some bottle throwing and other minor incidents but that everything was under control. It wasn't until Sunday morning that the two men spoke, briefly, via telephone. Again, Estavillo reassured the councilman that everything was in hand. Since that conversation, Washington Heights had been subsumed in chaos.

Watching from the other side of the dining room, Peter saw the discussion move beyond a greeting and exchange of formalities to something that seemed more substantive. He hoped it would be a productive conversation. It had been dismaying for him and Dave to watch the exploding strife on the streets of the neighborhood, with regular customers of theirs facing off in anger. In the years following the riot, a legend blossomed that a peace treaty was negotiated between Estavillo and Linares in Coogan's that night. That was likely a stretch. Both men were certainly motivated to bring an end to the violence and looting that had afflicted the neighborhood in recent days. Each had also previously advocated for the creation of a second police precinct for Washington Heights. There was furthermore an acknowledgment that communication between the police and the community needed to improve. Estavillo has denied on more than one occasion that any formal truce was negotiated that night, pointing out that the huge influx of police into Northern Manhattan had much more to do with the quelling of riots. For his part, Linares has spoken about the better relations that followed from the riots and credited the restaurant for its role as an agent of reconciliation. The saloon, he later said in Glenn Østen Anderson's documentary film *Coogan's Way*, "was a place that was instrumental in really getting us from that moment of crisis."

The Washington Heights riots all but ended the day after Linares and Estavillo shared a conversation in Coogan's, but it is unlikely that their conversation was directly responsible for quelling the unrest. (The contingent of three thousand additional cops remained deployed in the neighborhood through the remainder of the summer.) Rather, it was the beginning of a longer dialogue, one that would slowly improve police-community relations in Northern Manhattan.

The cumulative damage from the week was tremendous: 42 building fires; 121 vehicles burned; 11 police cars damaged; 125 arrests; 16 civilians and 53 cops injured. Garcia and Pichardo were dead. Drug sales, which had been severely curtailed since the night of Garcia's death, resumed on Friday. By the following Monday night, when Dinkins addressed the opening night of the Democratic

National Convention in Madison Square Garden, an uneasy peace had returned to Washington Heights.

Healing would take much longer.

That September, Robert Morgenthau issued a report on his office's investigation into the fatal shooting of Garcia by O'Keefe. The report found that ballistics evidence supported O'Keefe's version of events—that he had killed Garcia in self-defense. The accusations of police brutality made by witnesses could not be substantiated by evidence from the scene. Recordings of O'Keefe's radio transmissions revealed an officer who was, in Morgenthau's words, "desperate and frightened—not one engaged in an unprovoked assault and about to shoot an unconscious man." A week prior, a Manhattan grand jury had also cleared O'Keefe. Roger Parrino was likewise cleared in the death of Dagoberto Pichardo by both a grand jury and Morgenthau. The witness who claimed to have seen Parrino push Pichardo to his death admitted under oath that he had lied. The federal probe into corruption at the 34th Precinct eventually yielded only one conviction for perjury.

For many uptowners, the outcome of those investigations did not bring about the justice they thought they had been promised. Nor did Morgenthau's report resolve the longstanding grievances over poor treatment by the police that had spurred the protesters into action.

There was no large-scale unrest in Washington Heights that fall. Instead, less than two weeks after O'Keefe was cleared, thousands of police officers gathered outside City Hall to protest the mayor, using racist language and carrying racist signs. Rudy Giuliani, vying to succeed Dinkins, addressed the crowd of officers. "The reason the morale of the police department of the City of New York is so low is one reason and one reason alone: David Dinkins!" A mob of these officers, after failing to storm City Hall, rioted on the nearby Brooklyn Bridge. Eric Adams, who was sworn in as mayor of New York on January 1, 2022, was a transit police officer at the time. He told newspaper reporters, "We have been saying for years that the police department is comprised of racist Long Islanders who come into the city by day and leave at night with their arrogant attitudes and believing they are above the law. Well, finally, the entire city was able to see what we've been talking about."

In Washington Heights, which had been wrestling with that very problem for decades, officials announced that the 34th Precinct would be split in two. The southern portion, from 179th to 155th Streets, would become the 33rd Precinct, with a new station house on Amsterdam Avenue and 170th. This split would allow the cops to concentrate their energies on the higher-crime areas in the neighborhood. Linares helped coordinate the neighborhood's input into the creation of the new precinct, which opened in October 1994.

◦⌐◦

CHAPTER SEVENTEEN

Camelot on the Hudson

In Coogan's, the aftermath of the riots provoked an artistic response. Peter commissioned a painting from Sam Garcia to celebrate the return of relative peace to the neighborhood. He wanted something large and festive that evoked the style of the works collected at the Cloisters, something that would capture the boisterous spirit of the annual Medieval Festival that took place in Fort Tryon Park where Coogan's often set up a stand, the staff, dressed as monks and milkmaids, selling roasted turkey drumsticks. Peter, Sean, and Dave debated intensely over who should be pictured. Sam Garcia set about acquiring photographs and making sketches. Some of the featured locals were invited in for lunch so that they could be photographed. Garcia offered to paint Tess's portrait if she was willing to walk down to the Hudson with him and pose by the river. Tess, who worked mostly in the basement office at that time, hardly knew the artist and refused. For that reason, she didn't make the cut for the painting. To avoid getting political, the artist and the owners opted to leave politicians out of the picture. But they did include a handful of detectives from the 34th Precinct as well as precinct commander Estavillo.

Garcia worked on the canvas for weeks, and when he finished, the bar staged an unveiling party to which they invited all who were depicted. *Coogan's Castle* was painted in a High Renaissance style that paid homage to the work of Raphael, Bellini, and Piero della Francesca. It was a large painting. In the background, like a medieval keep, stood the turrets and slitted windows of the Cloisters. In the foreground, a carnival of knights, maidens, and friars celebrated a feast day, some three dozen figures in all.

The painting was an extended-family affair. A cherubic Dave Hunt, dressed in brown sackcloth, hoists a platter of wild boar. Joe Hintersteiner, clad in an ermine robe and a crown, occupies the center-left, beckoning regally to a white-robed Brenda Rosado. Peter and Sean are seated at a table in the middle of the painting, with Peter's wife, Suzanne, and their school-age twin daughters, Alice and Dana. Hector Santiago is next to Sean. Tim Muldoon, Joe Montori, Joel Potter, Gino Iocco, and John Bourges—all detectives from the 34th Precinct—are presented as knights with white tunics and red crosses. The bar's doorman, Joe Belton, stands near Dave. Leo Glueckselig and Bryan Dotson are also depicted along with a scattering of waiters, waitresses, and bartenders.

Once the canvas was revealed, it was hoisted into place high on the wall of the Gallery Room. Later, it would be moved to the main dining room where visitors would often pause, necks craned back, searching for themselves. From a distance, some of the faces were indistinct and, over the years, that ambiguity allowed many who were not in the picture to believe that they were.

Garcia's painting offered an idyllic vision of the little world the saloon was building uptown, a festive, multiracial

Camelot on the Hudson with plenty of round tables. The distance between that idealized vision and the gritty reality of Washington Heights was vast, of course, but it showed how far the owners of Coogan's wanted to go. It was not just a vision, but a vision statement.

CHAPTER EIGHTEEN

Boss Always Right

By the summer of the riots, Sean, Peter, and Dave had been in charge of Coogan's for two years. They had firmly put their stamp on the place, creating a safe and inclusive environment at the saloon. Business remained strong during the week but still flagged on the weekends. Their catering arm was thriving. Once they paid down the debt they'd acquired, the trio of owners looked for other ways to expand their reach beyond the corner of 169th and Broadway. The medical campus of the Ivy League university on their doorstep offered a lucrative potential. When the opportunity arose to provide food for the dorms and facilities of Columbia's medical campus, the owners formed a new venture, Fresh Express, to take on the task. It turned out to be more challenging than they expected.

Dave took the helm, largely because Sean and Peter didn't want the extra work. Fresh Express had coffee stands in Bard Hall, the library, and the William Black Building, as well as vending machines scattered around campus. It had a dedicated kitchen on campus as well as an office in Bard that overlooked the river. (When Dave needed help expediting a city permit for this new facility, Brenda Rosado came to the rescue, placing a call into the municipal bureaucracy that delivered the permit in three days rather than the expected six weeks.) Columbia was a unionized workplace, which entailed extra paperwork for Tess, who roved back and forth between the basement at Coogan's and the office at Bard Hall, managing the schedule, doing payroll, calculating accruals of sick and vacation time. In those pre-digital days, that meant lugging wide, heavy ledgers filled with columned pages and rows upon rows of figures. The work breaks mandated by the union contract meant that Tess sometimes had to step in and run the cash register herself or pick up other duties at the cafeteria, which, over time, became an annex of Coogan's. During quiet parts of the day, Peter would set up at one of the tables in the sun-splashed dining hall and work on a play.

A small, dedicated staff worked with Dave. One of the members of the Fresh Express team was a Lithuanian man named Vytas Rudys. Like a fair number of people who worked or congregated at Coogan's, Rudys came from a mixed family. But the mixture in his case was Russian and Lithuanian. He and his wife, Aliona, had immigrated to the United States just before the collapse of the Soviet Union. Aliona, a doctor in Lithuania, found a temp job with an agency that provided baby nurse and nanny services. The family that she worked for knew Peter Walsh and told Rudys that he should apply at Coogan's. His English was rudimentary, and his background was in sports and physical education, but he got the job.

Before dawn every morning, Rudys hauled supplies

(beverages, bagels, sandwiches, coffee, milk) on a pulley cart from Coogan's through the streets to Columbia's medical campus to set up and stock those various entities. Dave rode him hard, and thus Rudys learned to manage his time efficiently, to write everything down, and to rely on lists. Later, when Rudys took English lessons, his teacher had him keep a diary. The entries give us a picture of what it was like to work for Coogan's in the nineties:

> I worked in the food business field. I worked long hours in the coffee shop and restaurant in uptown Manhattan. . . . My boss was a very strict man. I respect him for that. His name is David Hunt. He was tall, six feet and fat about 280 pounds. Every day he wore old jeans with suspenders, good quality shoes and a woolen jacket. He was always unhappy and frustrated. Once he told me: "Vytas, rule No. 1—boss always right, rule No. 2—you are always wrong. If you do not know the rules, and you don't know what you have to do, use rule No. 1. After that your life will be fine and comfortable in this place." I didn't have another option. I accepted this statement not really seriously, but submissively. The boss was content with me.

There were two moderating influences on Dave's temper. One was Chef Miguel de la Cruz, the even-keeled Dominican who ran the kitchen at Coogan's. The other was Tess. Here is what Rudys wrote about her: "My boss has a lady manager from England. . . . Her name is Tess O'Connor. She is about twenty-six years old. She speaks very clearly and loudly so that it was very convenient for me." Rudys then describes Tess having her breakfast—a cup of tea and a chocolate muffin—followed by Dave arriving and making himself a ham and cheese sandwich with a mug of tea and a can of Coke. Rudys observes: "At this time, it is very important not to disturb these people, they are eating. They do not answer the phone calls. When I see the boss and Tess eating in the office quietly that means this day will be without trouble and problems."

One day, Tess introduced Rudys to the internet, showing him America Online, which she had begun to use for work. It opened a world of options. Rudys became convinced that he should pursue a career in information technology. He set his sights beyond coffee shops and restaurants.

Rudys worked at Fresh Express for two years, but Coogan's lost the contract with Columbia, and, much to Dave's ire, the coffee stations and vending concessions were taken over by a competitor. For all the effort they put into Fresh Express, it never met their lofty financial expectations, failing to generate the kind of income that their catering business did.

The shuttering of Fresh Express also revealed growing fissures between Sean and his two primary partners. Sean had long argued that they needed to broaden their offerings at the outlets on campus to include non-food items such as L'eggs hosiery, an idea that a female restaurant customer who worked at the medical center had suggested to him. Dave rejected the suggestion. Sean took the rejection and the disappointing performance of Fresh Express as a confirmation of his belief that he was smarter than his partners and better at business strategy. He questioned their emphasis on the community and made fun of Peter's artsy events. When Peter suggested that they all get pagers, Sean disparaged them as "Dick Tracy watches."

As irritating as these slights were, none of the owners viewed them at this stage as threatening to their partnership, but before long, as the irritants grew and the fissures widened, they would.

❦

CHAPTER NINETEEN

Up the Block

While Columbia's medical campus facilities turned out to be a disappointing source of new revenue, another nearby institutional neighbor provided a long-lasting windfall for the saloon. Up the block to the west, occupying nearly two acres of land between 168th and 169th Streets, was the Fort Washington Armory, a vast, squat, brick-and-limestone building with a curved, vaulted roof that had once housed the 22nd Regiment of the Army Corps of Engineers. The regiment departed after the Second World War, but from its earliest days, the structure had doubled as an indoor track and field facility, widely used by area high schools. The Armory had a flat wooden track that became notorious among runners for its lack of traction. Falls could result in splinters in the ass. (It was said that meet doctors kept alcohol and tweezers handy.) Nevertheless, when it was packed with spectators, the Armory transformed into a deafening crucible. The stands were very close to the track, giving runners the impression that the crowd was looming over them. With its jammed hallways and distinctive aroma of sweat, Bengay, and boiled hot dogs, there was no other athletic venue like it in the city.

As with much of Washington Heights, the Armory had fallen on hard times in recent years. As crime rose in the neighborhood, the number of meets held at the Armory—and the number of schools attending them—dwindled. In the 1980s, as the city housed larger and larger numbers of homeless men in the building, races were conducted with cots incongruously piled up in the track's infield. A tuberculosis scare in the city in 1987 brought an end to regular meets. From 1987 to 1992, no sporting events took place in the Armory as it was converted exclusively into a homeless shelter, housing as many as 1,400 men a night. The shelter was a source of anger and resentment in the neighborhood. The *Uptown Dispatch* called it "The Great Homeless Takeover" and railed against "the bum dump" on 169th Street. In the spring of 1992, the facility was used as a primary location for *The Saint of Fort Washington*, a film about two homeless men starring Danny Glover and Matt Dillon.

One afternoon, Peter chased a purse-snatcher from outside Coogan's into the Armory's back entrance. It was his first time inside the building, and he was astonished by what he saw. The infield of the wooden track was filled with hundreds of cots in evenly spaced rows. Unkempt men in shabby clothes moved about in a kind of daze. The smell was nauseating. It was how Peter had imagined prisoner-of-war camps. Unsettled, he gave up the pursuit of the purse-snatcher and went back out to 169th Street. There was no way for him to know it that afternoon, but in just a handful of years, the Armory would become a crucial partner for his saloon, ultimately collaborating with Coogan's on its most ambitious event.

Change arrived at the Armory in the form of Norbert Sander, a slim, energetic physician who led a campaign to partially reclaim the facility for track and field events. (The homeless shelter remained in the building, on the lower level, with a separate entrance.) Sander had raced at the Armory himself in the fifties while he was a student at Fordham Prep in the Bronx. He went on to win the New York City Marathon in 1974. Sander lobbied politicians and cajoled athletic apparel companies to support and fund his vision for the Armory as a thriving track and field facility. Once he got the keys to the track from the city, he became a regular at Coogan's, dining there as often as three times a week. He understood how useful Coogan's could be to his efforts to raise funds and political influence for his mission. In Peter Walsh, he found a fellow marathoner and a passionate fan of running. The two men hit it off. Their friendship was mutually beneficial but genuinely affectionate. The saloon offered Sander a connection point to meet with local politicians such as Denny Farrell and Stan Michels, who embraced his efforts.

Sander was able to raise more than $400,000 from municipal funds and the private sector. The athletic shoe company Saucony agreed to pick up the $170,000 tab on a new Mondo track—the state-of-the-art surface that was being used at the Olympics in Barcelona that year. Later in the decade, the Armory received an additional $400,000 in confiscated drug money via the New York/New Jersey High Intensity Drug Trafficking Area Program. Attorney General Janet Reno came to the Armory for a ceremony (and then paid a visit to Coogan's). The money funded the expansion of the Armory's activities to include after-school programs, SAT prep, and vocational training.

At the same time that Sander was driving the effort to bring track events back to the Armory, an association of community groups gained approval from the Dinkins administration to build a community center at the facility. The plan included a proposal to construct a high-rise building next to the Armory, which would provide housing to two hundred low-income or formerly homeless families, as well as office space for city services. However, after Dinkins lost his 1993 reelection campaign, the plan foundered. Meanwhile, Sander's vision to bring meets back to the venue became a reality late in 1993, when the Bishop Loughlin Games, the last event to leave the Armory, returned, bringing 5,000 athletes from 150 schools to Washington Heights. The meet happened just a few weeks after *The Saint of Fort Washington*, with its vivid and unvarnished depiction of life in the homeless shelter, opened in theaters.

In his efforts to revive track and field at the Armory, Sander was assisted by two men who had, like him, raced there during its glory days: Louis Vazquez and Ed Small. Vazquez, who coached at Bishop Ford High School and, later, Long Island University, organized meets for the Catholic High School Athletic Association. Sander recruited him to help lure those events back. Small, a retired supervisor in the city's welfare agency, was brought in to manage the day-to-day operations of the place, largely by himself. He often worked seventy hours a week, contending with the homeless men who found their way into the track from the shelter. Small's schedule didn't allow him much time to hang out in Coogan's, but he was a frequent visitor. In those early days, the Armory did not have an ice machine. Small would go down to Coogan's and fill buckets from the bar's supply. Eventually the bar's owners gave the Armory one of their ice machines and ordered a replacement for the restaurant.

They could afford to be generous. The resuscitation of

track and field events at the Armory had a profound and enduring effect on Coogan's. The day-long athletic competitions held there brought thousands of people to 168th and 169th Streets. For a long while, the nearest place to get a good meal was Coogan's. Aside from St. Patrick's Day, the big race days at the track became the busiest (and most profitable) on the Coogan's calendar. It was a huge source of business that had been utterly unimaginable when they took over the bar just a few years earlier.

Peter saw the Armory as much more than just a source of new business, however. He became a true believer in the power of running to transform lives. He read up on the history of the sport, talking to the coaches and athletes who dined at Coogan's every chance he got, and encouraged his twin daughters to become runners. He started to dream of an event that would combine athletics, showmanship, and community: a joint effort between the bar and the track, something no one in the neighborhood had seen before.

CHAPTER TWENTY

The Dance o' the Hop and the Barley

With races returning to the Armory and new customers coming into Coogan's, the bar's owners felt that it was an opportune time to reimagine their origin story. Their saloon was named after Coogan's Bluff, which, in turn, was named after James J. Coogan, the wealthy local landowner and former Manhattan borough president. Dave felt that Coogan's Bluff, once a sobriquet for the Polo Grounds where the New York Giants played, had lost its luster. After the Giants left New York for California in 1957, the stadium was razed to make space for low-income apartment towers. That's what Coogan's Bluff meant now: public housing. Dave believed that a majority of their patrons didn't care what or where Coogan's Bluff was. The closest association for some was perhaps the 1968 Clint Eastwood film of the same title, a framed poster for which hung high on the wall of the saloon's dining room.

For his part, Peter disliked the word "bluff," with its deceitful gambling connotations. Aiming for something more heroic, in the mid-1990s he created the fictional character of Jack Coogan, a swashbuckling, versifying nineteenth-century sea captain who also happened to be a master brewer. The owners commissioned a large painting from Sam Garcia to illustrate the legend of Captain Coogan. The new work, called *Coogan's Shipworks*, depicted a drunken dockside scene at sunset, with musicians, dancers, and revelers. At the center of this bedlam is Captain Jack himself (modeled after Peter, of course), in a heroic stance, one arm on his hip, the other thrusting a beer stein high in a salute to the partiers below. Behind him is his steamship, docked and ready to deliver its cargo of Coogan's Ale to the thirsty revelers. The legend was fleshed out in a sidebar on the wine list distributed to diners with the menu:

> At the top of Manhattan, in Washington Heights, near the east bank of the Hudson River in the City of New York, lies the pub named after Captain Jack Coogan, shipbuilder, navigator, artist and master brewer. Late in his illustrious career, Captain Coogan wrote of his passion for brewing: "Perhaps it was the foamy mists of the Irish Sea, or the quantities of the native brew I enjoyed off the distant China Coast, or simply the knowledge that nothing could ensure the loyalty of my crew more than the dance o' the hop and the barley . . . Whatever the cause, no pursuit has afforded me greater daily reward." Captain Coogan's private recipe has been followed to the letter by our own master brewer. The result is Coogan's Double Amber Ale. So gather 'round, wink at the stars, and share the fare!

The truth, of course, was much more pedestrian. The house ale came from the West End brewery in Utica, New York.

The fabrication of Captain Coogan, fun as it was, failed to remedy a longstanding problem: Saturday night. The busiest night of the week at most bars in the city remained stubbornly dead at Coogan's. It would take more than a swashbuckling story to draw people in. To address the issue, the owners hired a new weekend manager, James Fisher.

Fisher, who grew up in Greenwich Village, had been the morning bartender at Jimmy Day's—the daylight counterpart to Dave. When Dave contacted Fisher to see if he was interested in working as a weekend manager at Coogan's, Fisher was wary because of the neighborhood's reputation. After accepting the offer, he sought out acquaintances in the police force to ask if they had a spare bulletproof vest. But he found that the atmosphere in Coogan's was much less belligerent than in other places he'd worked. "In Jimmy Day's you had the bridge and tunnel crowd who figured they could do whatever the hell they wanted to do. You were in the street punching people, throwing people out, but I would say it was probably three times [total] at Coogan's, whereas at Jimmy Day's it could be three times a night."

Soon after starting, Fisher hired two young Saturday night bartenders, Brendan Straw and Chris Feci, and began putting out a free midnight buffet of leftover food from the day's catering orders. That proved to be a good lure. But the biggest draw came when Coogan's launched its karaoke night.

Though it is now as commonplace as brunch, in the 1990s karaoke was a relative newcomer to the New York City hospitality scene—especially to Irish bars. Karaoke (which means "empty orchestra") was invented in Japan in 1969 and became popular in clubs in Osaka in the early 1970s.

From there it spread throughout East Asia and, eventually, to the United States. The first English-language karaoke night in New York City was staged at the Lotus Blossom restaurant in Chinatown in 1987. By 1993, karaoke was on the cover of *New York* magazine, but the phenomenon didn't find its way to Washington Heights for another year or two.

Fisher first heard about karaoke from a friend who put on "song-a-roke" events at bars and nightclubs. Coogan's hired him for a one-off, and it proved to be popular. To create a weekly karaoke night, they turned to a neighborhood source. Around the corner from Coogan's, on 168th Street, was the Melbran Pharmacy. The pharmacy owner's daughter, Terry Odell, was a singer and entertainer who'd taken a course on being a karaoke hostess. Odell had dropped off a demo tape at Coogan's. After some discussion with Fisher and the owners, she and her boyfriend Ted were hired to stage karaoke on Tuesday nights in the bar. Odell, who was Puerto Rican and bilingual, was the emcee, while her boyfriend Ted ran the machine and cued up the songs.

As with other events, the owners wanted karaoke to be fun and inclusive but also structured. To wit, strict rules were established. Booing and trash talk were not allowed. There was no foul language or adult content permitted before 11:00 p.m. (If you cursed early in the evening, the mike was taken away.) Doormen were available to back these rules up. To promote this addition to the Coogan's calendar, Fisher went out and bought a mountain bike, a surfboard, and other items, which he hung from the bar's ceiling. Karaoke was launched with a ten-week competition, culminating during the

Christmas season, with prizes going to the winners. It was a smash hit.

Odell viewed the karaoke night as a cabaret in which the neighborhood's residents were the talent. Her job was to orchestrate, curate, and motivate—and sometimes to sing a song. During one of her regular numbers, "It's Raining Men," bartender Chris Feci would climb on top of the bar and do a striptease to the raucous delight of those in attendance. Peter would drop in and sing his favorite song, "The House of the Rising Sun." There were good-natured competitions between cops and firemen, doctors and nurses.

Karaoke brought in neighborhood folk who had been leery of entering an uptown Irish bar. Kevin Davis, who was Black and grew up in the southeastern Heights, said that he was suspicious of Coogan's because it seemed to serve the hospital and not the community. But he loved to sing, and when he heard that there were prizes for karaoke at Coogan's, he went in and competed, performing the ballads "I Believe in You and Me" by the Four Tops and "Lady" by Lionel Richie.

"I got Cooganized," Davis recalled. Inside the bar, "all your woes disappeared." His friends and neighbors started coming to see him perform, and before long they too became regulars. The word spread. Karaoke was such a splash that the owners added two additional nights, Thursdays and Saturdays. Finally they had a true weekend business. According to Dave Crenshaw, on karaoke nights, "you had to come early to get a seat. Karaoke might have started at nine o'clock. You had to come at six or seven to get a seat at the bar. It was packed." Bartender Brendan Straw recalled that the changes Coogan's put into place during those years increased the take on a typical Saturday night from $1,500 to as much as $10,000.

One karaoke night, the television newsman Ti-Hua Chang went to Coogan's to meet with a law enforcement source. Chang wasn't working on a story; he was simply checking in. By the time the meeting ended, karaoke had started. Chang put his name down on the list to sing, and when his turn came, he took the mike and gave a soulful rendition of "Can't Help Falling in Love" by Elvis. As was typical on a karaoke night, Coogan's was jammed with people, including a number of off-duty cops. Many of the people in the bar recognized Chang, whose reports were regularly featured on NBC News broadcasts. His Elvis impersonation was well received. The audience started calling out his name while he was singing: "Ti-Hua! Ti-Hua! Ti-Hua!" By the time he finished his song, it seemed like everyone in the place wanted to buy him a drink. Chang didn't realize until too late that what they really wanted was to get this celebrity drunk.

Chang had been coming to Coogan's for years for reasons that mixed business and pleasure. As a reporter, he'd covered the crack trade in Washington Heights as well as the 1992 riots, and had won a Peabody Award for "Passport to Kill," a documentary series about the lack of a functioning extradition process between the United States and the Dominican Republic. Though he wasn't much of a drinker, he had developed ties with the owners of a number of restaurants and bars all over the city. Coogan's was one of his favorites. Chang loved the corned beef. Dave and Peter reminded him of the parents of the Irish kids he'd grown up with in the blocks between Yorkville and East

Harlem. He was so comfortable at Coogan's, in fact, that he began to knock back the drinks that people bought for him after his karaoke performance. Before he knew it, there was another glass in front of him, and then another. The collective will of the bar asserted itself. The evening tilted and gained a headlong momentum as Chang became steadily more inebriated. The drinks kept coming: a beer, a whiskey, a beer *and* a whiskey, a shot of tequila, a beer, a beer, a whiskey, and so on. Suddenly, he was having the time of his life. All of the karaoke performances were sensational. Every conversation was profound and hilarious. He kept drinking, heading into uncharted territory for someone who imbibed as infrequently as he did. As the alcohol built up and his tolerance maxed out, the fluid, linear progress of time fragmented. The night turned into a series of garishly illuminated freeze-frames soundtracked with laughter and karaoke. *Click*. Another drink on the bar before him. *Click*. His fellow drinkers with their heads thrown back in laughter. *Click*. Applause for a performance. *Click*. Moving with urgency toward the restrooms. *Click*. The emerald-tiled men's room wall; vomit coming out of him. *Click*. Everyone trying to take his keys. "You can't drive like that." *Click*. "Don't worry, I'm not going to drive." *Click*. Chang in his Jeep, in a parking spot outside Coogan's. *Click*. Fade to black.

Sometime after seven the next morning, Chang was woken by the sound of tapping on the window. A police officer—one who hadn't been at Coogan's the night before—told him to move along. Chang drove back to his apartment in a kind of fugue state. When he got home, he tried to drink some water, but whatever he managed to swallow came right back up. He felt as though he'd been poisoned. Out of the recesses of his mind came the memory of his mother giving him ginger ale whenever his stomach was upset. He went out and bought himself a lot of ginger ale and that was the only thing that passed his lips for the next twenty-four hours. After that, Chang almost entirely stopped drinking alcohol. But he kept coming back to Coogan's to meet his sources, to eat the corned beef, and to sing karaoke.

CHAPTER TWENTY-ONE

৩

Spilled Milk

Approaching its tenth anniversary, Coogan's in 1995 was a thriving, growing business with a strong and stable staff and a loyal customer base. The owners had capable, trustworthy lieutenants in Tess, James, and Chef Miguel. They had overcome numerous challenges to get to this place of prosperity, but that did not mean that all was well in their partnership. After five years together, the stresses of the owners' differing visions for Coogan's began to take a toll.

Sean, as was his wont, had gotten into a dispute with the restaurant's dairy vendor. He requested that the dairy guy deliver the supplies to the Coogan's basement through the delivery entrance—a steep set of stairs that led down from the sidewalk. When the dairy guy refused, Sean stopped paying him. And when Sean stopped paying him, the dairy guy stopped delivering. The restaurant still needed dairy, of course. And Sean's solution was to drive to a distributor in the Bronx twice a week to pick up a standing order. It was cheaper, but much more trouble.

The new arrangement did not sit well with Dave and Peter, who had never liked Sean's tactic of trying to control

vendors by withholding payment. It was also emblematic of
the larger issues in their partnership. The dairy runs seemed
always to take place at the worst possible moment—often
in the middle of the lunch rush—which didn't appear to
concern Sean. They thought Sean's tiff with the dairy guy
was petty and shortsighted, hampering the efficient running
of the business. All because of Sean's need to get one over
on the vendor.

On Sean's part, those trips to the Bronx were an escape from a situation in which he felt he was slowly being
cornered. He saw himself as a survivor. He had outlasted
the McFaddens and KKS, but Peter and Dave seemed
far more entrenched than any of his previous partners.
Tess's arrival had also altered the dynamic among them.
In Sean's estimation, she was a more accomplished book-
keeper than any of the bar's accountants. They would have
to find a way to keep her around. As the self-described
"bean counter," he both admired her skills and felt redundant because of them. Sometimes he wished he could
have her as a business partner and be done with Dave and
Peter. He'd thought about trying the same gambit that
had rid him of KKS—walking out so that they had to run
the place without him—but it seemed much less likely to
work this time.

Bean counting, once again, was the biggest issue between Sean and his partners. With the rising income from
catering and an improving night business, Dave and Peter
had pressed Sean for a salary bump. Sean countered that
better business meant fatter envelopes for everyone, but
his partners were unsatisfied. Sean told them to bring it
up at the next owners' meeting, but he knew they would
be reluctant to do so in front of Vincent and Garry. Those
offsite owners, who were not on the payroll, would not

want to see their envelopes shrink in tandem with Dave's and Peter's salary raises.

On some level, as he drove to and from the Bronx to pick up their milk and eggs, he'd begun mentally preparing for a departure. He had no definite plan how or when that might happen, but he'd started saying to himself, *I have to get out of here. I could be doing this somewhere else. And with a lot less stress.*

It **happened** suddenly one weekday morning, and it was over spilled milk, figuratively at least.

Here's the scene: Dave, Sean, and Peter are sitting in the cramped, cluttered basement office, getting ready for the lunch rush, checking catering orders, looking over the list of large parties they're expecting that day, scrambling to find someone to cover a shift for an employee who called in sick. In the midst of all this, Sean announces that he is going to the Bronx to get the milk. He's done this before, but this time Dave and Peter object. "You can't go now."

Sean replies: "I can go whenever I want to."

"We don't want you to go during lunch," Dave says.

"Well maybe *you guys* can run this fucking place and I can stay at home."

Dave and Peter in unison: "Maybe we can."

And with that, the partnership ended. All that had been suppressed was now in the open. The negotiations to buy Sean out would go on for more than a year, and during that time, Sean would not work at Coogan's. He and his wife, Maureen, moved out of the Park Avenue apartment where Sean had once lived with Peter and Steve McFadden. They bought a house in Sayville on Long Island. Saul Victor represented Sean in the split from Coogan's, and the process turned out to be akin to a bitter divorce.

After the deed was done, Dave and Peter realized that Garry McAllister—unbeknownst to them—had added a tricky clause into the contract that would cost Sean at tax time. They gathered a sum of money and delivered it to Sean on Long Island. And they decided to buy out McAllister as soon as they could. By the end of it, though, Maureen—who had known Peter for years and who had helped Dave get his start at Coogan's—stopped speaking to them. And Sean only spoke to them when it was absolutely necessary.

For Tess and James Fisher, who worked most closely with the owners, the split came as a complete surprise. Dave and Peter sat Tess down and gave her the kind of speech that divorcing parents give their children. "Mummy and Daddy still love you, even though we won't be together anymore." Tess liked Sean and was sad to see him leave. Many of his responsibilities would be transferred to her. Looking over his shoulder at Coogan's as he went out the door for the last time, Sean figured that Dave and Peter would be all right as long as they kept Tess around.

A few years earlier, Sean had gone for a walk on the beach in Kismet, on Fire Island. The remains of a devastating hurricane had passed through the region, taking out a number of buildings in the Hamptons. Debris from the storm had been washing up on the beach for days. Ahead, Sean saw a large piece of turquoise-painted lumber. As he got closer, he noticed that there was a layer of peach-colored paint under the turquoise. It was a splinter from the Sandbox—the smaller of the two buildings that had once made up Tiana Beach Club. He and Steve McFadden had applied those layers of paint back in the late seventies. And now there it was, at his feet, washed up. Reflecting on it later—after the dissolution of his partnership in Coogan's—he recalled how devastated he had been when he and Steve had lost Tiana. But Steve had gone on to open McFadden's, and he had gone on to open Coogan's. Now he'd lost Coogan's. What would he open next? He didn't know, but the memory of that flotsam from Tiana prompted him to look forward, not backward.

Up in Washington Heights, Dave and Peter were also looking forward. With Sean out of the picture, they could finally put into place their shared vision for what Coogan's might become. They got to work immediately.

Part Three

A MORAL PUB

CHAPTER TWENTY-TWO

ᕫᕤᕦ

A New Lease on Life

In 1946, George Orwell published an essay in the *Evening Standard* describing the qualities of the ideal pub. It should be near to public transportation, but "drunks and rowdies" should never find their way there; it should have an inviting and pleasant atmosphere; the beer should be good, and a creamy stout should be among the options; the pub should be quiet enough to permit conversation; the staff should "know most of their customers by name, and take a personal interest in everyone"; one should be able to get "a good solid lunch"; and women and children should be welcome. As Olivia Laing pointed out in an essay in the *Observer* on British drinking culture, Orwell's ideal "was a harbour for enjoying drinking's best and most substantial magic: its happy knack for stimulating conviviality."

If one were to transpose this list of traits to the ideal New York neighborhood bar and grill, what would be added or subtracted? Certainly, you'd want good beer; proximity to mass transit; convivial atmosphere; attentive, personable staff; an affordable menu of well-made food. For football Sundays, the World Series, and March Madness, you'd want televisions, but, for the sake of good conversation, they'd be in places where you could ignore them the rest of the year. To be exemplary, though, the ideal New York City saloon would have to do more. It would feel like an essential part of the urban infrastructure and take some of its cues from the most democratic institutions in the city—subways, parks, and libraries—which are open to all and encourage the comingling of people from different backgrounds. The results would be simultaneously ephemeral and enduring. To paraphrase author and bookseller Jeff Deutsch's observation about bookstores: good neighborhood bars reflect their communities; exceptional neighborhood bars both reflect and create their communities.

In many regards, Coogan's met Orwell's criteria. It certainly had a happy knack for stimulating conviviality among regulars and newcomers alike. The bar, the dining room, and the Gallery Room could each sustain its own microclimate, from celebratory to solemn, allowing Coogan's flexibility in hosting its patrons. It could be three different establishments at the same time: karaoke at the bar; family dinners in the restaurant; and a nonprofit fundraiser in the Gallery Room. The memorabilia on the wall, which had accumulated steadily since 1985, spoke to the bar's shared history with its community, a visual representation of the neighborhood's social infrastructure. During the day, the dining room was filled with a welcoming natural light from the street. It was warm in the winter and cool in the summer. And you didn't have to run the gauntlet of a crowded bar area to get to the dining room. "In most places," Peter observed, "there are bar people, and there are restaurant people, and you don't get much crossover. But at Coogan's that didn't happen. Everybody sat everywhere."

Unlike the standard rail bar common in so many city saloons, the rectangular shape of Coogan's bar encouraged

The bar at Coogan's. The dining room is to the left.

The dining room, with the elevated bar in the background.

Holiday party in the Gallery Room, with the Christmas murals.

eye contact and interaction. There were no restrictive
booths in the dining room, which meant that tables could
be moved and combined easily to accommodate groups of
different sizes. The sight lines were unobstructed, giving
the place a performative atmosphere. Denny Farrell understood the theatrical possibilities of the Coogan's dining
room, putting on a show of interviewing candidates for
judgeships at his table. If you wanted something from Farrell, you made your way to Coogan's, waited your turn,
and sat before him. He continued to make it his spot not
least in part because he liked and admired Dave and Peter's
mission. "They are community activists who happen to be
bartenders," Farrell told a reporter from the *Baltimore Sun*
in 1998.

As they looked to the future, the principal owners, lib-
erated from their frustrating relations with Sean, began
putting into action a shared vision for a New York neighborhood bar and restaurant. That would be their spot in
the taxonomy. Their inspiration was part Schrafft's and
part Inwood saloon, but ultimately it descended from the
country pubs of Ireland. Peter liked to enumerate the traits
they had in mind: "The pub has a fireplace so you can
get warmed up. You find out the pig prices and the wheat
prices from your neighbor two miles down the road who
you only see at the pub. You also find out where the British soldiers are. You come in for warmth; you come in for
information; you come for social interaction. It's the whole
package: the christening, the wedding, and the wake." Peter
and Dave thought Coogan's should offer all of this, revised
and updated for their corner of New York. Pig and wheat
prices were not likely to be shared at Coogan's, but plenty
of other local intelligence was: Who was going to challenge
an incumbent elected official for their seat? Which piece

of property was the hospital acquiring and redeveloping? What current scandal was rippling through the community board? It was all fodder for the trough.

Coogan's also had a literary ancestor in Davy Byrne's, a Dublin pub mentioned in James Joyce's *Ulysses*. (Peter had drunk at Davy Byrne's during his time at Trinity College. Later he acquired a first-edition copy of Joyce's masterpiece.) In chapter 8—"Lestrygonians"—Leopold Bloom, hungry after a busy morning, looks for a place to get lunch. First, he enters the Burton Hotel restaurant, which is packed with "men, men, men." The scene assaults his senses: "Stink gripped his trembling breath: pungent meatjuice, slush of greens. See the animals feed." His gorge rising, Bloom abandons the Burton in favor of a light snack at Davy Byrne's on Duke Street. There he finds a much more salubrious atmosphere: "Nice quiet bar. Nice piece of wood on that counter. Nicely planed. Like the way it curves there." He orders a glass of wine and a gorgonzola sandwich. His relief is palpable. "Davy Byrne's," Bloom thinks. "Moral pub."

CHAPTER TWENTY-THREE

A Piece of the Pie

"**W**hat's going to happen today?" Dave and Peter would say to each other as they opened in the morning. In the mid-nineties, a series of events would display the versatility of Coogan's and help cement the bar's position in the political and cultural life of the neighborhood while at the same time extending its reach beyond Washington Heights. Here are a couple of highlights.

In September 1996, Vice President Al Gore gave a speech at Coogan's. The event was organized by Adelante con Clinton, the Latino outreach program of Bill Clinton's reelection campaign. It was attended by uptown business owners and politicos, including Denny Farrell, Guillermo Linares, and Charlie Rangel, and reportedly raised $60,000. Linares recalled Gore saying, "I thought I was coming to a Dominican restaurant." To which Linares replied, "Welcome to the heart of the Dominican community in one of our precious restaurants: Coogan's Restaurant!" It was another sign of the rising political muscle of the Hispanic community in Washington Heights and of Coogan's as a venue for the flexing of that muscle. A few years later, when Hillary Clinton was campaigning to become a sen-

Jim Dwyer at the Celtic Writers Night.

ator from the state of New York, she too would come to Washington Heights for a fundraiser.

The month after Gore's visit, Peter and Jim Dwyer organized a Celtic Writers Night, emceed by Dwyer, who had won a Pulitzer Prize the previous year for his *Newsday* columns. Among the readers were the *Daily News* columnist and novelist Mike McAlary; actress Moira Kelly; the Edgar Award–winning mystery writer and television producer Peter Blauner; Kevin Wade, the screenwriter for the film *Working Girl*; and journalist Peg Tyre, who had co-authored a book with Dwyer about the 1993 World Trade Center bombing. Between the readings there was music and singing.

Notably and typically, the Writers Night wasn't merely a literary event; it was a fundraiser for the Incarnation Children's Center, a skilled nursing facility for HIV-positive children. That connection between entertainment and altruism became a hallmark of the bar's programming. New

York City suffered the highest rate of pediatric AIDS in the nation during the eighties and early nineties. The ICC opened in 1989 to address the needs of HIV-positive children who were "abandoned, orphaned, or removed from their parents' care because of drug use, neglect, or abuse." Most of these children were unlikely candidates for foster care. Some of them, known as "boarder babies," had lived in hospitals for years, cared for by nurses.

In its first decade, the center served some seven hundred children, and it built relationships with the city's HIV-specialized foster care agencies. More than a hundred of those children died while in care of the ICC, but with advances in HIV treatments, many who were presumed to be terminally ill convalesced and were eventually placed with foster families.

The Celtic Writers Night was one of many fundraisers Coogan's hosted for the ICC over the years. The bar also threw an annual Halloween party for the children, who, accompanied by their caregivers, would walk the four blocks down Broadway in their costumes for lunch in the Gallery Room. "It's not just a restaurant or a pub," said Dr. Stephen Nicholas, who cofounded the ICC. "It works on many levels in a very complicated neighborhood that has a complex history. Those of us that have gotten to know the owners over the years, you know, we love them."

Dave later reflected that getting involved in community causes cut into the restaurant's profits but served something deeper. "I'm a capitalist with reservations," he said. "Everybody has to have a piece of the pie."

෴

CHAPTER TWENTY-FOUR

A Republican

On a bitterly cold winter night in 1996, Frank Hoare, who would become Denny Farrell's counsel the following year, stopped into Coogan's to have a drink and catch up with Dave and Peter. With auburn hair and pale skin, Hoare bore a passing resemblance to Danny Ainge of the Boston Celtics. He'd grown up in Washington Heights and became active in Democratic politics in the neighborhood after graduating from law school, quickly attaching himself to Farrell, who'd represented that part of the city in the state assembly since 1975.

During his conversation with Dave and Peter, the hot-button subject of Gerry Adams's impending visit to the United States came up. Adams was the president of Sinn Féin, the political wing of the Provisional Irish Republican Army, a paramilitary organization that had been waging a guerilla war against British rule in Northern Ireland for decades. He was a controversial figure. Though he has long denied it, Adams was a member of the IRA's command in his youth. He'd been in and out of jail in his twenties, but later adopted a more professorial image, eliding his revolutionary past and never admitting to any association with the IRA. In 1983, and then again in 1987, he was elected to represent West Belfast in the British Parliament, though in keeping with party policy, he did not take his seat. Many still saw him as a terrorist, but a growing number of political figures on both sides of the Atlantic—including Senator Edward Kennedy and the moderate Irish nationalist MP John Hume—had also come to believe that peace would not be possible in Northern Ireland without Adams's involvement.

Since February of 1994, Adams had made a series of trips to the United States. The trips were closely tied to the on-again, off-again Northern Ireland peace process and spoke to the increasing involvement of the Clinton administration in that process. In August of 1994, the IRA announced "a complete cessation of military operations" to allow for negotiations. The following year, Adams attended the St. Patrick's Day celebration at the White House, where he shook hands with Clinton. In a speech at the Guildhall Square in Derry later that year, Clinton said, "The time has come for the peacemakers to triumph."

Momentum appeared to be growing for a viable peace, but in February of 1996, a couple of weeks before Hoare dropped into Coogan's, the IRA ended their ceasefire, detonating a truck bomb outside the Canary Wharf Tower in London, killing two people and injuring dozens. This was a month before another scheduled visit by Adams to the United States. Over the objections of some in the State Department, Clinton agreed to grant Adams a visa but did not invite him to the White House for the presidential St. Patrick's Day celebration; Adams's staff was forced to hastily devise a more modest itinerary for him. In damage-control mode, Adams agreed to the visa stipulation of not fundraising while in the United States. Instead, he said that he intended to meet with "representatives of Irish America" and to offer "a measured message of hope."

Hoare, a member of the Brehon Law Society of New York—an organization that advocated for human rights in Northern Ireland—was connected to some of the people who were advising Adams on his new schedule, including Larry Downes, another Brehon member who headed the Friends of Sinn Féin, and Ciaran Staunton. Hoare had been told that Adams didn't want to only do the usual round of Irish bars and Hibernian Societies on this visit but was very keen on meeting diverse New York communities to whom he could deliver his message of inclusiveness.

Peter said, "Why don't you bring him here?"

It seemed like a passing remark at first, but Peter was serious. Hoare went away and mentioned it to Downes and Staunton, noting that the saloon was just a couple of blocks away from the Audubon Ballroom, where Malcolm X had been assassinated, and that Coogan's was in a district represented by a Black congressman, Charlie Rangel. The Republican movement in Northern Ireland had long aligned itself with other oppressed populations around the world: the Palestinians in the Middle East; Black South Africans under the apartheid regime; and African Americans in the United States.

Word came back to Dave and Peter through Hoare and Staunton: proceed. On short notice, the publicans threw together an event, assembling a roster of invitees that included Farrell, Rangel, Stanley Michels, Guillermo Linares, Brian Murtaugh, borough president Ruth Messinger, and public advocate Mark Green. They invited students from the Incarnation School on 175th Street and asked Dave Crenshaw to bring his Dreamers from PS 128. "Me and Peter have had many conversations about the similarities between the Blacks and Irish," Crenshaw said of the controversy surrounding Adams. "I talked it over with my people, and how they broke it down was, 'Dave, nobody gives up power without a fight. There's no transformations in history if you don't have a gangster.'" That was more than enough for Crenshaw. "You need people to show up? I'm showing up."

Press releases were faxed to media outlets around the city. Maria Luna and Steve Simon helped Dave and Peter orchestrate the event and the PR blitz, working until late at night in the paper-strewn basement office. Linares later said that he accepted the invitation as a way of honoring the longstanding Irish presence in Northern Manhattan and "embracing the community that was there before we were. When you learn about your neighbor's history, you enrich your understanding of your own."

The optics at Coogan's would end up being more statesmanlike than some other aspects of Adams's trip. On his first day in New York, Adams went to an Irish tavern in the Bronx where he was welcomed by a phalanx of bagpipers before addressing a crowd that chanted "Brits out!" That was precisely the scene that Dave and Peter did not want to emerge from Adams's visit to Washington Heights. While both publicans shared a strong desire for a united Ireland, they abhorred the violence and sectarianism that characterized the Troubles. They knew from their experiences in Northern Manhattan how damaging a blinkered tribalism could be. They also knew that a visit from Adams would generate a torrent of publicity for their restaurant—they wanted it to be favorable.

It was dark already when Adams arrived at Coogan's in the early evening of March 15. Hoare accompanied him in his limousine. A congregation of uptown schoolchildren, including the Dreamers, greeted them on the sidewalk out-side the bar, holding up handmade signs that read "Blessed are the Peacemakers" and "We love you, Gerry Adams." They cheered and waved Dominican, Irish, and American flags. Adams and his entourage shook hands and posed for photographs with the flag-waving children before going into the restaurant. Newspaper photographers and television cameras were there to capture it all.

Inside, Coogan's was thronged. Northern Manhattan turned out for the event. Members of the community board, bar regulars, staffers from the offices of elected officials, hospital workers, and Irish American businessmen from the area filled the dining room. The blackboard on the rear wall displayed the words "Coogan's Welcomes Gerry Adams on his mission of peace." A stage had been set up for the occasion. Peter introduced Representative Charlie Rangel, who formally welcomed Adams. Onstage with them were Linares, Michels, Murtaugh, Luna, and Messinger. As the Sinn Féin leader was about to speak, someone shouted, "How's the craic in Ireland, Gerry?" a question that some mistook as a reference to the drug that was still being widely sold in Washington Heights. Many others, however, recognized the Irish word for "fun" and laughed.

Adams was dressed in a dark suit and a burgundy tie, with an emerald-green ribbon pinned to his lapel. He wore round-framed glasses and a neatly trimmed beard that was beginning to gray at the chin. Gazing out at the diverse, integrated audience that filled the dining room, he looked delighted. Here was the kind of statesman-like setting he'd hoped for on this visit to New York.

Adams spoke in a practiced, deliberate tone, his Northern Irish brogue deep and cadenced. He did not directly address the peace process in his remarks but instead drew

Front: Charlie Rangel, Stanley Michels, Maria Luna, and
Gerry Adams. Back: Guillermo Linares (partly visible), Maria
Menendez (partly visible), Brian Murtaugh, and
Ruth Messinger (partly visible).

parallels between the shared struggles of Catholics in Ireland and immigrants to the United States: "I think it's entirely appropriate that there be a multiethnic event like
this. That people from all over who couldn't live in their
homeland—because of repression, because of economic
factors, because of occupation, because of all the diverse
injustices—that you can come here together. . . . We're all
the same. We want human dignity. We want the decency of
education or of health or of housing. That's what we want
back home in Ireland."

The speech was received with cheers and a long ovation.
Afterward, Adams was introduced to the elected officials
and others who'd been invited. He seemed particularly keen
to meet Rangel, who was on the House Ways and Means

Committee. Reporter Ti-Hua Chang, who was covering the event for WNBC, asked Rangel how he would respond to those who said that he had just welcomed a terrorist to the neighborhood. Unfazed, Rangel replied to the effect that he'd applied for the job where he only got to speak to the people he agreed with, but it was taken, so he took this job instead. Chang asked Adams about the Canary Wharf bombing and if he was in New York to raise money for the IRA. Adams didn't respond, walking away to look for more agreeable conversation. While Adams was glad-handing, most of the locals who were seated around the dining room ate, drank, and caught up on neighborhood gossip. It was now just another night at Coogan's.

Before leaving, Adams went into the kitchen and exchanged greetings with Chef Miguel and the staff, sharing that he had worked as a bartender earlier in life. As he stepped out of Coogan's, Adams was beaming. The schoolchildren were still there on the sidewalk, waving their flags and cheering for him.

The following day, Adams attended Mass at St. Patrick's Cathedral and marched in the city's St. Patrick's Day Parade. Dave had arranged to meet Adams at his Midtown hotel later that afternoon to deliver photographs from the Coogan's event. Adams didn't have time to talk though. He was on his way to Scranton, Pennsylvania, to give another speech, before returning to take his flight back home the next day. When he landed in Dublin, he had, in his pocket, the photographs of the Dominican children waving Irish flags in Washington Heights, ready to counter accusations that he'd only met with Irish Americans who supported violence and terrorism. For Dave and Peter, Adams's visit was a watershed, combining their Irish heritage and love of spectacle in an event that drew the Washington Heights community together and shone a bright and favorable public light on their bar. Eventually, it even garnered them an invitation to the White House.

The Good Friday Agreement between the United Kingdom and the Republic of Ireland was signed two years later, bringing relative peace to Northern Ireland. Dave and Peter watched the news from the office at Coogan's and felt proud of their own efforts in this pursuit of peace. The owners and their wives were invited to St. Patrick's Day parties at the White House in 1999 and 2000, where they met Clinton, Adams, Hume, and others involved in the peace process. Adams's visit also provided Peter with a handy quip when Mayor Rudy Giuliani came to Coogan's for an event not long after. Surveying the dozens of photographs of Democratic politicians on the walls, Giuliani remarked, "I guess I'm the first Republican who's ever been here."

Peter replied, "Nah, not really. Gerry Adams was here last week."

CHAPTER TWENTY-FIVE

In the Heights

Times Square, with its theaters, peep shows, and strip clubs was more than a hundred blocks south of Washington Heights, an easy train ride, to be sure, but still seemingly a world away. In the mid-nineties, though, as the effort to "clean up" the Deuce got under way in earnest, a little piece of Times Square made its way north to Coogan's. The Nat Horne Theater, home to Love Creek Productions, the off-off-Broadway company that counted Coogan's waiter Bryan Dotson among its members, was scheduled to be renovated as part of the larger makeover of Times Square. Love Creek would be homeless for at least six months. Its artistic director Le Wilhelm was left with a quandary for which Coogan's became the solution. Remembering how the bar's owners had snapped up tickets for Love Creek's production of *Touch Me, Touch Me Not*, Wilhelm suggested that they put on a show at Coogan's to keep the company active and to raise funds while they were displaced. They called it *Le and Sharon's Traveling Theater*, a showcase of one-act plays. (Sharon Fallon was a director with the company.)

Dave and Peter needed little persuading. It would be

another draw to bring people in at night; it would craft another identity for the saloon. An audience of fifty could be squeezed into the Gallery Room, with enough space left over for a makeshift stage. Dotson, who was still waiting tables at the bar, talked up *Le and Sharon's Traveling Theater* to customers, proffering promotional materials and selling tickets. Dave and Peter likewise did their best to drum up support. A week before the metaphorical curtain rose, every ticket had been sold. But there was confusion about the start time. Though the tickets said seven o'clock, many who'd purchased them showed up at the standard Broadway curtain time of 8:00 p.m. to find the back room already jammed and the show under way. A second show was hastily added. "Go sit at the bar," the latecomers were told. "The next performance starts in ninety minutes."

On the following Monday, when Dotson arrived for work, the owners told him that *Le and Sharon's Traveling Theater* had generated one of the biggest Saturday night takes in the restaurant's history. Encouraged by this success, Dotson began to think that there might be a future for a theater company based in Washington Heights. With the cooperation of local actors and the owners of Coogan's, he founded the Bridge Theatre Company in October of 1994. In November, they put on a weekend series of one-act plays at the bar. A few months later the company staged *The Book of Love*, a Valentine's-themed cabaret featuring the vocal talents of Peter Walsh.

Dotson wanted his troupe to be community based and representative of the neighborhood. The company's name was aspirational, not a reference to the George Washington Bridge. He and his artistic director Merry Beamer set a goal of filling at least half the roles for each production with actors who lived in Washington Heights or Inwood. Ivy Fairchild, Maria Luna, Brenda Rosado, and other members of the community board supported the company from its earliest days. Fairchild helped them gain access to the Alumni Auditorium at Columbia-Presbyterian Medical Center where, in the spring of 1995, Bridge staged its first full-length play, *Fools* by Neil Simon, in front of a paying audience of three hundred. The company used the ticket sales from small performances at Coogan's to fund the larger performances at Columbia. They held a series of gala fundraisers with shows that featured songs from current Broadway hits. Dotson also orchestrated a tribute for Dave and Peter at Coogan's. Jim Dwyer was the master of ceremonies.

With each successful production, Dotson's ambitions grew, but without a permanent home, those ambitions were hemmed in by mundane practicalities. The Alumni Auditorium was available on a limited basis, and the Gallery Room at Coogan's wasn't designed to be a theater; long-running full-scale productions just weren't feasible there. Peter and Dave helped as much as they could, donating lights and other equipment to the company. They permitted Dotson to build the risers and flats for his shows in the restaurant's basement. Over the next six years, Bridge Theatre Company somehow managed to stage more than seventy plays. Their production of *Dolorosa Sanchez* by Stanley Taikeff was selected for the Samuel French Off Off Broadway Short Play Festival and was published in the annual festival anthology. Despite these successes, the company was unable to secure a permanent theatrical venue uptown. Without that, they were ineligible for many large grants and limited in the projects they could take on.

After six years of waiting tables at the restaurant, Dotson had decided that he needed to leave Coogan's. While serving lunch to a table of regulars from the hospital he announced that it was his last day there. Among the diners was Marie Wallace, the former star of the 1960s soap opera *Dark Shadows* who now worked for Presbyterian as a photographer. She asked Dotson where he was going. "I don't know," Dotson replied. "All I know is that I can't wait tables any longer. I'll do anything." Before long, he was working in the media relations office at the hospital, serving as a liaison to journalists. When Columbia-Presbyterian merged with New York Hospital (affiliated with Cornell University) in 1998 to become New York–Presbyterian, Dotson took a full-time position, giving him financial stability but also significantly reducing the flexibility of his schedule. Nights and weekends he continued to run Bridge, building sets, sewing costumes, reading plays, and papering the neighborhood with flyers, hoping for a breakthrough.

In 1999, the community newspaper, the *Manhattan Times*, dispatched a young reporter—a local college student home on summer break from Wesleyan University—to write a profile of Dotson. His name was Lin-Manuel Miranda. Miranda interviewed Dotson in the dining room at Coogan's. The Miranda family lived in Inwood and dined at Coogan's frequently, celebrating birthdays and other special occasions there. Lin-Manuel's father Luís, who had cofounded the *Manhattan Times*, was a longtime prominent uptown power broker. In the eighties, he served as lead adviser to Mayor Edward Koch on Hispanic affairs; in the nineties, he became the founding president of the nonprofit Hispanic Federation, and a few years later, Giuliani appointed him chairman of the NYC Health and Hospitals Corporation.

More than six months after the profile was published, Dotson opened his mailbox to find a script from the young reporter. It was an early version of *In the Heights*, a musical about a bodega owner in Northern Manhattan. Dotson shared it with Merry Beamer. They agreed that it was the ideal project for Bridge. It was about the neighborhood, by a writer who'd grown up in Inwood, with a cast of characters that reflected the neighborhood's diverse populations. But, even as he was enthralled by the script, Dotson understood that his homeless theater company simply did not have the resources to develop and produce such an ambitious and complex piece of work. Despite its many successful shows, Bridge Theatre was still run on a shoestring budget, barely covering subway fares for its actors. Dotson had no choice but to turn down the play with regret, offering to look at it again later once the Bridge Theatre Company had more resources.

That day never came. About eighteen months later, Bridge was forced to close when the head of the nonprofit consultancy they'd hired to help manage their finances and apply for grants stole the company's savings—$12,000. When he saw the zero balance on the books, Dotson decided that his dream of building a community theater in Washington Heights was over. He offered his equipment and stage sets to a fledgling uptown company, the People's Theatre Project. Dotson left the stage behind and focused on his career at the hospital, ultimately rising to the position of director of media relations.

Meanwhile, after a student production at Wesleyan and a tryout at the Eugene O'Neill Theater Center in Waterford, Connecticut, *In the Heights* moved to the off-Broadway 37 Arts Theatre in 2007. The following year, the show made its Broadway debut at the Richard Rodgers Theatre, winning four Tony Awards, including Best Musical, Best Original Score, and Best Choreography. Coogan's held a watch party for the awards ceremony. When attendees left the restaurant that night, it was to the sound of firecrackers being set off in celebration.

~~

CHAPTER TWENTY-SIX

Could We Consider Other Options?

Vincent McDade came to New York City in 1991, after traveling across the country from California. Broke and in need of work, he went into an Irish bar and found a job with Big John's Moving. Friends from his hometown of Derry, hearing that he was in the Big Apple, put him in touch with a group of mostly Irish expatriates living in the city. Among them was a young woman named Tess O'Connor, who was working at a saloon in Washington Heights. That friend group went out on the town en masse and Tess soon developed a crush on the newcomer. She became so shy and nervous around Vinny that when he asked her out, she invited her roommate to chaperone the date. The three of them spent a long, enjoyable night at a bar, followed by an early morning breakfast at a diner. When Tess excused herself to use the diner's bathroom, Vinny asked the roommate if she wouldn't mind staying home for the next date.

Tess had been at Coogan's for more than a year by then, but she continued to regard her job there, and, indeed, her life in New York, as a temporary state of affairs. The bar was a fun place to work, sure, but was it really where she wanted to spend the rest of her life? Her home was across

Vinny and Tess at Coogan's with bartender Dan Daly.

the water. She had come to America intending to stay only a couple of weeks, and that continued to be her mindset even as, month by month, she took on more responsibility at Coogan's. Meeting Vinny didn't change that. But he soon left Big John's, putting his economics degree to use on Wall Street. He and Tess moved in together, got engaged, and started saving for a wedding. The young couple dreamed of moving to southern California to start a family once they were married.

The small wedding took place in August 1996. Tess and Vinny paid for it out of their own pockets, but they were helped enormously by their Coogan's family. The ceremony, at the Church of St. Elizabeth on the Upper East Side, was followed by a reception at the Convent of the Sacred Heart school, where Peter's wife, Suzanne, taught. Bryan Dotson and other staff from the restaurant worked as unpaid servers to save Tess and Vinny money—

their gift. To Tess's delight, Sean—who'd left Coogan's six months before—came to the wedding and exchanged civil greetings with his former business partners.

Tess and Vinny honeymooned in California to test out the idea of their dream life in the West. It was everything they'd hoped. The plan was set: She would resign from Coogan's. Vinny would get a transfer to the Morgan Stanley office in La Jolla. *Good-bye, New York. Hello, Southern California!* But within a week of their return from the West Coast, Vinny called her from work and said, "This paper-pushing bullshit, I can't do it. I'm going to quit."

"What the hell?" said Tess. "You couldn't have told me this three weeks ago?" But she heard the finality in his voice and knew there was no swaying him. "Well, then what are you going to do?" she asked. The only other occupation Vinny knew was moving, so he started a moving company—Upstairs Downstairs Moving. His first job was moving a friend's aunt. Coogan's supplied a steady flow of business. Jim Dwyer became a client. Eventually so did Peter and Suzanne.

Vinny's change of heart was a boon for Dave and Peter, who were well aware of what they would have lost had Tess relocated to San Diego. It had become hard to imagine running the place without her, so they took a series of steps that would allow them to offer Tess an ownership stake. Unhappy with Garry McAllister over his handling of the financial side of Sean's separation from Coogan's, they bought him out and offered to sell some of his share of the company to Tess. By that time, Tess and Vinny had a daughter, Hannah, with another child on the way. Vinny's business was beginning to thrive, and Tess was thinking about quitting Coogan's to be a stay-at-home mom. Sensing this, Dave and

Peter sweetened their offer. They knew that Tess didn't have the cash on hand to pay for an ownership stake, so they structured the deal in a way that would allow her to accrue the partnership in installments, through future profits. She could earn her way in without taking on debt. Tess was initially reluctant, worried that Coogan's would swamp her life and keep her from her children. But Dave and Peter talked her into it. With her signature on the agreement, she was also accepting that she would not be returning home to the British Isles anytime soon.

From the outset, she was clear in her own mind about her role. "For the most part, I am in the background," she observed. "This place is Dave and Peter's personality. This is who they are. I do my part. We all balance each other out. It definitely takes the three of us. When you walk around here, though, it's their vision. It's in them, deep in their hearts."

Though she never became the public face of Coogan's, Tess did take the lead in running the place on a day-to-day basis. Dave and Peter readily referred to her as "the boss." On the wall of the office there was a framed two-column diagram. The first column was titled "What the British Say." The second column, "What the British Mean." "I'll bear it in mind" was translated as "I will do nothing about it." "Please think about that some more" meant "It's a bad idea. Don't do it." And "Could we consider other options?" meant "I don't like your idea."

It was a helpful guide for Dave and Peter.

Tess not only oversaw the books and scheduling but was also involved in menu planning and the development of new dishes. On a quiet midweek afternoon, the three owners sat in the dining room, sampling some new party menu appetizers that Tess had brought out from the kitchen.

"This is the Reuben," she said. On the plate were stamp-sized squares of flatbread with sauerkraut, mustard, pastrami, and melted cheese on them.

"It's in two pieces," Dave said, lifting the pastrami and cheese off the rest of the appetizer. "Maybe we need a little cheese underneath to glue this to the bread?" He popped it in his mouth. "It's good."

"There's more," said Tess. On a separate plate were handmade crinkle-cut potato chips, each with a dollop of tartar sauce and a nugget of fried fish. "Fish and chips," said Tess.

"A pun!" exclaimed Peter.

"See, I can do words too," said Tess, smiling.

"But we have to think about the Reuben," protested Dave. "I want to make that work. Get puff pastry and press it into muffin pans, and put the sauerkraut—"

Tess cut him off. "No, because then they're all going to look like this." She pointed to another new appetizer, the mini chicken potpie. "I need something that's easier."

"My opinion means nothing," said Dave.

"No, I listen to it," replied Tess, laughing. "I evaluate it. And then I come to my own conclusion."

CHAPTER TWENTY-SEVEN

In the Middle of It

Dr. Mindy Thompson met her husband, Dr. Robert Ful-lilove, at UC Berkeley in 1986, when she hired him to be the statistician for research she was conducting on the HIV/AIDS epidemic. Though they met in California, they'd both grown up in Essex County, New Jersey—Mindy in Orange and Robert in Newark. Both came from activist backgrounds. Mindy's father, Ernest Thompson, was a labor organizer who fought to desegregate the schools in Orange. Robert was one of the first three Black students to attend Pingry, a private school in Elizabeth, New Jersey. In college, Robert worked for the Student Nonviolent Coordinating Committee, registering voters in Mississippi during the 1964 Freedom Summer. They were a charismatic couple: Robert was tall and stylish, a fast talker, like the leader of a jazz band; Mindy was soft-spoken and gentler of demeanor, with a steely intelligence and an impatience with fools.

The Fullilove came to Washington Heights in 1990 to join the faculty of the Columbia University School of Public Health. "We landed in the middle of a real community crisis," Robert recalled. Both of them viewed public health as an instrument of social justice. In their academic work, they focused on the intersection of health, racial inequality, and the urban environment. HIV/AIDS fit into that framework, and so did the crack epidemic, which became the focus of much of their research in the ensuing years. Studying the drug's effect on Washington Heights was more than just an academic pursuit for the Fulliloves; it was directly connected to their everyday lives. Their offices were located on 165th Street and Amsterdam Avenue—6 Block City, the heart of the drug market. More than once they arrived at work to find bullet holes in the building's front door. Mindy remembered that the "walk to the office was accompanied by the crunch of little plastic vials." Robert recalled doing an informal ethnography of the buyers, "just standing on the corner at two or three in the morning to see all of the cars with Massachusetts, Connecticut, Pennsylvania, DC license plates" coming to purchase cocaine. "We were literally right in the middle of it." In 1992, Robert's brother David died of a crack overdose. "We were an upper-middle-class family," said Robert. David "was not the usual guy who got caught up in this because of the cycles of poverty."

The Fulliloves were part of a team of researchers from the New York State Psychiatric Institute and Columbia School of Public Health that published a report on violence in Washington Heights in 1996. The report was the culmination of a yearlong effort, gathering responses from more than a hundred participants who lived or worked in the Heights. It's a grim document, delineating the ways that violence insinuated itself into the daily lives of the neighborhood's residents, undermining their quality of life and inhibiting the development of a shared sense of community. "Social networks are more implied than real [in

Washington Heights]," the report noted. "Relationships cannot be built overnight."

More than two-thirds of interviewees identified the drug trade as the primary factor in the violence in the community. Almost no one, it seemed, was beyond the corrupting reach of the dealers. A caseworker for a social services agency reported being offered $3,000 a week to make deliveries because the police were unlikely to suspect her. Children were aggressively recruited into the business because, if arrested, they would receive less severe sentences. Families who tried to protect their children ended up in "custody battles" with the drug dealers. "Drugs are tearing a neighborhood apart," the authors wrote, "stealing young lives, driving people behind locked doors and scaring them into silence."

The authors argued that two groups in particular were essential to any solution: immigrants and the police. "For immigrants to take part in solving the violence problem in the neighborhood, they must first feel welcomed by that community." At the same time, the relationship between the police and residents had to be rehabilitated. "What is missing are the bridges to link the people to the facilities and services that can help them." Retreatism was not the answer, the report's authors declared. "Social action requires more contact just at a time when people are trying to minimize contact. . . . Instead of each of us taking the position, 'I'm minding my own business,' we must all decide to 'mind OUR business,' that is the business of building a safe community." The report concluded with a list of action items:

- Foster a sense of community
- Provide care for people hurt by violence

- Link police and community efforts
- Create jobs and economic opportunity
- Prevent the spread of the drug epidemic

Coogan's never adopted a formal mission statement, but nearly all of these action items closely aligned with what Dave and Peter were trying to do. It was no coincidence that many of the people who worked on the report, including the Fulliloves, were regulars at the saloon. "In public health, the primary focus is the neighborhood and anchoring neighborhood institutions—and it was so clear that's what Coogan's was," Robert later said. It offered the Fulliloves a place to interact with the community, meet with students, hold faculty gatherings, and bring visiting scholars. "They knew me by name," said Robert. "They made me look good." The Fulliloves returned the favor. They were such generous tippers that servers fought over who would wait on them. They also mentored some of the young men and women who worked at Coogan's. Sully Gomez, a server in the dining room, recalled how Robert wrote her a letter of recommendation when she applied to nursing school. "It was easy to make those kinds of connections," Robert said. "They were more than just people who were serving me food and drink. They were my neighbors."

◠⁀◠

CHAPTER TWENTY-EIGHT

Rules of Order

The contrast between the warmth inside Coogan's and the sense of danger on the neighborhood streets was stark, but progress was slowly happening. Law enforcement had begun to make headway in thwarting the drug dealers, and the murder rate had declined dramatically. At the start of the decade, there were more than a hundred homicides a year in Washington Heights and Inwood. By the end of the decade, that number was in the teens. Two major crack-dealing gangs were successfully prosecuted by law enforcement: the Jheri Curls, in 1993, and the Wild Cowboys, in 1995. These gangs had been responsible for a spree of violence for over half a dozen years: murders (including of suspected informants), gun battles, drive-by shootings. While the convictions didn't bring an overnight end to the crack trade, it did help reduce some of the terror that Heights residents had described to the Fulliloves' research team.

Other approaches were also implemented to stifle drug sales. At the behest of Nicholas Estavillo, who'd been promoted to commanding officer of all Manhattan precincts above 59th Street, NYPD lawyers used the nuisance abatement law to shutter storefronts and buildings where drug sales took place, pushing the dealers out of their places of business. Another innovation was the model block program, instituted by Garry McCarthy, the commander of the new 33rd Precinct. The first of the four model blocks was on 163rd between Amsterdam Avenue and Broadway. Police raided the block, arresting drug dealers and setting up barricades at each end. All those entering the street had to show identification to prove they lived there or offer a valid reason for visiting. This went on for seven weeks, during which time city agencies were brought in to fix potholes, repair streetlights, paint over graffiti, and exterminate rodents. The program was effective at curbing drug sales and reducing crime, at least for a while, but it was also seen as an infringement on the freedoms of the area residents. "They were offering me a tree in front of my building so they could snatch my civil rights," said one community leader. Others complained that the model block program did little more than displace drug sales to other parts of the neighborhood.

Coogan's chef Miguel de la Cruz lived on a street where the model block program was implemented. On his way to work one day, he was detained by Detective John Bourges (one of the knights from Sam Garcia's *Coogan's Castle* painting). When Bourges learned where de la Cruz worked, he gave the chef his business card and said, "If anyone stops you again, contact me directly." Not long after that exchange, de la Cruz was shot. Gun violence was so pervasively used as an intimidation tactic by drug dealers that it was possible that de la Cruz had been shot for being seen talking to the police.

News of the shooting reached the restaurant quickly. It was a Friday night, and James Fisher, who was the manager on duty, ran over to the emergency room just in time to see de la Cruz being taken out of the ambulance and into the hospital. During the ensuing days, the restaurant sent food to the waiting room where de la Cruz's extended family was holding a vigil—and to the doctors and nurses responsible for his care. De la Cruz recovered from his wounds and went back to work in the kitchen, but the incident illustrated the risks that residents of Washington Heights took when interacting with the police.

Gun violence was just one of the challenges still facing the neighborhood. Northern Manhattan had long been underserved by city agencies. Schools were overcrowded. The streets were neither clean nor safe. Domestic violence was widespread and underreported. All of which deterred community engagement. Grassroots neighborhood associations arose to address this anomie. One of the oldest such organizations was the Community League of West 159th Street (later known as the Community League of the Heights, or CLOTH), which traced its origins back to the early 1950s, when a group of Afro-Caribbean women started gathering in building basements and apartment kitchens to discuss their shared needs. The members of the community league, led by Lucille Bulger, an immigrant from Guyana, worked to provide improved educational and recreational opportunities for the neighborhood's children. They began with volunteer after-school programs, neighborhood cleanup initiatives, and etiquette and social skills classes, raising money from fish fries and flea markets. Over the years, CLOTH grew significantly, gaining nonprofit status and being awarded municipal funding, expanding its services and its reach, opening a food pantry and a public school for sixth through twelfth graders, assisting women with reproductive healthcare needs, and providing small-business support, adult education, and affordable-housing development.

Yvonne Stennett, who succeeded Bulger as executive director in 1994, believes that she came to CLOTH through a form of divine intervention. As a young mother, unemployed and down on her luck, she was sitting on a stoop on 157th Street one day in the late 1970s, feeling despondent, when a gust of wind blew a piece of paper in her direction. It was a flyer advertising the position of property manager at CLOTH. This was a job she could do; out of college, Stennett had worked for the Bedford Stuyvesant Restoration Corporation in Brooklyn. But after interviewing with Bulger, Stennett was told that the position had already been filled. She burst into tears. The next morning she got a phone call from Bulger who said, "Young lady, I see something in you that I don't think you know you have. Come and I will hire you." She was brought in as a youth advisory counselor; her first task was to teach the young people that CLOTH worked with *Robert's Rules of Order*, the standard guide to parliamentary procedure and group decision-making. "At that point in time I had no idea who Robert was or what his rules were," Stennett recalled. She went to the library, studied, and was ready to instruct her charges by the following Monday morning. "I fell into my purpose," she said.

Stennett worked in many of the organization's departments, doing clerical tasks in the office, supervising youth programs, directing its substance abuse hotline. All the while, Bulger mentored her. As CLOTH expanded its reach in the neighborhood so did Stennett's influence. A petite, bespectacled woman who wore her hair straight and short, she spoke with the cadence, control, and rhetorical flourish of a practiced orator. It was Stennett who made the comment about her civil rights being snatched in return for a tree. She was a self-proclaimed "rebel," unafraid to cause a stir. "Because we need to."

Stennett believed that local small businesses were the key to building up the social fabric of the neighborhood. In Coogan's, she found an exemplary small business and a willing partner for community development activities. The bar catered events for CLOTH and collaborated with Stennett on attempts to create a business improvement district in the neighborhood. It was also one of the distribution points for the organization's community needs surveys. In Peter, she found a kindred spirit, someone who also liked to stir things up.

On April 6, 1997, yet another fatal encounter between the police and a member of the community showed how dysfunctional relations between law enforcement and local residents remained. A sixteen-year-old student at George Washington High School named Kevin Cedeno was shot and killed on Amsterdam Avenue near 164th Street. The incident occurred just after 3:30 a.m. Officers Anthony Pellegrini and Michael Garcia, responding to a 911 call reporting a brawl between dozens of Dominican and Black youths on Amsterdam, saw Cedeno running up the avenue. Cedeno was carrying a machete. Pellegrini jumped out of the patrol car and pursued him. Seeing Cedeno turn to look back at him and mistaking the machete's dark handle for a firearm, Pellegrini fired at Cedeno. Mayor Giuliani, relaying police claims, initially said that police shot in self-defense, but an autopsy soon revealed that Cedeno had been shot in the back.

Stennett knew Cedeno well. He had lived with his family

in the building where CLOTH's offices were located. The killing angered her. A teenage boy was dead for no good reason. Once again, it seemed, the police had shot first and asked questions later. A memorial display of candles appeared on the block. District Attorney Robert Morgenthau announced an investigation. The parallels with the death of Kiko Garcia were obvious to everyone, and there were fears of more rioting. Tensions were further stoked when the community learned that Pellegrini had been named the 33rd Precinct's Officer of the Month for April—the same month he shot Cedeno—by some of his peers. (An NYPD representative told media that senior officers at the precinct were not part of the club that had given the award to Pelligrini, but that did little to appease the outrage in the neighborhood.) Dave Crenshaw, who worked regularly with CLOTH, was so enraged by this news that he vowed never to have anything to do with the 33rd Precinct again.

In July, Morgenthau announced that a grand jury deemed Pellegrini's actions to be justified because the officer believed that his life was in danger. Once again, for those closest to the victim, the legal system had failed to deliver justice. At Stennett's invitation, Al Sharpton came to speak to local youths. Through lengthy discussions, he persuaded them that peaceful demonstrations were preferable to rioting and then led them in a protest march through the Heights. As Robert Snyder noted in his history of the neighborhood, "Five years after the rioting over the death of Kiko Garcia, Washington Heights was a different place. Not only was its crime rate lower, but its Dominican residents had elected representatives. . . . Once in office they reduced the sense of powerlessness that made so many people angry and edgy in the crack years." In Crenshaw's view, the difference in 1997 was that they had learned how to organize and channel their anger into protest and direct action.

Amid this turmoil, Stennett went to see Peter and Dave about an event that CLOTH planned to hold at Coogan's. She recalled that her organization's stand against the police "didn't make the rest of the community happy," and she was concerned that feeling might sour her relations with the two publicans for whom law enforcement was such a reliable source of income. The police "weren't happy with us returning" to host an event at Coogan's, said Stennett, but "Peter and Dave were sympathetic." They tried "to understand the issue and, in a way, to be a liaison" between the police and community members protesting against them, Stennett recalled.

"We believe in the importance of the police, but we also believe in the right to peaceful protest," Dave said. For Washington Heights to thrive, they felt, the neighborhood needed an effective police force *and* strong community activism. Coogan's could support both. Through directness, the force of their personalities, and the goodwill they had earned over the previous decade, Dave and Peter were able to maintain this balanced, communitarian position. They hosted the function for CLOTH, and their law enforcement regulars did not defect.

"Dave and Peter were objective and I respected that," Stennett recalled. "Because it was a really tough time. I really appreciated their ability to not take sides. They weren't looking at it through the lens of the business. They really looked at it as trying to piece together the community."

CHAPTER TWENTY-NINE

Salsa, Blues, and Shamrocks

In the late 1990s, Peter and Dave's ambitions for Coogan's began to outgrow the forty-two-hundred square feet inside their walls. As the case of Bridge Theatre Company demonstrated, even a space as adaptable as theirs had its limitations. While on a busy night it could seem that the entire neighborhood was in Coogan's, Dave and Peter wanted to take those good times out to the streets. Lou Vazquez of the Armory Track down the block had similar ambitions for his organization. Since its rebirth under Norbert Sander, the Armory had been criticized for being more interested in serving corporate clients and kids from the suburbs than the community right outside its doors.

One of Vazquez's ideas was to stage a 5K race at the track, literally bringing the neighborhood into the Armory as participants and spectators. He mentioned this to Peter, who said, "Why don't you run it through the streets of Washington Heights instead?" At first it seemed like a foolhardy idea, but they continued discussing it for weeks, and then months. Peter liked the concept of displacing the drug dealers from the corners, even if only for a day. And what about adding a kids' race? As he knew from speaking to Crenshaw about the Dreamers, so many children in Washington Heights were not allowed to play in the streets because their parents feared their getting involved in or hurt by violence. What if they could instead *own* the streets for a day?

The more Peter and Vazquez talked, the more excited they grew. It would be a huge logistical challenge, but as Vazquez pointed out, Coogan's had the political connections to surmount those obstacles. He also recognized that Peter, like Sander, could get almost anyone to do just about anything. Peter added his own touches to this evolving race plan. It would take place close to St. Patrick's Day, which was high season at the bar. A festival atmosphere was the goal, so musical groups would be placed along the race route. The music would reflect the cultural diversity of the neighborhood, from bagpipes to merengue to gospel. It would be called Coogan's Salsa, Blues, and Shamrocks 5K.

Peter discussed the idea with Dave and Tess, who had no frame of reference for the amount of work required to bring off what would easily be the biggest event in the bar's history. But they saw Peter's passion and expected that it would be a boon for the neighborhood. The money raised would go to the Armory Foundation, the Buczek Little League, and other child-focused charities in Northern Manhattan. With his partners' approval, Peter got to work. Vazquez would be the race director. Denny Farrell agreed to be co-chairman of the race with Peter. The affiliation with Farrell opened doors for the organizers. Farrell's chief of staff, Ilene Zucker, gave Peter a list of likely corporate sponsors, calling her contacts at those companies in advance of

Peter to let them know that Farrell was fully behind the race. Banco Popular, Chase, Pepsi, Revlon, Presbyterian Hospital, Bell Atlantic, and Con Edison all gave money. Time Warner signed on as the lead sponsor.

Peter and Dave would draw on nearly a decade's worth of goodwill and partnerships to make the event happen. They assembled a board comprising neighborhood representatives. Brenda Rosado, Charlie Rangel, and the commanders of the 33rd and 34th Precincts all agreed to put their influence behind the event, expediting permits and cutting through red tape. Nicholas Estavillo helped solve a last-minute snafu over a sound permit. Vazquez acted as liaison with New York Road Runners, which sanctioned the 5K and partnered with Coogan's in planning it. Sam Garcia created art for posters, leaflets, and T-shirts.

A glaring issue was the condition of the roadways around the George Washington Bridge, which were potholed and crumbling. That presented runners with the possibility of sprained ankles and broken legs. Rosado coordinated with the city department of transportation to have the holes filled prior to the race. Some areas were resurfaced. Peter put on a lunch for the crews that would be doing the work. One of the lasting legacies of the race would be improved road conditions along Fort Washington Avenue.

In early February 1999, just before he was due in Florida for spring training, Manny Ramirez, the slugging right fielder for the Cleveland Indians, came into Coogan's for a beer. Ramirez, who was broad-shouldered, thickarmed, and easygoing, had grown up in Washington Heights and attended George Washington High School, where he set records on the baseball field. The Indians drafted him in 1991. Two years later he made his major league debut. By 1998, he was one of the elite hitters in baseball, finishing sixth in the voting for the American League MVP, amassing 45 home runs and 145 RBI while earning $2.85 million in salary.

While not a regular at the bar, Ramirez was a neighborhood celebrity. People remembered seeing him during his high school years, running on the streets with a truck tire around his waist. That day in February, Peter buttonholed him as soon as he entered the bar and started bending his ear about the 5K. "Come with me, I want to show you something," he said, leading Ramirez up the block. They went in through the back entrance of the Armory. It was late afternoon, and the track was full of student-athletes training. Sun beamed in from the high windows. Peter let Ramirez take in the scene for a moment. "Can you imagine if there'd been a place like this in the neighborhood when you were younger?" Peter said. He then asked Ramirez to donate $5,000 to the race. The slugger agreed, and Peter immediately regretted not asking for twice that sum. Some of the donation was used to fund the Manny Ramirez High School Open, which would award the winning boys' and girls' teams $1,000 each for their athletics programs.

Through Sander, the legendary PR man Joe Goldstein was hired to run publicity for the race even as Peter was engaged in his own campaign. Peter spoke to just about anyone who entered the bar, touting the 5K. He went around to small businesses on the race route, talking up the event and offering the business owners modest sums of money to allow musicians to run extension cords from their amplifiers to the stores' electrical outlets. There were T-shirts to order, brochures to print, trophies to commission, medals to mint and thread onto ribbons. Dave Crenshaw and Al Kurland distributed thousands of leaflets and organized volunteers from the Police Athletic League and the Uptown Dreamers, who set up the race course before dawn.

Race day was Sunday, March 14, 1999. It was partly cloudy and cool, temperatures in the thirties, a steady breeze coming off the Hudson River. Five hundred runners from all over the city had registered for the race, and thousands of locals had turned out to watch. Up and down Fort Washington Avenue, they lined the streets or looked out their windows. Just as Peter was about to make his pre-race speech to the runners, he spotted Nicholas Estavillo lurking nearby. He was out of uniform, wearing a trench coat and hat. "You did it, kid," he said to Peter and shook his hand.

At 9:00 a.m., Sybil Dodson-Lucas, the newly elected chairperson of CB 12, started the race with a blast from an air horn. Two vintage pace cars, a 1931 Studebaker and a 1934 Ford, led the runners up the incline of Fort Washington Avenue toward the George Washington Bridge. A trio of bagpipers egged them on. Further up the avenue, the pipes gave way to the driving rock and roll of a local band, Men Without Hope. The racers continued, passing the well-appointed apartment buildings of upper Fort Washington Avenue to Margaret Corbin Plaza and the entrance to Fort Tryon Park. Once in the park, they followed a circular route that took them around the walls of the Cloisters, looping them back in a southward direction, the Hudson on their right with the cliffs of the Palisades visible in the distance. For newcomers to the Heights, the sublime vista was a surprise and a suggestion that there was more to the neighborhood than its reputation for drugs and crime. The Good Shepherd Folk Choir sang them through the park.

As they exited back onto Fort Washington Avenue, they were welcomed by the salsa and merengue of the District 6 school band. The cheers of the crowd mounted as the runners descended along Fort Washington to the finish line. Rachid Razguaoui, a Morocco-born Brooklynite, was the first man across. Bishop Loughlin Memorial High School took home both the boys' and girls' prizes in the Manny Ramirez High School Open.

The women's winner was Kim Griffin, a thirty-seven-year-old intensive-care physician at Mount Sinai Hospital, who'd been a decorated high school and college runner. Later that year, she was the twelfth woman to cross the finish line at the New York City Marathon.

At 10:00 a.m., once the 5K was over, the kids' races were staged on Fort Washington Avenue, just south of the finish line, in front of the Armory. More than a thousand children ran the pavements that morning in a series of sprints, their friends and families cheering them on. Every child who participated received a shirt and medal presented by local elected officials—Farrell, Rangel, Stanley Michels, and Guillermo Linares. Amid the crowd and the music and the pageantry, Peter found Lou Vazquez, and the two men hugged. Somehow, their plan had worked better than they'd dared hope. They had taken Coogan's and the Armory out into the neighborhood, and the neighborhood had taken back its streets, at least for a day.

CHAPTER THIRTY

The Apostrophe

Dania Zapata was a latchkey kid, raised by a single mother, an immigrant from the Dominican Republic, who worked as a seamstress; but Zapata was also raised by the neighborhood. She grew up on 191st Street and Audubon Avenue. Family friends who lived on her route home would notify her mother if she was late returning from school. In their building, the woman in the apartment closest to the street kept keys for many of the children of working parents who lived on the floors above. When the children arrived home, she would see them safely to their apartment, wait for the door to be locked from inside, and then head back downstairs to her post.

Zapata graduated from George Washington High School. While studying business in college, she got a part-time job doing the books for a caviar purveyor. She was warned, "Once you have food on your résumé, nobody else looks at you." This proved to be the case. After graduation, she went to work at the Baby Watson Cheesecake company, which produced confections sold in supermarkets all over the East Coast. Later Zapata worked at Steve's Mom, a rugelach maker in Brooklyn, before moving on to Spoonbread, Inc., a restaurant and catering company in Harlem started by the former model Norma Jean Darden. Zapata supervised staff, managed catering orders, and helped oversee the development of a second outpost, Miss Mamie's Spoonbread Too. Though she loved working with Darden, she was by this time in her late twenties with a young son to look after. She'd never had health insurance, and it suddenly became imperative to find a position with health benefits.

One of Spoonbread's vendors mentioned that there was a restaurant in Washington Heights that was looking for a manager.

"What place in Washington Heights?" Zapata asked.

"Coogan's," said the vendor.

"You mean the funeral home?"

Zapata went past Coogan's almost every day on her way to and from Spoonbread, but she rarely spent any time on or near 169th Street. She found the black doors and windowless walls off-putting, and, if you didn't drink—as she didn't—the "Tap Room" sign was not enticing. When she finally went in through one of those black doors for her interview, she was astonished at the full-color world within, the gleaming wood, the high ceilings, the famous faces that adorned the walls. *This has been here my whole adult life, and I didn't know about it?* she thought. She interviewed with Tess, then very pregnant, who was looking for someone who could take on many of her duties while she was on maternity leave and then remain as a manager when she returned. (James Fisher had departed for a job on the Jersey Shore and Coogan's had gone through several managers since, with mixed results.) To Tess, Zapata came across as knowledgeable and assured and someone whose personality would fit with theirs: she was strong enough to complement the three of them without upsetting the careful balance. Zapata laid out her minimum salary requirement, along with the expectation that she would receive health insurance and two weeks' paid vacation a year. Tess nodded, and said, "I'm going to have to discuss this with the boys." Before Zapata had even made it back to Spoonbread, she got a call asking her to come for an interview with Peter. They offered her a thirty-day trial. On the thirtieth day, Dave arrived at the office with a box of business cards bearing Zapata's name.

She would work at Coogan's for the next seventeen years and become integral to the daily functioning of the restaurant. Her extroverted, sunny personality immediately endeared her to Coogan's customers. And she developed almost instantly a close friendship with Tess; they formed a female pairing to counter "the boys." They checked on each other to make sure they each got home safely if it was late or if the weather was inclement. Zapata's fluency in Spanish, her ties to the neighborhood, and her Dominican background helped her fill an important gap in the management team. She could relate to the experiences of employees who'd also grown up in the area. When needed, she served as a translator for Spanish-speaking customers and staff. When the owners considered adding brunch items to their menu, she warned them that Dominicans would not pay restaurant prices for eggs, a staple of the Dominican diet. "You know they sell them by the dozen at the supermarket?" she said, and she was right; pancakes proved far more popular.

Zapata took her role seriously and pushed the owners to try new things. She had instructors from a local firehouse come in and teach the staff CPR and the Heimlich maneuver. It paid immediate dividends. The following Saturday,

Zapata was eating with her mother in the dining room when a waitress who had not attended the Heimlich tutorial burst out of the Gallery Room doors, saying, "Someone in there is choking!" Dania hustled to the table and deployed her newly acquired skill, sending a piece of steak flying through the air. Then she went back to dinner with her mother. When the family members of the choking victim came out to thank her, she waved them off. "It was nothing. I just want to get back to my pork chop."

Expanding the bar's community outreach, Zapata created a mentoring program for girls in the neighborhood, which ran for six weeks at Coogan's during the summer vacations. Its focus was on improving confidence and self-esteem, as well as to redress the challenges that many girls in the neighborhood faced, having been raised in immigrant, often single-parent households, where education and career development were secondary concerns. The participants, aged between seven and fourteen, were taught table manners, interview techniques, conversational etiquette, CPR, and yoga. A session was organized for parents in which they were introduced to the technology their children were likely to be using; they were also taught how to monitor their children's online activities.

Dave started referring to Zapata affectionately as "the apostrophe in Coogan's"—possessive, clarifying, essential. Every year, on the anniversary of her start date—August 15—the owners brought her flowers. When Dania's mother was admitted to Presbyterian Hospital, they sent over coconut shrimp and chicken fingers to the doctors and nurses looking after her. All of this bound her to Coogan's in a way that was more like family than a traditional employer-employee relationship. The joshing, friendly exchanges she enjoyed with Peter, Tess, and Dave had one downside though: the steady flow of conversation could be distracting. Zapata got in the habit of arriving an hour early so that she could get some work done before the jokes and chatter started.

⚓

CHAPTER THIRTY-ONE

God Forgives You

For years, Peter had been working on a musical about the final day of business at an Irish saloon in a changing New York City neighborhood. The play was a repository for his thoughts and fears about the bar business, a warped mirror through which he reflected on his own career and thwarted artistic ambitions. It began life as *Pudding's: The Last Saloon,* then became *Coogan's Castle,* and finally *The Castle Bar.* Peter wrote the book and the lyrics; the music was by Franklin Micare, a singer-songwriter who'd had a regular Friday night gig at Pudding's.

Peter spent more than a decade trying to get his play produced. The irony, of course, was that Peter already had a long-running show on Broadway—Coogan's itself—in which he was the producer, the director, and the singing star. Nevertheless, in uncanny ways, *The Castle Bar* anticipated events that would occur some two decades later at Coogan's. On the cusp of the twenty-first century, Washington Heights was edging toward a transformation that would have been near unimaginable when Peter, Dave, and Sean took over the bar. Crime was falling, rents were on the rise, and the neighborhood seemed to be getting whiter by the day. In Peter's play, the bar is saved by an eleventh-hour twist of fate. It was hard to imagine, but Coogan's would one day need a similar intervention to stay in business.

Getting a play produced in New York is likely one of the few enterprises even more challenging than opening a restaurant there. In both cases, you needed connections and good luck. Peter at least had the former. During his time working at the performing arts nonprofit HAI, he had befriended the actress Geraldine Fitzgerald, who became a guiding light for the play. The Irish-born Fitzgerald had a long and distinguished career that included an Academy Award nomination for the 1939 adaptation of *Wuthering Heights*. A trusting bond formed between the aspiring playwright and the great actress. For a star of her stature—someone who counted Laurence Olivier and Charlie Chaplin as friends—she struck Peter as generous, smart, and surprisingly low-key. One of the final performances of Fitzgerald's career was an evening of songs and stories at Coogan's.

Early in the nineties, Fitzgerald arranged a reading of *Coogan's Castle* in her apartment, with Milo O'Shea, Malachy McCourt, Moira Kelly, and Bryan Dotson all taking roles. Peter, who was rarely dumbstruck, sat mute at Fitzgerald's table, watching and listening with amazement as the actors ran through his script. When it was finished, he said to Fitzgerald, "I'm going to take a walk around the block so they can tell you what they really think." When he returned, Fitzgerald chided him for false modesty: "You will not stop doing this play!" But even with that encouragement, Peter would not be able to land a full-scale production. There would be other readings of the play over the years, including one at Coogan's in 1996 and another at the Church of the Incarnation. But a production of selections from *The Castle Bar* mounted in the dining room at Coogan's in 2000 was the closest the play ever came to a full staging.

To cast that production in 2000, Peter drew on the full spectrum of his connections, from neighborhood regulars at Coogan's to people he'd performed with when he owned Pudding's. Many of them did not know each other, and during rehearsals there was a stunning revelation of a hidden connection between the man playing the saloon's chef and the leader of the gospel choir that sang in several of the musical numbers.

The choir leader was Darren Ferguson, a newly ordained minister who was in the process of rehabilitating his life after a long prison sentence. His Voices of Faith Missionary Church choir had sung at the finish line of the first Salsa, Blues, and Shamrocks race. Peter had been impressed with their performance; he and Dave were also drawn to Ferguson's story of personal and spiritual redemption.

Ferguson, a tall, charismatic Black man, grew up in Northern Manhattan and the Bronx. He dabbled briefly in stand-up comedy, but his true passion was singing. His goal was to be an R&B and gospel superstar like his idols Luther Vandross and Lionel Richie. By his early twenties, he seemed well on his way to achieving that goal, recording songs and performing regularly in clubs in Midtown and Harlem. But there was one major impediment; as he later wrote in his memoir, *How I Became an Angry Black Man*, it was a "White Lady Called Cocaine." For six years, cocaine was his "confidante and closest companion."

He knew his addiction had gotten out of control when he broke one of his own cardinal rules and got high before a performance. All the money for rent and utilities for the apartment he shared with his grandfather had disappeared into his bloodstream. Facing a seventy-two-hour eviction notice, he went on a bender, combining his usual drugs of choice with Bacardi Dark and expired Valium. In his memoir, he described that morning:

> I walked back and forth in the house. I paced, and punched things. I muttered to myself, and then, all of a sudden, everything got really simple: If the apartment were no longer there, I would not have to pay the rent. If the apartment burned down, for instance, I would be relived of all of this pressure, and we would be free to go and live somewhere else.

He made a pyre of the eviction notices and past-due bills on top of his grandfather's dresser, doused it in kerosene, and ignited it with a lighter. As the papers burned, he put on his coat, grabbed his bag and left the apartment. When outside, he wrote, he turned and looked back at his bedroom window. There was no smoke. Figuring, hopefully, that the blaze had put itself out, he proceeded south to the Macombs Dam Bridge, crossing into the Bronx where his girlfriend lived. At 2:00 p.m., his mother called to say that the police were looking for him.

When he turned himself in to the 34th Precinct, Ferguson learned that an eighty-seven-year-old woman named Marjorie Styles, who lived in the apartment above his, had died from smoke inhalation. Ferguson recalled, "I got down on my knees, right there in the interrogation room at about 10:00 PM on February 5th, 1990 and did something that I had never done before. I prayed."

He spent the next eight and a half years behind bars—sixteen months on Rikers Island and seven years in Sing Sing. It was while he was at Rikers waiting for his case to be heard that he found his faith. At Sing Sing, Ferguson enrolled in college courses, directed the prison choir, led Bible study, preached his first sermon, and generally tried to be an agent of peace and reconciliation. The year before his release, he appeared in a C-SPAN documentary about the prison. In one scene, he reflects, "The bottom line is when you go in that cell at night. It's just you and yourself and the problem is there's a lot of guys that can't deal with themselves. They feel guilty for what they did but they don't know how to express it. They don't really understand what true remorse is. When you go in that cell late at night, you're in there by yourself. It's just you and your crime."

Ferguson had graduated in 1995 from Bronx Community College with an associate's degree in paralegal studies. A year later, he obtained a master's degree in theology from the New York Theological Seminary. A parole board approved his early release, and Ferguson returned to civilian life in the fall of 1998, finding work in faith-based social services organizations.

The following year, he learned that an Irish bar was organizing a 5K race in Washington Heights and needed a gospel choir to sing at the event. Ferguson had been licensed for ministry for less than a month. He was stunned by the scale of what Coogan's pulled off with the 5K. "I fell in love with Dave and Peter," he said.

A year or so later, Peter got in touch with Ferguson about *The Castle Bar*. "Around this time," Ferguson recalled, "Peter started talking to me about this guy named Taz, saying 'He really reminds me of you.'" Taz, a karaoke regular with

Kevin "Taz" Davis, Darren Ferguson, Peter Walsh, and actor
Mickey Kelly at the performance of *The Castle Bar*.

a deep and rich bass voice, had been cast as the saloon's
African American cook.

When Ferguson arrived at Coogan's for rehearsal, Peter
welcomed the pastor, saying, "Oh, great, Taz is here." Ferguson looked across the room and saw Kevin "Taz" Davis,
the neighbor and schoolmate who'd been raised by Marjorie Styles, the woman who died in the fire he'd set. Though
not related by blood, she had been like a mother to Davis.
Ferguson was frozen. While in prison, he'd received messages from Davis warning him that, "If I see you, whatever
happens *happens.*" Ferguson had made up his mind that he
was not going to defend himself. "I was going to put my
hands in my pockets. Whatever he did, I deserved it." At
Coogan's though, Ferguson was conflicted, thinking, *Am I
really going to put my hands in my pockets? Is he going to
kill me? Does he have a* right *to kill me?*

Davis, who had bleached his beard and mustache for his role, approached Ferguson and said, "Come here. No, *come here*." He took Ferguson's head in his hands, kissed Ferguson on both of his cheeks, and said, "God forgives you, and so do I." The two men embraced each other and wept. (Davis later reflected that his response might have been different if they'd met anywhere but Coogan's.)

A few days later, Davis and Ferguson took the stage together to perform in *The Castle Bar*.

❧

CHAPTER THIRTY-TWO

Every New Yorker's Nightmare

It was the end of April but already uncomfortably warm and stuffy amid the press of bodies in the Midtown subway station. Tired after working a long day, the thirty-seven-year-old copy clerk consoled himself by thinking ahead to dinner with his wife and children, followed by that night's Yankee game. He heard a commotion coming from down the platform; a man was behaving oddly, spouting nonsense. He and everyone else in the station did what you do at such times: try to ignore the man and hope that nothing happens. He heard the distant rumble of an arriving train. With the determination of a veteran straphanger, he shuffled and edged for position, trying to guess where the doors would be when the train stopped. If he was lucky, he might get a seat. Just then, a shove from behind sent him down onto the tracks as the broad metal face of the train emerged from the tunnel.

That horrific event—every New Yorker's nightmare—happened to Edgar Rivera in the spring of 1999. In the 51st Street and Lexington Avenue station, Rivera, on his way home to the Bronx, was pushed onto the tracks by a man who had been behaving erratically, just as the train pulled into the station. The train operator applied the emergency brake, but it was too late; Rivera was struck and dragged some fifty feet down the platform. When the train finally came to a stop, Rivera was caught between the second and third cars. Both of his legs had been severed.

A pair of FDNY men, Fred Ill and John McLean, soon arrived at the scene. Rivera's eyes were still fluttering with life, and the two firefighters managed to maneuver him out from under the train. He was taken to Bellevue Hospital where an attempt to surgically reattach his legs failed. However, Rivera survived and was later widely admired for how he responded to the ordeal, not with anger and despair but with gratitude for getting another chance at life.

Moved by Rivera's stoic bravery, Captain Ill, a twenty-two-year veteran of the fire department, did something he'd never done before: he went to the hospital to visit someone he'd helped save. A bond developed between the two men. Ill assisted the Riveras in their search for wheelchair-accessible housing. He offered to pay for Rivera's son to attend his alma mater until a foundation stepped in and offered him a scholarship. "He's gone, in a sense, above and beyond the call of duty," Rivera told the *Daily News* in October of 1999.

Reading that *Daily News* story on a Monday morning in the office at Coogan's, Peter Walsh felt awestruck. He was still riding high from the success of the first Salsa, Blues, and Shamrocks race, and the story resonated deeply with him. It represented the spirit he wanted Coogan's and the race to embody—of service and fellowship. Peter got in touch with someone he knew at the fire department who told him where Ill worked. He went down to the firehouse and introduced himself to Ill, taking an immediate liking to the fireman. "He had a Gary Cooper aura about him," Peter later recalled. "Like a western hero."

He invited the Ills and the Riveras to Coogan's for dinner. At that dinner, Peter asked Ill and Rivera if they would be the official starters for the second Salsa, Blues, and Shamrocks 5K, which he was already in the process of planning. Both men agreed. They would become the faces of the 2000 race, featured in local television news coverage and articles in the *Times* and the *Daily News*. The second race was an even bigger success than the first—more runners, more people lining the route, more media attention—and confirmed what Peter and Lou Vazquez had hoped from the beginning: that it would become an annual celebration for the neighborhood, one that united the community as it took back its streets.

"In a section of New York City made up largely of black, Latino and Irish people, even a running race goes beyond just exercise, becoming an exercise in race relations," wrote Corey Kilgannon in the *Times*. "And at a time when ethnicity is frequently discussed as polarizing, the harmony in this neighborhood might surprise anyone who has glimpsed it only through police blotters and media dispatches."

～➘

CHAPTER THIRTY-THREE

Ballad of the Spirit

On the morning of September 11, 2001, Dave heard the news of the first plane strike on the radio while he was parking his car on Broadway. In the basement office at Coogan's, Peter and Dania were watching the television coverage. (Tess was on vacation.) Dave soon joined them and when the second plane struck, he momentarily thought that he was watching a replay of the first. Then Peter, who'd recently read the book Jim Dwyer had cowritten about the 1993 World Trade Center bombing, shouted, "This is an attack! They've come back to finish the job!"

Much as they felt compelled, the trio could not stay in the office watching TV. There was a business to run. The housing office at Columbia called and asked if Coogan's could provide two hundred lunches for the students in Bard Hall. Dave and the kitchen staff scrambled to assemble the meals. As he crossed Haven Avenue to deliver the boxed lunches, Dave saw fighter jets roaring overhead, heading south. People on the street cheered, raising their arms at the planes. Back at the restaurant, they learned that the Armory was being readied as a secondary triage area. They prepared for a possible crush of business as people came to Washington Heights to search for their loved ones: the Cop Shot Protocol, but exponentially larger. A few neighborhood folk came in, mostly to check on the bar's staff and to exchange looks of astonishment. Because of the shutdown of the subways, there was a stream of pedestrians walking past the bar, bringing in some newcomers. All the TVs in Coogan's were tuned to the news, with the volume up—a rarity. The repeated images of the second plane crashing into Tower 2; the black specks of people jumping; the fire trucks and police cars; ashen-faced survivors. Some customers were riled up, shouting at the screens, "These fucking guys! We're going to get back at them!" But most people watched with a trance-like stare. As the day wore on, it became clear that there would be no crush at the Armory, or at the bar.

In the afternoon, Dave drove to Fordham Prep to pick up his son. The George Washington Bridge was closed; they made it home to River Edge in a roundabout fashion, via the Tappan Zee. That evening there was an emergency Mass at their church. Rumors had been circulating that Joe Esposito, the NYPD's chief of department (and a former 34th Precinct commander), had been killed at Ground Zero. Only days earlier, Dave, Peter, and their wives had been with Esposito at a birthday party in the city. Now Dave and Kathleen prayed for him. Later, they would learn that it was the FDNY's chief of department, Peter Ganci, a thirty-three-year veteran, who had perished. Ganci had rushed to the site after the first plane strike. He was directing rescue efforts in front of 1 World Trade Center when the building collapsed.

The next afternoon Peter received news that Captain Frederick Ill had also been killed at Ground Zero. A mutual friend drove to the bar to tell Peter. That brought the attacks home to Coogan's in a way that the television images had not. In the days that followed, Peter wrote a song, "Ballad of the Spirit," which he dedicated to Ill's memory. These are the final stanzas:

> You'll see me in the eyes
> Of a neighbor on the road
> You touch me in your heart
> When a stranger shares the load

> I'm the ballad of the spirit
> A firefighter's pride
> The song of our fathers
> The days that never die

> So raise your hands together
> And take ol' glory high
> Through the smoke and the rubble
> The towers will arise.

Over in Europe, Vytas Rudys had woken from an afternoon nap. Bleary-eyed and hungover, Vytas turned on the television and could not believe what he saw. After leaving Coogan's, he'd gotten a certificate in database management and then a job at the Port Authority of New York and New Jersey headquartered in the World Trade Center. But he'd proved to be a terrible database manager and had been fired in August. He'd recently returned with his wife to Lithuania to celebrate his forty-first birthday on the tenth. It was their first visit back since leaving for New York. They gathered all of their old friends and family members for a huge bash that went late into the night. Vytas woke up just in time to see the second tower collapse. He scrolled through the list of contacts on his cell phone and realized that several of the people he knew with a 212 telephone number—some of them his former colleagues at the Port Authority—were possibly dead. He could have been one of them if he had not been fired. His incompetence as a database manager had likely saved his life.

September 11, a Tuesday, was Primary Day for New York City. Among the slate of races were the Democratic and Republican primaries for mayor, as well as several high-profile contests for city council and borough president. The polls opened at 6:00 a.m., but Governor George Pataki suspended voting not long after the attacks. Coogan's would customarily host a party for local campaign staff and poll workers as they watched the results come in. Steve Simon, the chief of staff for councilman Stanley Michels, who normally didn't get to Coogan's until well after the polls closed, was at the bar much earlier than he could ever have predicted. "Where else was I going to go?"

All votes cast that day were nullified, and polling rescheduled for two weeks later. Giuliani, who was dubbed "America's Mayor" in the days following 9/11, ended up endorsing billionaire political newcomer Michael Bloomberg. The devastating strike at the heart of the Financial District caused many voters to fear that corporations would flee the city, bringing about an economic collapse like the one New York faced in the 1970s. For just enough New Yorkers, 9/11 made a successful businessman such as Bloomberg suddenly seem like a more suitable candidate for mayor than a career politician like the eventual Democratic candidate, Mark Green. The consequences of that mayoral election for the city would be significant and long-lasting. Gentrification had been ongoing for years, but it would accelerate sharply under Bloomberg, transforming the city through the rezoning and redevelopment of neighborhoods. Inevitably, that transformation would work its way toward Northern Manhattan and Coogan's.

September 11 had also been a scheduled karaoke night at the bar. It was of course canceled and resumed only at the end of the month, offering those who came a chance to escape from the grim news for a few hours. Many of the cops and firefighters who had regularly participated did not immediately come back. However, as fall turned to winter, several of them did return, and each time one of them got up to sing, they were greeted with a hero's welcome.

Part Four

HOMECOMING

CHAPTER THIRTY-FOUR

Regulars

In the wake of the attacks, what many New Yorkers wanted more than anything else was comfort, familiarity, and a return to normalcy. Coogan's was there to provide that comfort to its regular patrons, and perhaps no patron was more regular (and more comfortable) at Coogan's than Steve Simon. Over the years, he'd become so close to Dave, Peter, and Tess that they sometimes treated him like an honorary staff member. In fact, he did have a quasi-official position as menu proofreader, a post he was given after repeatedly complaining about typos in the menu.

That familiarity could become a problem. Simon's favorite dish at Coogan's was a dessert special, the brandied peach crepes. He evangelized for those crepes, but sometimes this passion got him into hot water with the bar's owners. One evening Simon discovered to his dismay that the crepes were not on the menu. Refusing to be deprived, he got up from his table and went into the kitchen to speak with Chef José Ynoa. José—who had succeeded the now retired Chef Miguel after years of working the line—was in the midst of preparing dinner for a large party in the

Gallery Room. Mild-mannered and affable, he was used to visits from Simon. Simon asked José if he could make the peach crepes for him. José said he'd be happy to, but he had no peaches.

"What if I go get you some peaches?" Simon asked. "Could you make the crepes then?"

Nodding tolerantly, José said he could. Simon walked to the nearest supermarket only to discover that there were no peaches available. Undeterred, he bought a bag of nectarines and headed back to Coogan's. He presented the fruit to José and asked if he could make the crepes with nectarines instead of peaches. José said he could. Simon returned to his table to await the delicacy. In the meantime, Dave was in the Gallery Room fielding complaints from the diners still waiting for their meals. He stormed into the kitchen to ask what the hell was causing the delay only to find José slicing nectarines and mixing batter for the crepes instead of preparing dinner orders.

The crepes were already a source of tension among the Coogan's owners. Tess despised them as an anachronism from the 1970s. "Nobody buys them but Steve!" she said. "We should put something more contemporary on the menu." Dave wanted to keep them in the rotation of specials out of loyalty to their most regular customer. For his part, Peter noted that he was getting fat from eating the unserved portions of the dessert; no one but Simon ever ordered them.

Matters came to a head one night when Simon was eating in the dining room. Next to him was a large party for whom Coogan's had created a special, limited menu. Simon got to talking to those sitting nearest to him and raved about his favorite peach crepes. These were not a dessert option on the special menu, but a number of the

diners got curious and placed an order for them. The waitress relayed the request to the kitchen. Other meals were
delayed as José and his team worked to make the crepes.
Again, Dave stormed into the kitchen, demanding to know
what the hell was causing the delay.

After that, the crepes were removed even from the specials menu—at least for a while.

Unlike Simon, Cletus Hyacinth, who worked at the medical
center, had for many years done his best to stay away from
Coogan's. He was motivated by a sense of propriety; he
didn't want to bump into people he supervised when they
were drinking. But Coogan's—known to some as "Area
C" of the hospital—was an almost unavoidable part of
working at the medical center. On one of his occasional
visits to the bar, Hyacinth spied Cathy Subervi-Taylor, a
tall Latina, poised and familiar, sitting alone. He invited
her to join him for a drink. Subervi-Taylor recognized Hyacinth from the hallways of the medical center—a dap-
per Black man who wore bow ties and always said hello
whenever they crossed paths. She accepted the invitation.

Meeting Subervi-Taylor rid Hyacinth of his caution regarding Coogan's. As they grew closer, Friday happy hours
at the bar became part of their weekly routine. Before long
they were bonding with some of the other end-of-the-week
regulars. There was Joe Riley, a security consultant who
umpired local high school baseball games; Dago Remy
Suarez, an officer in the police auxiliary; Jenny Mercado,
a longtime hospital employee, and others. Subervi-Taylor
said that just thinking about going to Coogan's lifted the
weight of the workweek from her shoulders. "You feel
at home," Hyacinth recalled. "We tried other bars. It just
didn't work."

Hyacinth discovered that Coogan's was more than just a place to have fun. It was also a support network for difficult times. When he was out of work for a period, the other regulars would stand him drinks. And when one of the Friday night bartenders, Bremi Ramos, learned that he was going to be alone for Thanksgiving, she invited him to join her family for the meal. On Hyacinth's forty-fifth birthday, Ramos, who was pregnant at the time, said, "Let's do a shot together." When Hyacinth raised an eyebrow, Ramos replied, "Mine'll be water."

Even after Hyacinth got a new job in Brooklyn, he still headed across the city to Coogan's when he got out of work on Friday. He and Subervi-Taylor moved into an apartment together in the Bronx, but they fretted over who would get Coogan's if they broke up. Neither was willing to be separated from it. "I hope we're mature enough that we would both come in and sit at opposite ends of the bar and still have a good time," Hyacinth said.

Another pair of regulars, Evamarii Johnson and her husband, Cal Pritner, had bought an apartment across the street from Coogan's in 2000, relocating to New York from the West Coast. They moved in with little more than an air mattress and a coffee maker. The bare cupboards sent them across Broadway to Coogan's for dinner. That first night they found a group of politicians seated around a table deliberating intensely. "OK," Johnson decided on the spot. "This is our joint."

Both Johnson, who was Black, and Pritner, who was white, worked in theater—Johnson as a voice and dialect instructor and Pritner as an actor, professor, and artistic director. In Peter Walsh, they found a welcoming fellow thespian. Before long, a framed photograph of Pritner—

dressed as Mark Twain in his celebrated one-man show—
appeared on the restaurant's wall.

Pritner was from the Midwest, but for Johnson, who
grew up in and around New York City, the move east was
a sort of homecoming. Raised by a stepfather who was a
barfly, she felt at home in saloons in part because she had
done her homework in them while her stepfather played
the numbers. Her drink of choice was an ice-cold Tito's
martini, *very dry*, with a twist. "The first time I came into
Coogan's, I told the bartender to 'imagine the vermouth.'
He got it down." As her drink arrived, Johnson would exclaim, "Thank you, Doctor!" Pritner, a teetotaler, preferred
an Arnold Palmer—or just plain water.

Peter and Pritner discussed the idea of mounting a production of the Twain play at the bar, but before they could
make it happen, Pritner was diagnosed with brain cancer.
He was treated at New York–Presbyterian, undergoing
operations and chemotherapy. Johnson would stay in Pritner's hospital room as late as she was allowed to do so and
then head over to Coogan's for a drink. At Thanksgiving,
she and her family ate dinner at the bar and then took the
dessert to Pritner at the Isabella Geriatric Center. He died
on the first of December.

After Pritner's death, Johnson continued coming by
Coogan's about once a week. The restaurant's staff knew
to seat her at her regular table across from her husband's
photograph. At the start of every meal, she'd raise an ice-
cold martini to toast him and their life together.

CHAPTER THIRTY-FIVE

The Dreamers

No list of regulars would be complete without Coach Dave Crenshaw, who seemed to be everywhere in the neighborhood yet always in Coogan's. Coach Dave's favorite items on the menu were the chicken wings and the ice cream special. The portions of both dishes were generous, and they were made for sharing, which was good because Crenshaw frequently showed up at Coogan's with a gaggle of Dreamers in tow. They might arrive after spending the morning cleaning up the playground in Edgecombe Park, putting a new coat of paint on a neighborhood building, or plucking litter off the pavements. Going to Coogan's was the carrot Crenshaw offered his kids—a carrot shaped like a dish of ice cream.

The bar's owners wanted to support Crenshaw's work with the Dreamers and knew that he ran the program on a shoestring. Crenshaw never asked for a discount, but Dave, Peter, and Tess accommodated him in other ways. They let him pay his tab off over time or they changed the plating of items to be more suitable for large groups. The Coogan's ice cream special was supposed to have two scoops of ice cream in each serving, but when Crenshaw and his kids arrived, each scoop was delivered in a separate bowl, so every kid got their own, cutting the price in half. Likewise, the chicken wing special (three dozen wings), which was only supposed to be available during football games: no matter the month, if the Dreamers showed up, it was football season at Coogan's.

When the Dreamers went on their trips to Washington, DC, or camping in New Jersey, they usually boarded the bus in front the Shabazz Center (formerly known as the Audubon Ballroom) on Broadway and 165th Street. But the departure times for these trips were so early in the morning that the center was often closed. There was no access to bathrooms or to warm interiors while the kids waited for the bus. Hearing Crenshaw mention this at the bar one evening, Dave offered Coogan's as a departure point. The night porter would let the Dreamers in, and they waited in the Gallery Room until the bus arrived. Coogan's also would pack a lunch for them for these trips: sandwich, chips, fruit, and a cookie. Crenshaw liked the symbolism of leaving from the Shabazz Center, but the amenities offered by Coogan's were beyond compare.

One night, Crenshaw was in Coogan's without his Dreamers. It was late, after 11:00 p.m., and he was drinking at the bar. He ended up talking to Detective Christopher Stoll, the newly appointed community affairs officer from the 33rd Precinct. Stoll was paying his bill when the conversation started, but he ended up staying at Coogan's for another couple of hours. There was an open seat on the Precinct Community Council, and he thought that Coach Dave would be a good fit. Crenshaw, who had sworn off all dealings with the 33rd Precinct after Kevin Cedeno's death, initially rejected the idea. But Stoll was persistent. "I'm not from Long Island or upstate. I grew up in the Bronx. I'm from here, man. I'm from here." Crenshaw recalls Stoll saying, "We really want people like you on the council. We know what you do and how you carry yourself. We want to make a change." Crenshaw said that if he joined the council, he would speak his mind, and he would bring other people to the meetings who would speak theirs. He questioned how serious the precinct was about changing its approach to community relations. "I can bring folks on my street in," said Crenshaw, "but it doesn't mean you're going to like what they say." Stoll replied, "We want to work on this. Good relationships are where it starts."

"We talked and talked, and he convinced me that this is what I had to do," recalled Crenshaw. He agreed to become a candidate for the empty seat. Not everybody approved: Crenshaw got called a sellout. But, as promised, once Crenshaw was elected, he started bringing in people who spoke their minds, people like Robert Fullilove. People like his brother, the Reverend Jeffrey Crenshaw. He also brought in kids from his program to speak and listen, to play the violin in meetings, and to show the cops a different side to neighborhood youth than they might see on the street. A dialogue opened up. The police listened to Crenshaw's advice about how to handle situations that might arise at freelance block parties without resorting to violence or mass arrests. Eventually, Crenshaw became the vice president of the precinct community council, and relations between the police and the community in 6 Block City slowly improved. "That block has a strange relationship with the 33rd Precinct. A long history, not a good history," said Crenshaw. "But it's been getting better."

Coogan's had become a venue where relationships like

that could begin, a place where a community activist like Crenshaw and a police detective like Stoll both felt comfortable. "I'm not sure that conversation happens anywhere else," Stoll later reflected. "I don't think Dave would have let his guard down anywhere else."

CHAPTER THIRTY-SIX

Changes

As the crack epidemic faded and the neighborhood changed, so did the exterior of Coogan's. The funereal black entrances were replaced with a series of aluminum-framed French doors that admitted light as well as curious glances. The renovation—and the newfound ease with which snooping passersby could peek into the dining room—was the cause of dismay for at least one of the bar's regulars, who was in the habit of bringing his mistress to Coogan's during the week and his wife on the weekends. But most other patrons welcomed the changes. In the spring and summer, there were tables and chairs out on the sidewalk in front of the restaurant, a sight that was unimaginable in 1985. On the bar's façade, stately pewter letters spelling out COOGAN'S had displaced the venerable lasso logo. Inside, however, the saloon remained largely the same. A couple of years earlier, the fire marshal had forced them to take down the array of track singlets that were hanging from the rafters. The owners continued to mount photographs, artwork, awards, posters, news clippings, and book jackets to their walls, leaving almost no open space. There were a few other signs of the times, too: the cigarette machine was gone; so was the pay phone. But if you spoke nicely to the bartender, she'd lend you one of the house charging cords.

The streetscape around Coogan's had been altered too. At the southern end of the block, where Bab's, a mom-and-pop clothing store had once operated, there was now a Starbucks. Next door, a Chipotle and a Sbarro. Broadway, between 165th Street and Dyckman, boasted a string of new nightlife options: the Fort Washington Public House, Apt. 78, the Buddha Beer Bar, and the Tryon Public House. At the western end of Dyckman Street, past a flourishing restaurant row, there was La Marina, an indoor-outdoor resort-style party venue that sometimes felt more like Cancun than New York City. Yellow taxicabs, once rarely seen north of 125th Street, were now commonplace, fighting for fares with the local gypsy car services as well as Ubers and Lyfts. The neighborhood, which had once deterred prospective medical students from attending Columbia's College of Physicians and Surgeons and its School of Nursing, had in recent years, because of *In the Heights* and *Hamilton*, seemed ever more attractive.

On Haven Avenue, in 2016, Columbia University had erected the fourteen-story Vagelos Education Center, a harbinger of the future. Designed by Diller Scofidio + Renfro in collaboration with Gensler, it stood out among the five-story brick apartment buildings like a slice of wedding cake on a table of oatmeal cookies. All the while, New York–Presbyterian Hospital and Columbia University continued to acquire and develop uptown properties. Rumors started spreading that the hospital had "big plans" for the stretch of Broadway around Coogan's.

There had also been some turnover among the political class. Charlie Rangel and Denny Farrell had retired, replaced by Adriano Espaillat and Al Taylor, respectively. Former councilmember Stanley Michels had passed away in 2008. Maria Luna, however, remained a presence in the district and in the restaurant's dining room. The new Manhattan borough president, Gale Brewer, who assumed office in January 2014, was a frequent visitor and a friend to the bar's owners. Other familiar faces had also moved on, though. Brenda Rosado, the onetime district manager at the community board, and her husband, Bob Tracy, now lived in Wilmington, Delaware, where Tracy was chief of police. Artist Sam Garcia, while still painting at a feverish rate, had moved to Puerto Rico. Sybil Dodson-Lucas, who'd once worked front-of-house at Coogan's, was in Florida. Bryan Dotson, who'd run the Bridge Theatre Company out of the Gallery Room, had left the hospital and started a communications firm.

Though Norbert Sander had died in 2017, the close ties between the Armory and Coogan's remained intact. In 2012, Sander had spearheaded a successful effort to relocate the storied Millrose Games and its featured event, the Wanamaker Mile, from Madison Square Garden to the Armory. Each February thereafter, at the post-meet party, if you happened to be dining at Coogan's, you could see world-class athletes such as Matt Centrowitz and Bernard Lagat perform karaoke before a crowd of their peers. Every March, the neighborhood still turned out for the Salsa, Blues, and Shamrocks 5K, but since 2016 it had been managed by New York Road Runners, and not the bar. The dessert menu at Coogan's paid tribute to the ongoing special relationship between the bar and the sport, touting confections named after star athletes such as Eamonn Coghlan, Alan Webb, Joe Kovacs, and Ajeé Wilson.

It seemed that riots and gun battles were things of the

past in Washington Heights. These days, the police were far more likely to be summoned for a noise complaint than a homicide. The pressing challenges facing the community were those of gentrification: rising rents, the displacement of longtime residents, and the shuttering of local small businesses. An analysis published by the CUNY Dominican Studies Institute in 2018 quantified those trends. The price of housing in Washington Heights and Inwood appreciated sixfold between 2000 and 2015. Also, as the population of Northern Manhattan grew during those years, the number of Dominicans living there had dropped, many of them relocating north to the Bronx and Yonkers. Though the Heights was still seen as the heart of Dominican New York, since 2000, the majority of people moving to the neighborhood were Asian.

Of course, Peter, Dave, and Tess were still at Coogan's, running the joint. Over two decades, their partnership had been largely free of the strife that characterized earlier ownership teams. A test of their trusting and stable relationship had come in the mid-aughts, when Coogan's opened a second location, Coogan's Parrot Bay, on Third Avenue between 93rd and 94th Streets, not far from where Peter lived at the time.

Parrot Bay was a folly, ill-conceived and ultimately short-lived. Unlike Coogan's, Parrot Bay did not have a captive target audience such as the medical center; unlike Coogan's, it had plenty of competition. Yorkville touted an abundance of established bars and restaurants. It was also a neighborhood where the Coogan's name carried little cachet. The new saloon's identity was a muddled hybrid—a Caribbean sports bar—partly inspired by Peter's regular vacations to Turks and Caicos. "Tropical atmosphere with an Irish touch," the promotional materials promised. "Runners, surfers, and wildlife welcome." Peter was to be the guiding spirit of the place, but he found himself overwhelmed. He still had plenty of responsibilities uptown. Eventually, a manager was hired to run Parrot Bay, but by then it was a lost cause. With no steady daytime business and a tepid nighttime trade, it bled money fast. Realizing that they had a turkey instead of a parrot on their hands, Tess, Dave, and Peter quickly sold the property. The entire escapade lasted less than two years.

In previous iterations of the Coogan's ownership, the consequences of such a failure would have been disastrous. Finger-pointing and blame would have been the order of the day. Arguments would have ensued. But there were no such recriminations among Peter, Tess, and Dave. There was still a business uptown to run.

And there were other hurdles to surmount. Coogan's had helped turn the neighborhood around, but that success had brought it competition—the bar scene was also gentrifying. Every time a new tavern or restaurant opened nearby, Coogan's would lose a piece of their regular business. Some drinkers and diners might return, eventually, but not everyone did. Catering, which brought in as much as $700,000 a year, kept them afloat, but in 2015 and 2016, finances became increasingly tight. Then, manager Dania Zapata quit in 2017. After nearly two decades of harmonious collaboration, she and the owners had a falling-out. Zapata, now married, had moved out of Washington Heights to live with her husband in New Jersey. The commute was long and expensive and, with the restaurant struggling to make payroll each week, the owners were not able to offer Zapata much overtime, which would have helped allay those high commuting costs. Feelings were hurt, but once

Zapata found a job in the Garden State, she patched things up with Dave and Peter and Tess, returning every March to run the charity brunch on the morning of the 5K.

Also weighing on all of them was an ongoing class-action lawsuit brought against the owners and Coogan's on behalf of current and former employees in November 2016 and refiled with additional plaintiffs in May 2018. The employees were represented by C. K. Lee, a notorious "shakedown" lawyer. The suit accused the bar owners of stiffing the employees in a variety of ways, including time shaving, not giving them their full tip credit, failing to pay overtime, and denying them meal credits. Plaintiffs said that they were expected to eat leftover food from catering events instead of being given a proper staff meal.

Following the advice of their lawyer—the uncannily named Jane Jacobs—the bar's owners, after months of negotiating, settled the suit in January 2019 without admitting any wrongdoing. They decided to settle after being advised that the cost of taking the case to court could run as high as half a million dollars—an untenable sum given their recent financial struggles. The settlement left Tess, Dave, and Peter feeling angry and frustrated, but also relieved that it was over.

"We do not believe we have done anything wrong, but had to make a business decision," said Jacobs, on behalf of the owners, to the *Daily News*. "We are looking forward to putting this behind us and continuing to be part of community that we have served for more than 30 years."

And beneath all of these concerns, there was another, bigger, issue ticking away like a time bomb—an issue the owners wouldn't be able to settle on their own.

CHAPTER THIRTY-SEVEN

How Stupid Could You Be?

If you walked out the front door of Coogan's, crossed to the median strip on Broadway, and looked south, you could see the silhouettes of the cranes that were being used to build the towers of Hudson Yards on the western edge of Midtown—reportedly the most expensive real estate development in U.S. history. With a property developer in the White House, a spree of acquisition and construction had accelerated all over New York. Supertall skyscrapers were sprouting near Central Park, and uptown, all around Coogan's, long-established small businesses began closing at an alarming rate. Seven of them had been evicted in recent years from Broadway between 162nd and 163rd Streets after Coltown Properties bought the building that housed them, along with four other buildings in the area. The enterprises that lost their leases included a tax and business service center, a barbershop, a sporting goods store, and Punta Cana, a Dominican restaurant that had been in operation since the 1980s. Liberato Foods, which had served the neighborhood on the adjoining block for four decades, saw its rent triple to $30,000 a month, forcing it to shutter. And in 2017, New York–Presbyterian

Hospital began emptying out the block just north of Coogan's, putting a pharmacy, a shoe repair store, a dry cleaner, and a supermarket on month-to-month leases in anticipation of building a new thirteen-story mixed-use structure on the site. One of the casualties was the Reme lunch counter, which stood opposite Coogan's on the northwest corner of 169th and Broadway for most of the bar's existence. The two hostelries had a mutually respectful relationship; for years, Coogan's didn't serve breakfast because that was a big draw for Reme. The residents of the building above the lunch counter were pushed out of their apartments long before the new development got under way. (Demolition permits for the block were not filed until 2020.)

Reflecting on the eviction of Reme and the tenants from the apartment building across the street, Dave said, "If you've got a big project in the works and your calculations are off by three years, maybe you suck at what you do." The harshness of that assessment stemmed at least in part from Dave's own dealings with Royal Charter—the real estate arm of Presbyterian Hospital and the bar's landlord. As they watched the tide of small business closures, Dave and his partners were in extended talks to keep their own small business open.

In 2003, they had signed a fifteen-year lease extension with the hospital. The negotiations had taken five years, during which time they'd asked for and received letters of support from Denny Farrell and Stanley Michels. When finally in place, the extension called for annual rent increases of between 2.5 and 3.5 percent. That lease was scheduled to end on May 31, 2018. As early as 2013, when they were paying nearly $20,000 a month in rent, Coogan's owners had started the process of negotiating a new lease with

Royal Charter. They wanted to sign another fifteen-year extension with a similar range of rent increases. What went unstated was that they planned to sell the business midway through the new lease in order to fund their retirements, or, in Tess's case, a transition to her long-delayed post-Coogan's life as a stay-at-home mom. "People think we have some kind of pension," Dave often remarked. "We have a cash register. And when that cash register stops, our income stops."

Royal Charter, which had held holiday parties at Coogan's, rejected the owners' proposal of continuing with the previous pace of rent increases. Their job, they told Dave, was "to maximize the real estate potential" of the location. Such modest hikes no longer reflected the market rate for the rapidly gentrifying neighborhood. What they had in mind was doubling the rent to $40,000 a month. For Coogan's owners, that sum was not even remotely viable. They felt that the hike was so extreme that it did not even seem like a negotiating ploy; it was clearly intended to put them out of business.

Talks broke down. The Royal Charter representative the owners had been dealing with left his position. Months went by. Subsequent exchanges between tenant and landlord proved fruitless. At one point, Coogan's turned the tables and suggested that the hospital buy them out, but Royal Charter's offer was well below what the owners thought their business was worth. Relations continued to deteriorate until the summer of 2017, when Winick Realty began advertising and showing the space that Coogan's occupied. A listing also appeared on the commercial real estate website LoopNet. The bar's owners heard through connections that the asking price for their space was now $62,000 per month, more than triple what they were paying. Prospective tenants started showing up at the bar with realtors to look around the property. Peter, Tess, and Dave were forced to lie to their employees, saying that the unexpected visitors were city inspectors of one stripe or another.

On December 6, 2017, a mere six months from the end of their lease, Dave made a last-ditch attempt to reopen negotiations with Royal Charter. By this time Peter and Tess had thrown in the towel, but Dave was not ready to give up. He persuaded their partner Vincent Walsh to accompany him to a meeting with Kenrick Ou, the corporate director of real estate for New York–Presbyterian Hospital. They were offered a $5,000-a-month reduction from the market rate—that is, a new rent of $57,000 per month, a vertigo-inducing $37,000 increase on what they were currently paying. Dave calculated that in order to make that rent, Coogan's would have to raise their prices beyond the budgets of their regular customers. Vincent and Dave left the meeting frustrated and despondent. It seemed inevitable that by June, Coogan's would be out of business.

As the negotiations with Royal Charter foundered, the owners decided to share their worries with their friend Jim Dwyer, who wrote the "About New York" column at the *Times*. In mid-November 2017, when the bar's closure had come to seem like a strong possibility, Dwyer composed a hasty tribute in the Notes app on his phone:

> They were running races for everyone.
> They were open when the riots were going on.
> People were chanting "Whose street?" And it was their street.
> And then people visiting relatives, keeping vigil in the hospital. And if you knew ahead of time, you'd tell them, when you want to take a break, there's this place down the block.

For Dwyer, who had lived in Washington Heights for three decades, the news was troubling. He saw Coogan's as a keystone of the neighborhood; its ongoing existence made it possible for him to imagine that all of his "best hopes for New York were not delusions." When he learned that the owners were going to tell their staff about the closure, he wrote an article about these developments for the *Times*. It appeared online the evening of Tuesday, January 9, and in print the following morning. Not wanting their staff and regulars to be blindsided by Dwyer's article, Peter, Tess, and Dave immediately began notifying the people closest to them.

The reactions ran a narrow spectrum from outrage to anger. Former CB 12 district manager Brenda Rosado recalled thinking, "It was like a death. The thought of Coogan's not being there was terrifying." Dave Crenshaw was defiant. "You can't close Coogan's! There's some things that are untouchable. Coogan's is untouchable." Representative Adriano Espaillat said much the same thing: "No, that can't happen. We've got to figure this out." From Florida, Sybil Dodson-Lucas sent an irate message to the hospital: "Are you nuts?" Ivy Fairchild, who'd left Columbia's community affairs office and was now working as a political consultant, called up her old contacts at the hospital and asked them, "How stupid could you be?"

Yvonne Stennett received a phone call from Peter, asking if she wanted Sam Garcia's Christmas murals to hang in CLOTH's school. In the midst of a busy day at work, the content of what Peter was saying didn't fully register. "Coogan's called and said they were going to close. They said, 'Do you want the piece of artwork? To put in the school?'" Stennett remembered. "And I said, 'Sure, I'll take the artwork.' It wasn't until I got off the phone, that I said, 'Did he just tell me that Coogan's is closing?' I tried to call him back and it went to voicemail. I started calling people. 'Is Coogan's really closing?'"

For Stennett, the news didn't really sink in until she got home that evening. "I was decompressing. And I got to this dark place. Like, *No, that can't happen! That's not allowable. That makes no sense.* It was a feeling of being in a dark spot for a moment. Having been here forty years, I know what it means when important people are snatched out of the neighborhood. I know what that feels like, and I know what it means. And I've seen the consequences when we lose something like that, and they're not good. It's like taking away a piece of the whole. That absence. You cannot fill that absence with something that you just throw in there. Because it's part of how you grew. You grew into that wholeness. So you can't just snatch it out and think that it can be replaced.

"That was a dark feeling."

~✺~

CHAPTER THIRTY-EIGHT

Why Are You Crying?

Belgica Borges, the daytime bartender, had worked at Coogan's since 2002. Dominican by birth, she'd grown up in Aruba, raised in what she thought of as a soup of languages, learning Spanish at home and Dutch and Papiamento—Portuguese creole—in school. Since immigrating to New York, she'd picked up English too. Belgica (or Bel or Belgy as she was often called at work) started out as a server in the dining room, but when the daytime bartender left to go work at the short-lived Parrot Bay, she took over, and there she had been ever since, from 10:00 a.m. until 7:00 p.m., Friday through Tuesday. Her warm personality and unperturbable demeanor made her a favorite of her bosses as well as her patrons. Borges and her husband had no children; she thought of the bar as her home, the staff and regulars as her family.

Once she arrived at work, Borges had an hour to set up for the day: an hour to get cash for the register; to get the sliced lemons, limes, and oranges from the prep kitchen; to get the ice from the ice machine; to get clean glasses from the dishwasher; to put out the rubber mats and the bar towels; to check the rail drinks and request new bottles from the liquor safe, and test the beer taps to make sure that there were no empty kegs from the night before. She'd barely gotten started on her tasks that morning in January 2018 when Peter appeared and said, "I need you in the back room for five minutes, Bel."

It was an unusual request. After all, there was nobody else in the bar. Each morning, the owners normally came out and talked to her about the day ahead as she set up. Something big must be happening. She wiped her hands on one of the bar towels and followed Peter across the dining area and into the back room, where Tess and Dave were sitting at their usual table. José was there, too, and she could tell by his face that something was up. "We're going to have to close Coogan's," they told her. (Later, she wouldn't be able to remember which of them said the words.) "Don't worry, we've got another job for you."

She started crying. And then Tess was crying. They explained to her the issues with the lease and the rent increase. She couldn't believe it. Coogan's was her home, and now it was going to be taken away from her. Almost immediately after hearing the news, she started thinking not about herself but about Dave. Peter had his singing and Tess had her family. They would be all right, she felt. But Coogan's was Dave's life.

Back at the bar, trying to keep her composure, she watched as other employees—Martín, Emily, Omar—went into the back room and returned looking shocked. The bar opened as usual, and the customers began to arrive—to them it was just another day. She poured the pints, mixed the drinks, put in the food orders, but throughout the day, it was difficult for her to keep her emotions under control. In the middle of mixing a drink or pouring a beer, she would start crying again. During a break, she went and found Chef José, who was normally unflappable. "I don't want to work anywhere except Coogan's," he said, shaking his head.

Then she was back out at the bar. "What's the matter?" her regulars asked. "Why are you crying?"

Tess, Peter, and Dave had waited as long as possible to break the news of the bar's closure to their staff. It had been a rough winter for Peter as his health declined in tandem with the bar's chances for survival. He was waiting on the results of a biopsy, and he'd been told that his prostate would need to be removed. On this particular morning, he was also suffering from the flu. If not for the business at hand, he would have stayed in bed. Psychologically, he had already begun to move forward, to put this stinging loss behind him. He and Suzanne had sold their apartment on the Upper East Side. They were planning to move out in the spring, relocating permanently to a vacation home they owned in Water Mill on Long Island. Peter had vague ideas about managing a restaurant out there, or writing another play.

Dave was still drained from the run of the holidays and the failed lease negotiations, but he was otherwise engaged and focused on the tasks that lay ahead of them: all that needed to be done in the coming months to close down Coogan's. Though he was past retirement age, he had no intention of hanging up his saloonkeeper's apron. He'd already begun reaching out to his network of fellow bar and restaurant owners in the city inquiring about jobs for his soon-to-be unemployed staff and for himself.

Tess's feelings about the impending closure were decidedly mixed. For the preceding twenty-six years, Coogan's had been a focus of her life, providing her with a good income and the company of many people she had come to love. Her children had grown up there, celebrating birthdays and other rites of passage. It was impossible for her to imagine not going there every day, not seeing Dave and Peter, not hearing the latest from the bartenders and busboys and waitresses and patrons whose lives had become bound with her own. And yet, she was excited at the prospect of having the weight of this place lifted off her, excited by the thought of having the whole summer at home with her daughters. Her eldest, Hannah, would be back from college in Virginia. The yearning for domesticity was especially strong because Tess had been working extra hours this past year. Fearing that the lease might not be renewed, the owners had held off hiring a replacement for Dania. Tess picked up a lot of that work and did so willingly, knowing that there would be the reward of time off after the bar shut down. That thought, that promise, had helped her get through this tumultuous time. She knew she was going to have to find another job, but there would be time to worry about that, after the summer was over and the dust had settled. Since Dave and Vincent's failed last-ditch attempt to cut a deal with the hospital, a mixture of anticipation and melancholy had filled her waking hours. Now she no longer needed to keep those feelings bottled up.

Jim Dwyer's article, "Coogan's, an Uptown Stalwart, Makes Its Last Stand," was published online in the early evening of January 9. Soon after, the *Manhattan Times* ran a story by Gregg McQueen, "Closing Time at Coogan's." Peter Walsh was quoted in it: "They say they want to maximize rents. They're a hospital, but they're pulling the plug on us." Luis Miranda, the cofounder of the newspaper, tweeted out McQueen's story, saying:

> @CoogansNYC is a special place where I did @LinManuel
> birthdays, political & community events. Closing, NO WAY.

A few minutes later, Lin-Manuel Miranda retweeted his father's message to his 2.1 million followers with the accompanying note:

> One of the true Washington Heights mainstays, and has embraced
> every wave of neighborhood changes. I love Coogan's. My stomach
> hurts from this news.

At the time McQueen's story was published, an Inwood resident named Graham Ciraulo was attending a community board meeting, and it was there that he heard the news that Coogan's was closing. Board meetings often adjourned to Coogan's and, when that evening's official business was completed, some of the attendees said that they were going to head over to the bar for "a last drink." Ciraulo, who generally preferred to drink *before* community board meetings, was too angry to join them. Rather than commiserating with the others, he decided he was going to do something. "I love Irish pubs," he later recalled. "But I don't have any patience for the Irish wake mentality." He went home and created a Change.org petition called "Save Coogan's Irish Pub and Restaurant" with the following blurb:

> New York Presbyterian is forcing Coogan's to close by raising
> its rent by an astounding $40,000 more per month than it
> currently pays. Coogan's is a beloved community institution
> and we the residents of Northern Manhattan demand NYP
> offer Coogan's a renewal lease at a rent that will allow them
> to remain open.

Ciraulo tagged Royal Charter Properties and New York–Presbyterian's CEO, Steven J. Corwin, and then posted a link to the petition on Facebook, sharing it with friends and spending fifty dollars to promote it among users in nearby zip codes.

Ciraulo believed Coogan's could be saved. That belief came not from blind optimism but from professional experience. He worked in fundraising at NYU-Langone Medical Center, interacting with the hospital's public relations and real estate departments. He was convinced that if enough of a stink could be made about Coogan's closing, New York–Presbyterian's executives would cave and force its real estate division to change course. The petition was just the first step in what he saw as an escalating campaign to save the bar.

Ciraulo was also on the board of the Metropolitan Council on Housing, a sixty-year-old tenants' rights organization, and had cofounded Northern Manhattan Is Not For Sale, which he and his partners established specifically to fight Mayor Bill de Blasio's administration's plans to rezone and redevelop parts of Inwood. In Ciraulo's mind, there were two competing ideas of what makes a good neighborhood. "The community side sees a neighborhood as providing support networks and stability, with long-term residents and families. Then you have this other idea of neighborhood as *lifestyle*. There are economic and demographic forces behind it. You have young people flooding into the city. They are transient, and what they're looking for is *amenities*. And what you're seeing is an amenity boom within communities. The neighborhood has become a lifestyle vehicle. Are there good restaurants? What can I eat, and where can I spend my money? That's ultimately what people opposed to the rezoning are fighting against."

For Ciraulo, though, Coogan's was both *community* and *amenity*. When he woke up on the next morning, Ciraulo checked on the petition. He was astounded to see that thousands of people had signed it overnight. His Facebook post had been shared widely. It was all happening much faster than he'd expected.

That Wednesday morning, Tess left her house in the Hudson Valley town of Dobbs Ferry, dropped her daughters at school, and headed south to Washington Heights. It had been a frantic night. When the *Times* article went up, she and Peter and Dave were deluged with texts, emails, and phone calls. The Coogan's community experienced overnight the beginnings of the bereavement process that Tess and her partners had worked through during the previous months. In many of the calls and text exchanges, she and Peter and Dave found themselves in the strange position of consoling the people who'd reached out to console them. Among the callers was Steve Simon, who told them that it wasn't over and that they should fight the hospital. Hollywood had also responded. The actor Jared Harris, who'd once worked as a busboy at Pudding's, called to offer his help, as did Kevin Wade, now the showrunner for the cop drama *Blue Bloods*, which had filmed scenes at Coogan's. But by then, Tess, Peter, and Dave were resigned.

Also that morning there was still a restaurant to run. Tess was focused on a big catering order for the Columbia School of Public Health. She parked her car, and as she approached the front door of Coogan's she was startled to be greeted by a man holding a microphone. "Hi," he said. "I'm Glenn Schuck, from 1010 WINS. We just need a mo—"

"No!" said Tess. She hated microphones, hated public speaking. She invited Schuck in and offered him coffee while she called Peter, who was scheduled to work later that day, flu or no flu. "You need to get your ass up here, now!" she whispered into the phone. Then she told Schuck he would have to wait for one of the other owners to arrive.

"You're going to have a lot of interest in this story," Schuck replied. "It's out on the wire services."

⟡

CHAPTER THIRTY-NINE

#Yeeeeeeeeaaaaaaaah-BOOOOOOOOOOOOOOIIIIII

S chuck was right. In an ironic reprise of the days when the restaurant was full of television news crews reporting on drug-related crimes in the neighborhood, PIX 11, NY1, and the local affiliates of NBC, CBS, and ABC all dispatched correspondents to the bar to file stories about its impending closure.

Customers arrived in droves too. Every day that week, Coogan's was jammed with press and punters. The phone calls, text messages, emails, and social media posts did not stop. Peter equated it to a drumbeat that kept getting louder and faster as the week went on, an escalating, uncontrollable rhythm of sympathy, rage, and protest.

The story radiated out in pulsing waves over the various networks the bar had built over the decades. Neighborhood news sources such as *Uptown Collective*, *Harlem World*, the *Amsterdam News*, and the *Washington Heights Patch* reported on the closure, as did the free commuter paper, *amNewYork*. *The Irish Echo*, which bills itself as the nation's most widely read Irish American newspaper, ran an op-ed arguing that the hospital needed to give "care and consideration" to the restaurant. The

Dominican American news site *Listin USA* also covered the story, featuring a photo of Hillary Clinton at the bar. Anti-gentrification activist Jeremiah Moss published a post on his *Vanishing New York* blog, arguing that the closure of Coogan's was "another brick in the wall of the sterilized, de-urbanized, hyper-gentrified zone that New York is becoming." *Runner's World* and *Running* published stories lamenting the loss of one of the world's great track and field bars. They were picked up on running blogs as far away as Scotland, France, and Japan. Jim Dwyer's article was republished in newspapers across the country.

Local government quickly got involved. City councilmember Ydanis Rodriguez called for Community Board 12 to convene a brainstorming session to figure out how to save Coogan's. A public demonstration led by Espaillat, Gale Brewer, assemblywoman Carmen De La Rosa, and state senator Marisol Alcantara was scheduled for Sunday, January 14. The topic even came up during Mayor de Blasio's weekly appearance on Brian Lehrer's radio program on WNYC, a mainstay of the city's airwaves. When Lehrer asked the mayor about the closing of this "iconic New York establishment," de Blasio replied, "I think it's a huge mistake. I did not know the landlord was a hospital, and that makes me even more upset. I think they should reconsider immediately, that . . . Coogan's is an extraordinarily important institution in that community and a link to the past, and some things are more important than money."

By this point, Ciraulo's petition had garnered more than fifteen thousand signatures.

New York–Presbyterian had gone into damage-control mode. Earlier in the week, the hospital had refused to

answer reporters' requests for comments. But now it released a statement, signaling some flexibility: "Coogan's is
a very special gathering place for those who live and work
in our Washington Heights community. We are willing to
continue those negotiations in an effort to reach a fair and
reasonable resolution."

That was news to the bar's owners. "I'm hearing this
for the first time right now," Peter Walsh told Fox 5. "Nobody has called me."

The next morning, Luis Miranda and Congressman
Adriano Espaillat met with New York–Presbyterian CEO
Stephen J. Corwin. The public relations fallout from the
impending closure of a neighborhood bar had reached
such a pitch that the head of one of the city's largest
hospitals, with $6.32 billion in revenue in 2018, took a
hastily scheduled meeting with a U.S. congressman and
a Latino city power broker to discuss a $40,000 rent in-
crease at a minor property in his organization's vast real
estate portfolio.

The results of that meeting were immediate. Joe Ienuso,
the hospital's senior vice president for facilities and real
estate, was dispatched to the bar to negotiate a lease extension. Peter was still sick, so Dave and Tess received him. It
was clear to them that Ienuso had been instructed not to
return to the hospital without a deal in hand. They rejected
Ienuso's initial offer of a 20 percent increase on the current
rent. After some back and forth, they agreed on a more
modest annual increase. The extension was for three years.
Ienuso went back to the hospital to have the contract
drawn up. By the time he returned, late in the afternoon,
many of the people who had helped bring this about—
Brewer, Espaillat, Dwyer, state senator Robert Jackson,
and the Mirandas—had gathered at Coogan's. Ienuso had

Dave Hunt, Adriano Espaillat, Gale Brewer, Luis Miranda,
Tess O'Connor McDade, Lin-Manuel Miranda, and Peter Walsh
on the night Coogan's was saved.

to walk past them to get to the Gallery Room where Peter, Tess, and Dave signed the new contract. For the deal to be completed, Vincent Walsh, who was in Southampton, New York, also had to sign. Ienuso indicated that he was willing to drive out to the Hamptons that night if necessary, but in the end, a signature by fax proved sufficient.

At 6:36 p.m., Espaillat tweeted out the news that a handshake deal had been struck between the bar and the hospital. Lin-Manuel Miranda retweeted it with a yawping hashtag:

#YeeeeeeeeeaaaaaaaahBOOOOOOOOOOOOOOOIIIIII

Revelry broke out in the restaurant as the news spread. There were hugs, toasts, backslaps, and fists raised triumphantly. They whooped and cheered and sang. In the middle of the impromptu celebration, a waitress approached Dave. "The ladies at table 228 are having a birthday party, and they're wondering if Lin-Manuel would sing happy birthday to them." Dave's initial, unspoken, response was, *Are you out of your mind?* There was no way he was going to ask Lin-Manuel Miranda to sing for a stranger. But, upon further reflection, he did feel comfortable raising it with Luis, who in turn asked his son. Lin-Manuel agreed.

He and Peter Walsh approached the table of delighted women and sang "Happy Birthday." Dave followed with a candle-illuminated cake. Miranda finished the song with a flourish of his wrist, shouting, "Coogan's!"

◦──◦

CHAPTER FORTY

Saved by a Neighborhood

Peter, Tess, and Dave had gone through that wild week in a kind of fugue state, carried along by forces that were out of their control. Once the new lease was signed, they began to reckon with what had just happened. Not only had Coogan's been saved from going out of business, but forty jobs had also been saved and incomes preserved for all of those individuals and families. It had also generated vast international attention to their business. A PR analysis commissioned by Peter calculated that the publicity value of the *New York Times* coverage alone was in excess of $170,000. What would they do with all of that goodwill?

The owners created a banner, printed on yellow vinyl, with a stylized four-leaf clover and hung it on the bar's exterior, to thank the community.

When they spoke about the events of the previous week, they began to frame them within the larger context of national politics. The lease extension had been signed almost exactly a year after the inauguration of Donald Trump, who was widely reviled in Washington Heights for his xenophobic and anti-immigrant policies. "The neighborhood

came to us," Walsh said to a reporter. "Here we are, a group of Irish immigrants being saved by the newer immigrants that the president of the United States is trying to keep out of the country. We were *saved* by these people. The children of immigrants being defended by today's immigrants: Dominican, Haitian, Caribbean, African. It's thrilling." Peter saw the near-death experience of the bar as a call to further action. "We have to be more concerned about what's going on with our neighbors and with New York and our country. We've got to be even more involved now."

Yet, there were also practical considerations arising from this sudden twist of fate. Peter, who'd already shifted into retirement mode, was suddenly faced with the prospect of commuting to Washington Heights from Water Mill: two and a half hours each way on a good day. He also needed to schedule surgery on his prostate. Dave, who had been the most determined to keep Coogan's open, understood that Peter and Tess were, on some level, accommodating his wish to continue. And even he had finally given up after the December 6 meeting with Kenrick Ou. His focus had shifted from running Coogan's to looking for work and placing his staff in good positions. With the impending closure in mind, he had suspended regular maintenance on some of the mechanicals at the bar and, in the coming months, there would be leaks and failures to contend with. Tess faced the most emotional challenge of the three. Gone was the promise of a summer at home with her girls; returned was the weight of all that responsibility. The news that had brought joy to so many was a source of deeply contradictory feelings for her. There was no way she would put her personal needs ahead of the widespread demand for Coogan's to remain open, but there was also no denying that she was mourning the loss of all that long-awaited time with her family. It would take months to absorb that loss and fully reengage with her work. As a means of coping, Tess added a countdown app to her phone. She labeled it "Freedom" and set it for May 31, 2021, the last day of the new lease.

The gentrifying forces that had threatened Coogan's could not be kept at bay for everyone. A week after Royal Charter buckled to popular demand and negotiated an affordable lease renewal for Coogan's, another neighborhood institution announced that it was facing eviction: La Galicia, a restaurant just three blocks north on Broadway. The owner, Ramón Calo, had immigrated to New York from Spain in 1985 and become part owner of Galicia in 1990. His friends downtown thought he was crazy and told him he was going to be murdered. "I'm only going to sell food," he answered. "I'm not going to do harm to anybody." Galicia featured dishes from Latin America and the Iberian Peninsula. The food was flavorful, affordable, and generously portioned, making it a popular spot among the locals. The restaurant boasted a similar heterogeneous clientele to Coogan's: MTA employees, medical students, and police officers ate shoulder to shoulder in the cramped dining room.

Galicia's long-term lease expired in October of 2017. Since then, Calo had been renting the space on a month-to-month basis. Calo, who had been trying to renegotiate an affordable lease renewal for the past two years, was told that the monthly arrangement could continue until June 30, 2018, at which point the rent would rise from $5,000 to $25,000 a month. Calo told the landlord that $7,000 was the most he could afford.

Many of the same people who rallied for Coogan's voiced support for Galicia, including Manhattan borough president Gale Brewer, state senator Marisol Alcantara, and city councilmembers Ydanis Rodriguez and Carmen De La Rosa. A petition gathered sixteen hundred signatures. At a rally outside the restaurant in late January, Peter Walsh addressed an animated crowd, saying, "Shut stores bring drug dealers. Shut stores endanger our children. . . . We made this neighborhood attractive for families. And now they want to take it away from us."

The rally, the petition, and the pleas from local elected officials did not save Galicia, which closed in June. Galicia's landlord was simply not embarrassable like the hospital. Calo was disconsolate. "The location itself is part of the family. It's where my sons grew up," he told the *Village Voice*, adding, "It's just tough knowing that one person can just say, 'This is the end for you. You have to start over.'"

◞๛◟

CHAPTER FORTY-ONE

An Attack on the Urban Ecosystem

Though Coogan's had been saved, the closure of Galicia and other local businesses was a reminder of what was at stake. The fear of gentrification remained widespread in the community. One evening, not long after the new lease for Coogan's was signed, Dave left work and walked over to 165th and Amsterdam for a discussion about those anxieties at Word Up Community Bookshop/Librería Comunitaria. Word Up was born in 2011 as a pop-up store, opened on Broadway and 176th Street in a storefront that had once been a pharmacy. It was the brainchild of Veronica Liu, a Canadian who came to New York to study at Barnard; she later moved farther uptown to pursue an MFA in fiction at City College. Cheerful, diminutive, and deep-voiced, Liu had a radical heart and an entrepreneurial drive. She once ran a pirate radio station (Washington Heights Free Radio) out of her apartment. Later she turned her hand to independent publishing, helping to create the Fractious Press. "I was always trying to connect with the neighborhood," she recalled.

Liu had noticed that there wasn't a single general-interest bookstore between Columbia University and

Riverdale in the Bronx, a stretch of more than a hundred blocks. The pop-up store emerged from collaborations with the Northern Manhattan Arts Alliance and Vantage Properties, a landlord making amends for violations in its residential and commercial holdings in the area. The initial agreement was for a one-month rent-free run, but when the space remained unleased at the end of the month, Word Up stayed there rent free for an additional four months, and then for another year at a below-market-rate rent, building itself quickly into a neighborhood hub staffed by a corps of volunteers. More than a hundred people gave their time to the store, and some thirty thousand books were sold, often at heavily discounted prices. A good portion of the stock originated from the defunct Occupy Wall Street library; other books were donated or sold on consignment. Word Up would become a venue for open-mic nights, art shows, storytimes, musical performances, poetry readings, and activist meetings. It was run as a collective, with members voting on important decisions. In the fall of 2012, Vantage informed Liu that they had found a market-rate tenant for the storefront. Word Up was given thirty days to leave.

Liu thought that might be the end of it—a better run than she had hoped for. She and some volunteers boxed up the stock and stored it across the street in the basement of the United Palace Theater (a bunch of boxes also ended up in her living room). Liu had a day job as an editor at Seven Stories Press but tried to figure out what to do next regarding her year-long venture into bookselling. As would later happen with Coogan's, the community stepped in and wouldn't let Word Up go away. An Indiegogo campaign raised more than $60,000 of seed money; an additional $10,000 came from other donations. A permanent location was found in a building owned by CLOTH. The store reopened in the summer of 2013 and continues to be a vital, essential presence in the neighborhood.

The event that Dave went to at Word Up was a discussion led by Jeremiah Moss, the author of *Vanishing New York*, and Claudia de la Cruz, a pastor and community organizer. It was part of a series of readings on gentrification that Word Up had programmed that season. The scruffy, beloved little store, with children's art on the walls and every nook and cranny stuffed with books, was at standing-room-only capacity, an indication of the community's concern, which had become focused in recent months on the Inwood rezoning plan. Introducing the event, Liu noted that many of the empty storefronts she'd scouted as possible locations for Word Up in 2011 were still unoccupied. She observed that "the tension between the crowded and the empty" remained a big problem in New York. Moss, bald, red-bearded, and wearing owlish spectacles, read from his book and spoke about the "sociopathic character" of the current wave of hypergentrification, its omnivorousness, and the way it targets people of color, queers, and artists. The discussion broadened to consider what could be done to preserve the communities of Northern Manhattan. De la Cruz said that social media had only a limited impact and that face-to-face communications were essential to community organizing: knocking on doors, engaging in discussions, listening to opinions that were different from yours. There was a need for spaces where people could meet and speak to each other freely—places like Word Up; places like Coogan's.

During the Q&A session, Dave rose to thank Moss and others in the room who'd helped save the saloon. "We knew we were appreciated in the neighborhood, but not on that level," he said. He had brought coupons to the reading as a gesture of gratitude. Anyone who purchased a copy of Moss's book got $5 off their next meal at Coogan's.

De la Cruz's comments on the importance of in-person communications echoed the 1996 Columbia School of Public Health report on violence in Washington Heights, which had called on the often-fractious uptown enclaves to find "the ways and means to talk . . . to each other." The principal author of that report, Dr. Mindy Thompson Fullilove, appeared at Word Up a few weeks later in conversation with Coach Dave Crenshaw. Fullilove had recently republished *Root Shock*, her 2004 book about the trauma suffered by communities displaced by urban renewal and gentrification. At the store, she gave a distilled presentation of her work and ideas. "The most important thing I want to say to you is that gentrification is not a neighborhood problem. . . . It is an ecological catastrophe." She compared it to an invasive species and to a virus. "It is an attack on the urban ecosystem of the United States." The solution to this ecological problem, she argued, was not a local one, but a systemic one. "Being a good neighbor does not stop at your neighborhood border," said Fullilove, "because ecological problems do not stop at political borders." Citywide networks were required, along with a nationwide effort.

Fullilove and Crenshaw offered a small-scale example: City Life Is Moving Bodies (CLIMB), a grassroots organization focused on the outdoor spaces in Upper Manhattan. CLIMB hosts an annual event called Hike the Heights, which invites people from all over New York City and its suburbs to walk to Highbridge Park for a day of festivities. One-third of Northern Manhattan is parkland, Fullilove observed. Hike the Heights aimed to get people involved in the maintenance and preservation of those parks.

Fullilove and Crenshaw then described how CLIMB was part of the coalition of community groups that successfully campaigned to have the High Bridge—the oldest standing bridge in the city—reopened to the public. The bridge was constructed in 1848 as part of the Croton Aqueduct system, which brought water to the metropolis from upstate New York. It also served as a pedestrian walkway over the Harlem River, connecting Washington Heights and the Bronx. The High Bridge and its adjacent parks were popular spots for walking, boating, and other leisure activities in the nineteenth and early twentieth centuries. Hotels, restaurants, and amusement parks sprang up nearby; pleasure cruises would bring tourists from other parts of the city. The construction of the Major Deegan Expressway and the Harlem River Drive (both part of Robert Moses's master plan for the city) made it much more difficult to access the waterfront and the bridge and ruined the unspoiled riverine landscape. The High Bridge fell into disrepair and was closed to the public in 1970, severing a pedestrian link between the two boroughs. It remained closed for forty-five years.

When the city reopened the rehabilitated bridge in 2015, Crenshaw and Fullilove were working to renovate the playground on Edgecombe Avenue. After years of advocacy at community board meetings and applying pressure on the Parks Department, the playground was slated for a $15 million makeover. In preparation for the renovation, Crenshaw and Fullilove had been getting local residents involved in the park's upkeep, organizing litter collection, weeding, and other beautification activities so that when the makeover happened, the community would already be invested in maintaining the space. Those activities also nurtured connections between neighbors who might not otherwise have gotten to know each other. Healthy parks, like bookstores and bars, could be community hubs, places where networks were created and nourished.

Crenshaw brought up Coogan's during the Word Up event. The bar had hosted fundraisers for CLIMB and Hike the Heights. "Coogan's got saved, but they didn't get saved just because of *our* community. They were saved because of all the other people that come from all over the city and the world [to drink there]. We need places like that in our community." After the event, Crenshaw headed to the bar for a drink. He continued his earlier thought. "Deals get started in offices, but deals get closed at Coogan's. We're going to need this place if we're going to win this fight."

CHAPTER FORTY-TWO

Life Is a Vacation from Death

The twenty-first Salsa, Blues, and Shamrocks 5K took place on March 1, 2020. It was a frigid day, twenty-six degrees at race time, which kept the number of spectators down but didn't deter the runners. Nearly five thousand men and women crossed the finish line that morning. The race had continued to bring newcomers to the neighborhood: that day more than a thousand of those who'd run came from outside New York City. Since taking over management of the race, New York Road Runners had discontinued the tradition of lining the course with musical acts, though a DJ did provide an up-tempo soundtrack at the start and finish lines. At the post-race reception back at Coogan's, Peter Walsh stood before a table of ruddy-faced runners as they tucked into their corned beef and Guinness. Peter, who'd recently stopped drinking alcohol, raised a glass of club soda and cranberry juice and offered a toast: "Life is a vacation from death, so let's stay on vacation!" There were cheers around the Gallery Room and pints hoisted in response.

Two years after the bar had been saved, the party continued at Coogan's, but it would not last forever. Later that day, Governor Andrew Cuomo announced the first positive test for COVID-19 in New York State.

By the end of the week, there were more than one hundred cases of COVID-19 in New York. The owners of Coogan's, like many people around the world, got a crash course in virology and epidemiology. Just as the events surrounding the rent increase had reeled out of their control, so did their attempts to manage their bar and restaurant through the early days of COVID.

On the afternoon of Friday, March 13, Dave, Tess, and Peter held an emergency strategy meeting to formulate a plan for this rapidly changing situation. With astonishing speed, the virus had gone from being a public health issue in China to being an existential threat not only to their business but to the entire hospitality industry. It was happy hour, St. Patrick's season, and only three of the twenty-four tables in the dining room were occupied. At the rectangular bar, half a dozen drinkers exchanged *can-you-believe-this-shit?* looks. On the TV screens, where March Madness and spring training baseball should have been, the president was declaring a national emergency. "It feels like a storm's coming," Peter said, surveying the scene. "It's going to blow over us, and we'll see what's standing afterward."

Out of that Friday meeting, the partners planned to reduce their salaries, trim employee hours, and cut every nonessential expense, in the hopes of staying afloat. That plan lasted the weekend. On Monday, March 16, Governor Cuomo ordered all bars and restaurants in New York to close to the public at 8:00 p.m. and shift to providing only takeout and delivery service.

CHAPTER FORTY-THREE

The Suspension of Everyday Life

When Steve Simon heard the news about the governor's order, he knew he needed to get to Coogan's one more time. The pandemic had made for a busy day at the Parks Department, and Simon got out later than he'd hoped. Yet there it was, the beacon on the corner, the familiar white façade, green awning, and pewter letters. The lights were still on. He went in through the front entrance. It was the eve of St. Patrick's Day. Normally the place was jammed every night in March. You opened the door to a wall of sound, a delectation of the senses: the smell of grilled beef and fresh beer; the comforting sight of so many familiar faces; the feel of smoothed wood and brass fixtures; the engine-like roar of conversation, laughter, and music. All of those taken-for-granted comforts and sensations now seemed evanescent. Coogan's was nearly deserted. A handful of people were up at the elevated bar, observing the social distancing practices that were quickly becoming routine. Irish music played on the PA, but the mood was restive, not festive. Everyday life had been abruptly suspended. A catastrophe was unfolding in slow motion; for now it was offstage, away from the bar, but you could sense it bearing down.

Dave, dressed as ever in a green Coogan's polo shirt, greeted Simon and showed him to a table in the large dining room. The same room where Stan Michels had thrown that party for him more than thirty years earlier. There were plenty of tables to choose from; only one was occupied, by Tess and her family, who were eating dinner. She had summoned Vinny and their daughters to the restaurant that afternoon, saying it might be their last chance to have a meal at Coogan's. A pair of waitresses stood near the front windows chatting. A busboy lurked in the back service bar, waiting for something to do.

Simon hung his baseball cap and trench coat in their accustomed places, set down his briefcase on a chair, and ordered chicken piccata with penne and vegetables—a favorite item from the menu—along with a Corona Light. Then, as was his custom, he went to the men's room to wash his hands. On a normal night he would have exited the restroom and gone straight to the bar to greet other regulars. Often, he got so caught up in conversation that one of the owners would have to summon him back to the dining room before his food got cold. This evening, however, he returned directly to his table where Dave soon joined him.

They exchanged remarks about the strangeness of the moment. "What are you guys going to do?" Simon asked. Dave shook his head and gave a helpless shrug. "We'll have to cut hours," he said. "We'll try to get by on delivery and takeout until this passes. But as you know, that's not our business model."

Coogan's preferred business model was bringing people together over food and drink, connecting networks and communities. Takeout was anathema. Simon looked around the dining room, which was decorated with Bud Light and Guinness banners. Cardboard shamrocks had been hung in every window and among the pictures on the wall. It all seemed unreal, like a deserted movie set. He figured that he'd eaten at least three thousand meals in this room over the past thirty-five years. He'd dined with congressmen and borough presidents, medics and professors, community activists, neighbors, friends, and political rivals. And plenty of times, he'd dined alone. Was this his final meal at Coogan's? Would there ever be another St. Patrick's Day celebration here? It was too terrible to contemplate.

The food arrived and Simon ate slowly, savoring each bite. Tess and her family departed, saying their farewells. By the time eight o'clock rolled around, he was the last customer. He paid his tab, left a generous tip, put on his coat, and picked up his briefcase. Dave had already dismissed the rest of the staff. He turned out the lights and he and Simon walked out together. "Normally, I'd offer to drive you home," said Dave. "But we don't want to be too close to each other." They touched elbows and then they parted.

As he made his way home, Simon thought back to his first visit, in the fall of 1985. He remembered all that the bar and the neighborhood and the city had undergone since then: the savage violence of the crack years; the AIDS epidemic; the riots; the September 11 attacks; the 2008 financial crisis; gentrification; and the resistance to the wave of bigotry that had followed Trump becoming president. During each of those crises, Simon and others in Washington Heights had been able to turn to Coogan's for safety, community, and solace. But now the city was facing a crisis unlike anything that had come in the past century, a crisis that had turned bars and restaurants from places of refuge and comfort into vectors for the spread of disease and death. The very essence of urban life seemed to be under threat.

How would they survive without Coogan's? And how would Coogan's survive without them?

❦

CHAPTER FORTY-FOUR

A Strange Farewell

Coogan's and its owners were ill prepared for this sudden new pandemic reality. Although the restaurant had long provided catering and takeout service, delivery of individual meals had never been a part of its business. The restaurant had only a rudimentary website, which lacked an online ordering system. Nor did they have arrangements with Seamless or Grubhub or any of the other meal-delivery apps. The owners had decided early on that these services took too big of a cut to be worthwhile. There was also no squad of bicycle couriers standing ready to dispatch meals to every corner of the neighborhood. In fact, food made up a little less than 10 percent of the average daily take at Coogan's. "Food is 10 percent of our profit and 90 percent of our problems," Dave often noted. They made their money on booze, and the booziest, busiest day of the year at Coogan's was St. Patrick's. (The Millrose Games was a close second.) The prospects for this St. Patrick's Day had been especially good. "Middle of the week and rainy," Peter observed. "Rain chases people into restaurants and bars. This would have been the *biggest* day for us." Normally, a full staff would have been on hand to serve the boisterous clientele. But, on Tuesday, March 17, there were five employees working at Coogan's, plus the owners. A few workers from the medical center showed up, wearing masks, to collect lunch orders. Meanwhile, Tess was on the phone, helping staff file for unemployment. Down in the office, Dave was cajoling vendors into allowing him to return unopened cases of liquor and other nonperishable goods. "I don't need to have ten thousand paper napkins on hand right now," he said. Stocking up for a busy month that never materialized left them overextended and vulnerable.

The shutdown came at a particularly unlucky moment for Coogan's. On March 16, the owners made their monthly sales-tax payment. (Failure to do so would have incurred stiff penalties.) And, at midnight on the seventeenth, the restaurant's insurance policy came up for renewal, with a substantial premium due, and it would face significant fines if it failed to pay. The owners had requested a three-month extension of the previous policy from their insurer but were turned down. "Two monster payments going out the door," Peter said. "That's cash we could have used." All of this left their coffers depleted. "We know we can go to this week. We probably can go to next week, but after that . . ."

None of them questioned the drastic actions that civic leaders were taking. "Everything is secondary to fighting this disease," Peter said. But their shared sense of loss was palpable. "The big, raucous community of Coogan's is now just four walls and forty-two hundred square feet of empty space," Dave observed mournfully. Later, as the place would normally have been filling up with revelers decked out in green, Tess texted out a photograph of the dining room to friends. All the chairs were turned upside down on the tables. Not a soul was in the picture. "Saddest St. Patrick's Day ever," she wrote.

On Friday, March 20—exactly a week after the emergency strategy meeting, which now felt like a decade ago—Coogan's ceased operations. The restaurant had done about two hundred dollars' worth of takeout and delivery business on Wednesday. On Thursday, it took in eleven hundred dollars, with sales boosted by a charitable customer who'd bought twenty boxed lunches for the emergency room staff at New York–Presbyterian. Friends of Tess's had also ordered cases of wine, which she delivered on her way home. Despite the bump, the economic reality was irrefutable. Preparations for a prolonged shutdown began the next morning. Ice machines were emptied and drained. Beer lines were disconnected and cleaned. Anheuser-Busch, Coors, and other distributors came to pick up untapped kegs. Those credits to the bar's accounts helped it meet payroll for that final week. "We *are* going to run out of money," Dave said. "But, hopefully, we will run out of money when we run out of bills." At this point, all three owners still hoped that Coogan's would reopen after a lockdown period of a few weeks or maybe, at worst, a couple of months.

Staff were instructed to come in on Friday morning to pick up their checks. Arrival times were staggered to enable everyone to keep a safe distance. First came the kitchen workers and porters. Then the waiters, runners, and busboys; and finally the bartenders. All the perishable food and drink in the house was laid out on tables in the dining room: carrots, eggs, milk, apples, onions, potatoes, greens, and jugs of pre-made sangria—a momentary cornucopia. Peter sat at a table nearby with the paychecks and unemployment letters. The employees were invited to help themselves to as much food as they could carry. Whatever was left over would be donated to a local charity.

In order to keep herself from weeping, Tess found busy-work, restocking items on the table. It was hard to watch them come in: Chef José; Martin, the quiet, hardworking prep cook; Rob McDonough, the nighttime bartender who'd grown up across the street from Dave's house in River Edge. One by one, they filled bags with food and departed. Notable for his absence was Quincy Lopez, the "most fired (and rehired) waiter in Coogan's history," according to the owners. Quincy was easily distracted, but also a favorite among some of the bar's regulars. He once called out sick on a day he wasn't scheduled to work. He'd mess up, lose his job, stay away a week or a month or three and then come back and they'd take him on again, because he was family now. Another server, Amanda Kisic, came in and announced that she somehow had ended up with Quincy's phone, which meant that there was no way to reach Quincy. No one knew where he was or when he would show up. It was typical Quincy. In the moment of levity, Tess poured out a glass of sangria for Amanda and one for herself. They drank and talked, laughing quietly.

It was a strange farewell. They had all worked long hours in close quarters together, and now they couldn't hug one another or even shake hands to say good-bye. Several staff members, including two who were pregnant, were too worried to leave their homes and asked that checks be mailed. Those who did come choked back tears or went through the motions in a kind of stupefied trance. Peter told them all, "We love you. Keep in touch. Let us know how you're doing. We'll help if we can." Dave advised them not to look for work in the hospitality business. He was already figuring that it would be at least a

Tess, Dave, and Peter, in the dining room, March 2020.
Photograph by Cristóbal Vivar

year before the city's nightlife returned to normal. The last to arrive was Belgica. She said she would apply for unemployment the next day. In the meantime, she was sending money to family in Aruba and the Dominican Republic, where the virus's spread was just beginning. "I hope we'll be back by April," she said, standing in the door and waving good-bye.

"You'll be the first one we call when we reopen," Peter replied.

As Belgica left, the news broke that the governor was ordering all nonessential businesses to close and that all gatherings of any size would be banned. That included Peter, Tess, and Dave standing around in the empty dining room at Coogan's. They fretted about what would become of the neighborhood during the weeks ahead. "A lot of businesses aren't going to make it," Dave said.

"The streets are beginning to feel very threatening now that there are fewer pedestrians," said Tess. They were adamant that they wouldn't board up their windows.

"We didn't board up for the riots; we're not boarding up for this," said Dave.

Ever the optimist and ever the party planner, Peter said, "We're New Yorkers. We're getting through this. And, when we reopen, we'll have our own St. Patrick's Day parade around the block, with bagpipes, salsa, and merengue."

∽

CHAPTER FORTY-FIVE

A Bar Full of Life

There would be no parade. But, as March wheezed into April and the COVID cases in New York continued to rise exponentially, it still seemed possible—*just* possible—to Dave and Peter and Tess that they might be able to reopen if the city were somehow able to flatten the curve soon. Royal Charter gave Coogan's a three-month moratorium on the rent. There was no longer a staff to pay, but there were still recurring expenses that accrued whether the restaurant was open or not: equipment rentals, vehicle payments, taxes, insurance, and utilities. It added up to more than $20,000 per month. "We're bleeding blood we don't have," Peter remarked after a phone call with the bar's accountant. With their longstanding connections to nonprofits and elected officials, it was conceivable that some financial aid might be forthcoming to tide them over. The most likely source was the Northern Manhattan Emergency Recovery Fund administered by the Hispanic Foundation and New York–Presbyterian Hospital. Much of the aid offered by the federal and state governments—including the Paycheck Protection Program—came in the form of loans, only some of which could be turned into grants if certain requirements, such as rehiring employees, were met. But it seemed foolish to rehire staff when the return to normal life kept getting pushed back. With their unemployment benefits enhanced by COVID relief funds, at least some former Coogan's employees were likely to prefer staying safe at home. The end of the restaurant's lease extension was now just over a year away. The owners were unwilling to assume much debt because they would have only a narrow window in which to repay it.

Coogan's applied for $250,000 from the Northern Manhattan Emergency Recovery Fund, supplying reams of paperwork, copies of invoices, payroll documentation, and a reopening plan. Tess, who compiled the application, thought the grant might see them through six months of barebones bills, just enough to tide them over until things settled down. On April 8, they were awarded $25,000. It was the maximum grant amount, but still only a tenth of what they'd hoped to receive. The grant came with the stipulation that it had to be spent on payroll. "I knew, we all knew, it was game over," Tess said. "Our weekly payroll averaged $35K. A 250-seat restaurant in Manhattan is a big boat to float: $25,000 wouldn't buy us any time." They gave the money back and started thinking seriously about the process of closing for good. Until that moment, Tess had thought they would be able to get back up and running. "None of it seemed real to me. It was incomprehensible." But when Mayor de Blasio announced on April 11 that New York City schools would remain closed for the rest of the academic year, Tess said she knew without a doubt, "We were done."

Ten days later, they made it official, posting a letter in the restaurant's windows and on their social media feeds. It read, in part:

> Coogan's was a public house, a meeting place, a table to
> break bread and solve problems. We were a place of cel-
> ebration and remembrance. We were a bar full of life . . .
> a place to listen and a place to talk . . .
>
> We were people of different races, creeds, and ideas,
> all with the same dream to be secure and love. . . .
>
> Now it is your turn to complete our story.

The lease agreement with the hospital required the owners to turn the space over "broom clean," and Dave, who
led the breakdown operation, intended to do just that.
He and Chef José and the porters took down every item
from the bar's walls. They contacted the people in the pictures—or their living relatives—and began to disperse the
items among their patrons, a piecemeal redistribution of
their history. An auctioneer sold off their appliances and
catering equipment for pennies on the dollar. A wholesale
restaurant supplier bought up the plates, glassware, and
other items left after the auction. The Christmas murals
were delivered to the CLOTH school. Peter drove in and
emptied his desk. Tess hauled away the financial history of
the bar and stored it in her garage.

They worked, masked and gloved, interrupted by a
knock at the door and a familiar face—or at least a set
of familiar eyes. Dave would invite them in and let them
stand in that space one more time, feeling the emptiness
and the quiet, looking up at the ceiling, and the ghostly
rectangles of paint on the walls where the photographs
had been, staring at the empty bar, peeking into the Gallery Room where the debris was piled, waiting to be taken
away. Coogan's had hosted so many wakes for others, and
now it was holding one for itself. "Our customers were
at the service of the staff as much as the staff served the

The bar at Coogan's, May 2020.

customers," Peter reflected. But each day that went by they were more and more convinced that they'd done the right thing.

"Most bars hang on too long, and sell too late," said Peter.

Just before Memorial Day, Dave met with Kenrick Ou at Coogan's to hand over the keys. He walked out the door, no longer having to worry about whether it was locked behind him. He was seventy years old. He'd been working since the age of fourteen. And now his work was done.

Afterword

My own Coogan's story is a modest one compared to those that have gone before. Grecia Solano, the Dominican immigrant whose journey to Washington Heights is described in chapter 4, is my mother-in-law, and it was from Grecia's apartment on Haven Avenue that I made my first foray to Coogan's. On a hazy, hydrant-draining day in the summer of 1998, I was sitting in Grecia's living room staring out at the view of the George Washington Bridge. Beside me was Grecia's son, Jansel Botex, who would, a few years later, become my brother-in-law. Both of us were dressed in suits for a wedding later that afternoon. There was a baseball game muted on the TV—some hapless visiting team getting mauled at Yankee Stadium. From the adjoining window, a buzzing box fan vented the stultifying outside air into the apartment like an exhaust. There was only one air conditioner in Grecia's apartment, and it was in the bedroom. Also in the bedroom that afternoon were two domed hair dryers. Sitting under the dryers, two women: Jansel's fiancée, Eva, and his sister Zoraida, my girlfriend at the time, later my wife. With gossip magazines in their laps and cold beverages in their hands, they had turned the bedroom into an impromptu salon. Jansel's twin sister Wilma was in the kitchen, cooking with Grecia. On the radio, bachata. On the stove, pieces of chicken frying in oil. Thick and starchy sancocho bubbled in a steel pot. Food for the week.

The wedding was still hours away. Hours of hair and makeup. Hours of primas and tias coming and going. Hours of family bochinche. The apartment would only get hotter as the hair dryers blew and the stovetop burned and the bodies assembled.

"Fuck this," said Jansel. "Let's go to Coogan's."

We grabbed our suit jackets. Jansel went into the bedroom where the whirring of the dryers sounded like a pair of outboard motors. He said something to Eva as she brought her head out from under the white plastic dome. Eva nodded. Zoraida lowered her magazine and waved at me. I blew her a kiss, and then we were out the front door and into the echoing tiled foyer.

"What did you say to them?" I asked.

"I told them Mami needed some yucca and verdura. They think we're going to the market."

We exited the building, gleeful with truancy, and walked south along Haven Avenue, past the towering medical school dorms. It was quiet, almost eerie. The academic year wouldn't start for a couple of weeks. A gypsy cab went by with salsa playing from its open windows. Two lean men on bikes pedaled north toward the bridge. Turning left on 170th Street, we crossed Fort Washington Avenue and headed for Broadway. Even though we were walking in the shade, it felt no cooler out here than it had in the apartment.

Northern Manhattan, with its undulating pavements and clifftop parks, its vibrant street life and criminal reputation, was a foreign land to me in 1998. I'd been in New York since 1991, itinerant in Chelsea, Brooklyn, and Queens, hungry for the city's history. But since meeting Zoraida, I'd been spending most weekends uptown, at her apartment on Seaman Avenue in Inwood, which was far airier and more spacious than my lightless basement studio in Astoria. I was falling hard for her and almost as hard for her neighborhood.

On Broadway, there was hustle and noise—bodegas and fruit sellers and pedestrians fanning themselves as they walked. Traffic honked and roared along the street. Up ahead on the corner, I saw the awning: *Coogan's* in white cursive, the letters surrounded by a lasso. Jansel led me in through the front door, and we were immediately embraced by the air-conditioning. Nobody looked twice at us, a sweaty white guy and a Dominican man, both dressed in suits. Straight ahead was the wide-open dining room. Jansel elbowed me and nodded at one of the tables farthest from us.

"You see over there? Denny Farrell."

"Who's Denny Farrell?" I asked.

"The assemblyman. Represents us in Albany. Went to G-dubs like me," he said, referring to George Washington High School.

Handsome, mustachioed, distinguished-looking, Farrell was in animated conversation with the people at his table.

"Seems like he's always here. You could go over and complain about something if you want to."

"Maybe another time," I said.

I followed Jansel up the three steps to the bar, a round-cornered rectangle of mahogany, clusters of glasses hanging upside down from the ceiling fixtures. The same

Yankees game was on a couple of TVs mounted high on the walls. There was music playing. I felt immediately at home, as if I'd been coming there for years.

"I remember when this place first opened," said Jansel. "I looked in the window and saw the tablecloths and thought, *No way*. This was the eighties when there was nothing like this up here. But then I came in one night, and I could see that it was cool. I started telling all my friends, 'Man, you got to go to Coogan's.' Now it's our joint. Everybody in the family drinks here. And you know what? They got rid of the tablecloths. For a while it was butcher paper. Now it's nothing, just the wood."

He took a sip of his beer and looked around. "Eva comes in for her job! Can you believe that shit?" Jansel's fiancée worked in the community relations department at Columbia-Presbyterian. Her boss, Ivy Fairchild, liked to have meetings in Coogan's whenever possible.

I loved bars, especially Irish pubs. I'd spent my teenage years in Northern Ireland during the Troubles. From the age of fifteen, one of my main weekend activities was drinking in Belfast's saloons and gin palaces—the Shakespeare, Lavery's, the King's Head, Robinson's, and the Crown. When I moved to New York, I learned the metropolis partly through its drinking establishments: McSorley's, the Old Town Bar, Puffy's, the Ear, McHale's. In Astoria, I'd taken a shine to the Bohemian Beer Hall. Up near Zoraida's apartment there was the Piper's Kilt.

And now here was Coogan's.

Very little happened at the bar that afternoon. Jansel and I talked, getting to know each other, building familial bonds; by the time we finished our drinks and headed back to the sweatbox on Haven Avenue, I'd been Cooganized.

A few weeks later, when my brother Josh and his Peruvian girlfriend, Jessica, came to visit, Zoraida and I took them to Coogan's for dinner. It was a Saturday night, and the place was thronged and electric. We were worn out from touring the city, but the energy in the bar, along with a round of drinks, revived us. We ordered food. I couldn't help but notice the easygoing warmth of the place. People dressed up for a night on the town next to people in hospital scrubs. The two guys with the thick shoulders and close-cropped hair over there had to be off-duty cops. Near them a cluster of middle-aged Dominican and Puerto Rican women laughing uproariously, holding their hands up, trying to fend off the hilarity. The group next to us—regulars from the way they talked to the bartender—suddenly included us in their banter, the conversation slipping freely between English and Spanish.

"We don't get many Peruanas up here," one of them remarked to Jessica. "Welcome, hermana."

Then the karaoke started.

It was the main event, the reason the place was so full. Unbeknownst to us, people had been adding their names to a signup sheet at the front of the bar, and now, Terry Odell, the doyenne of the karaoke night, began summoning the singers. Madonna's "La Isla Bonita," "Baby Got Back" by Sir Mix-a-Lot, "Come to My Window" by Melissa Etheridge, Gloria Estefan's "Turn the Beat Around," and Michael Jackson's "Beat It." There were whoops and cheers, rounds of applause. My brother put his name down, and before long he was called. His song was "Wonderwall," by Oasis. Josh is a good singer, and he nailed the song that night. By the end, half the bar was singing along with him:

> *I said maybe*
> *You're going to be the one that saves me.*
> *And after all*
> *You're my wonderwall*

A few years later, Zoraida and I moved to New Jersey, but Coogan's was a necessary stop whenever we brought our sons into the city to see their abuela. Later, during a family health crisis, when Zoraida and I were changing jobs and residences, I lived for a time with Grecia on Haven Avenue. I was in Coogan's most nights. The warm welcome and happy mood at the bar helped get me through that difficult period.

In January of 2018, when I heard the news of the impending closure, I felt I should write something. I went back to Broadway and 169th Street for what I expected would be a fifteen-minute interview with the owners. I spent more than two hours with them, running out to St. Nicholas Avenue twice to feed the meter. Woozy with stories, I went away and wrote my article, but that was just the beginning of a four-year conversation with Peter, Dave, and Tess. A conversation that led to this book.

Acknowledgments

Dave, Peter, and Tess welcomed me into their lives, answering questions, making introductions, and solving problems without once telling me how their story should be written. As I hope the book shows, they have a true gift for collaboration. Sean Cannon likewise invited me into his home and talked to me with bracing honesty about his life in the bar business. This book would not exist without their active participation and I am grateful to all four of them.

Thank you to Michael Agger at *The New Yorker*, who edited the articles from which this book grew; thanks also to David Remnick, Pamela McCarthy, and David Haglund for their unstinting support. My literary agent, Eric Simonoff, who stood by me through a very lean decade, embraced the idea for this book, helped me craft a proposal, and then found it a home. Many thanks to Taylor Rondestvedt, Jessica Spitz, and Criss Moon at WME.

Tim Bartlett was exactly the tough-minded yet kindhearted editor this book needed. Thank you, Tim, for your belief in this story, your vision, and your patience. At St. Martin's, I'm also grateful to Sally Richardson, Kevin Reilly, Gabrielle Gantz, Michelle Cashman, Susannah

Noel, Adriana Coada, Ervin Serrano, Devereux Chatillon, Ryan Masteller, and Meryl Levavi for their enthusiasm and hard work on this book. And thank you to Jeffrey L. Ward for the beautiful maps. My early readers, Atar Hadari, Robert Snyder, and Led Black, provided invaluable feedback, helping to shape the book. Sameen Gauhar fact-checked the manuscript and made crucial editorial suggestions. (Any errors are mine alone.)

The late, great Jim Dwyer was generous and encouraging during the early stages of my reporting; I wish he had been around for the finish. I also owe an enormous debt to Glenn Østen Anderson, my fellow traveler on Coogan's Way. The extended Coogan's family and so many others in Upper Manhattan embraced this project and enriched it enormously, making it feel like a community effort. Thank you to everyone who spoke to me for this book. (A list can be found in the Notes on Sources.)

Throughout the writing of this book I have leaned heavily on the three pillars of my life in Maplewood-South Orange: my SOMA family (Liz and Nick Testa-Licata, Joyce Paton, Jackie and Brad Newman, Patricia and Jim Canning, Trenesa and Chris Danuser, and Marty and Eddie Remy); the Maplewood WTF (Jay Pingree, Arthur Moorhead, Woodie Keenan, Lara Tomlin, Ian Pagan, Barry Echtman, George Chin, Mark McLaughlin, Mitsuko Ueda, Eyrique Miller, Patrick Ravix, Patrick Ruppe, Deryck Rugbeer, Stephanie Ortiz-Cidlik, Robert Langreth, Mohamed Abdel-Moniem, Tom Puryear, and Ivano di Gennaro); and the SOMA Gucci Mane Society (Pamela Erens, Anne Fernald, Karen Shelby, Laura Sims, Corey Mead, Karen Gevirtz, Joanne Fisher, Nicole Rudick, Helen Wan, and Matt Thomas). I must also give a big shout-out to my colleagues at the Millburn Free Public Library.

For various and sundry favors and good deeds, special thanks are owed to Dwyer Murphy, Joe Bonomo, Sarah Lester, Mike Fitelson, Adrian McKinty, Aneiry Batista, Veronica Liu, Cristóbal Vivar, Sam Garcia, Joe Riley, Tim Muldoon, Debralee Santos, Mary Norris, Susan Orlean, Rosie Schaap, Kia Corthron, Ed Park, Nelson DeMille, J.T. Molloy, Martin Collins, Liz Miller-Boose, Insha Fitzpatrick, Mike Banick, and Sarah Pardi.

I would never have gone to Coogan's were it not for the family I was lucky enough to marry into. Love and gratitude to Grecia Solano, Jansel Botex, Wilma Botex, Eva Matos, Alex Matos, and Sara Gustaffson. Thank you to my family: Josh, Jason, Cassandra, Jessica, and Michael Michaud for years of support and encouragement.

My wife, Zoraida, and our sons, Marcus and Thomas, give purpose to my days and meaning to my life. This book is for them, with love.

Notes on Sources

Last Call at Coogan's is based on four years of research and reporting. Most of the details in the book come from interviews conducted with the owners of Coogan's, their employees, and their customers, as well as current and former residents of Northern Manhattan. Unless otherwise noted, quotes from individuals in this book are from personal interviews. In some cases, the quotes have been edited for clarity and concision.

In addition to numerous in-person, email, telephone, and text exchanges with Dave Hunt, Tess O'Connor McDade, and Peter Walsh, I conducted interviews with the following individuals:

Led Black, aka Leo Fuentes (February 2019, in person)
Belgica Borges-Zapata (August 2018, in person)
John Bourges (February 2022, phone)
Mary Jo Buczek (April 2019, in person)
Ann Burack-Weiss (September 2020, Zoom)
Sean Cannon (December 2019, in person, plus numerous subsequent phone calls and emails)
Ti-Hua Chang (November 2021, phone)
Graham Ciraulo (May 2019, in person)
Kim Clark (March 2021, phone)
Patricia Conlan (April 2020, phone)
Dave Crenshaw (May 2018 and August 2021, in person)
Gus Cruz (April 2022, in person)
Kevin "Taz" Davis (July 2022, phone)

Margaret Day (July 2021, phone)

Dickson Despommier (June 2020, phone)

Franklin Diaz (April 2019, phone)

Sybil Dodson-Lucas (September 2021, phone)

John "Chick" Donohue (March 2021, phone)

Bryan Dotson (November 2018, in person)

Jim Dwyer (October 2018, in person)

Patrick Dwyer (March 2022, phone)

Adriano Espaillat (April 2019, phone, and August 2021, Zoom)

Nicholas Estavillo (November 2019, in person)

Ivy Fairchild (June 2018, phone)

Darren Ferguson (April 2019, in person)

Rita Finkel (March 2018, in person)

James Fisher (October 2021, phone)

Mike Fitelson (March 2018, in person)

Robert Fullilove (September 2021, Zoom)

Maria Guzman-Colon (May 2018, in person)

Jared Harris (May 2020, phone)

Carina Herrera (March 2022, phone)

Frank Hoare (January 2021, phone)

Brian Hunt (October 2019, in person)

Kate Hunt (August 2021, phone)

Cletus Hyacinth (July 2019, in person)

Evamarii Johnson (August 2018, in person)

Bridget Kiniry (March 2019, in person)

Corey Kilgannon (February 2021, phone)

Al Kurland (April 2022, phone)

Mary LeBlond (June 2021, phone)

Guillermo Linares (July 2021, phone)

Veronica Liu (April 2018, in person)

Maria Lizardo (May 2018, in person)

Tom Lockhart (August 2021, phone)

Quincy Lopez (December 2019, in person)

Eva Matos (October 2021, in person)

Gregg McQueen (April 2021, phone)

Franklin Micare (March 2021, phone)

Luis Miranda (September 2018, in person, with Glenn Østen Anderson)

Pranoy Mohapatra (July 2020, Zoom)

Johnny Moynihan (April 2019, in person)
Shiva Mozaffarian (July 2020, Zoom)
Tim Muldoon (December 2019, in person)
Walt Murphy (December 2019, phone)
Stephen Nicholas (March 2018, in person)
Terry Odell (July 2021, phone)
Cathy Oerter (April 2021, email)
Norm Ogilvie (March 2018, phone)
Michael O'Keefe (July 2019, phone)
Carolina Pichardo (January and April 2018, phone)
Sarina Prabasi (May 2019, in person)
Nanette Ramkisoon (March 2022, phone)
Daniel Reardon (June 2018, in person)
Joe Riley (March 2022, phone)
John Roe (May 2020, phone)
Juan Rosa (August 2019, in person)
Brenda Rosado-Tracy (September 2019, in person)
Maxine Rosaler (March 2019, in person)
Vytas Rudys (November 2018, in person)
Rodrigo Sanchez (May 2018, in person)
Hector Santiago (May 2020, phone)
Jonathan Schindel (March 2018, in person)
Arlene Schulman (January 2019, in person)
Larry Siegel (March 2019, phone and in person)
Steve Simon (May 2020, phone)
Ed Small (August 2020, phone)
Robert Snyder (October 2018 and January 2019, in person)
Yvonne Stennett (March 2019, in person)
Christopher Stoll (June 2022, phone)
Brendan Straw (March 2022, phone)
Cathy Subervi-Taylor (July 2019, in person)
Al Taylor (August 2021, phone)
Milton Tingling (November 2021, phone)
Sully Torres (August 2021, phone)
Robert Tracy (September 2019, in person)
Lou Vazquez (October 2020, Zoom)
Billy Wall (September 2020, phone)
Suzanne Walsh (May 2021, phone)

Vincent Walsh (September 2018, phone)
Sheila McFadden Waters (January 2020, phone)
Suzana Williams (August 2021, phone)
José Ynoa (September 2018, in person)
Dania Zapata Green (March 2019, in person)

As I was reporting this book, the filmmaker Glenn Østen Anderson was shooting his documentary *Coogan's Way*. Glenn and I shared leads, transcripts, and other materials. Several lines of dialogue in this book are taken from *Coogan's Way*. I hope readers of this book will be inspired to seek out Glenn's film.

For the history of Washington Heights and New York City, I relied on the following books:

Tyler Anbinder, *City of Dreams: The 400-Year Epic History of Immigrant New York* (New York: Houghton Mifflin Harcourt, 2016)

Ronald H. Baylor and Timothy J. Meagher, eds., *The New York Irish* (Baltimore, MD: The Johns Hopkins University Press, 1996)

Thomas Dyja, *New York, New York, New York: Four Decades of Success, Excess, and Transformation* (New York: Simon & Schuster, 2021)

Jesse Hoffnung-Garskof, *A Tale of Two Cities: Santo Domingo and New York After 1950* (Princeton, NJ: Princeton University Press, 2008)

Robert Jackall, *Wild Cowboys: Urban Marauders & the Forces of Order* (Cambridge, MA: Harvard University Press, 1997)

Kenneth T. Jackson, ed., *The Encyclopedia of New York City* (New Haven, CT: Yale University Press, 1995)

Robert W. Snyder, *Crossing Broadway: Washington Heights and the Promise of New York City* (Ithaca, NY: Cornell University Press, 2015)

Silvio Torres-Saillant and Ramona Hernández, *The Dominican Americans* (Westport, CT: Greenwood Press, 1998)

On the crack epidemic, I am indebted to David Farber, *Crack: Rock Cocaine, Street Capitalism, and the Decade of Greed*

(Cambridge, UK: Cambridge University Press, 2019); and Philippe Bourgois, *In Search of Respect: Selling Crack in El Barrio* (Cambridge, UK: Cambridge University Press, 1995).

On Gerry Adams and the Northern Irish peace process, I relied on Francis M. Carroll, *The American Presence in Ulster: A Diplomatic History, 1796–1996* (Washington, DC: The Catholic University of America Press, 2005); Patrick Radden Keefe, *Say Nothing: A True Story of Murder and Memory in Northern Ireland* (New York: Doubleday, 2019); and Ulster University's CAIN Archive (https://cain.ulster.ac.uk/).

Much of the demographic and economic data about Upper Manhattan came from research papers produced by the CUNY Dominican Studies Institute.

On the subjects of community and gentrification, I am indebted to:

Jeff Deutsch, *In Praise of Good Bookstores* (Princeton, NJ: Princeton University Press, 2022)

The work of Mindy Thompson Fullilove, especially *Main Street: How a City's Heart Connects Us All* (New Village Press, 2020), and *Root Shock: How Tearing Up City Neighborhoods Hurts America, and What We Can Do About It* (New Village Press, 2016)

Eric Klinenberg, *Palaces for the People: How Social Infrastructure Can Help Fight Inequality, Polarization, and the Decline of Civic Life* (New York: Crown, 2018)

Jeremiah Moss, *Vanishing New York: How a Great City Lost its Soul* (New York: HarperCollins Publishers, 2017)

Ray Oldenburg, *The Great Good Place: Cafés, Coffee Shops, Bookstores, Bars, Hair Salons, and Other Hangouts at the Heart of a Community*, 2nd ed. (Cambridge, MA: Da Capo Press, 1997)

Sarah Schulman, *The Gentrification of the Mind: Witness to a Lost Imagination* (Berkeley, CA: University of California Press, 2012)

Jim Dwyer's many columns and reports about New York City were essential to my research and writing.

The description of the 1992 police protest at City Hall is based in large part on Laura Nahmias's article "White Riot," published in *New York* magazine (October 4, 2021).

My account of Ramon Calo and the closure of Galicia relies on reporting by DJ Cashmere published in *The Village Voice*.

The account of Steve Simon's last meal at Coogan's draws on reporting by Arlene Schulman published at *Medium*.

The notion of Coogan's as a "moral pub" like Davy Byrne's was first suggested by Andy Merrifield in a conversation with Mindy Thompson Fullilove.

Other important resources include the archives of:

The New York Times
The New York Daily News
The New York Post
New York Newsday
The Manhattan Times
The Amsterdam News
New York magazine
The Uptown Collective
Washington Heights *Patch*
Newspapers.com
MyInwood.net
Back issues of the following local newspapers held in the collections of the New York Public Library and the New-York Historical Society: *Uptown Dispatch*, *Uptown Press*, *The Bridge Leader*, and *Heights-Inwood*

The interviews conducted by Arlene Schulman for the New York Public Library's Washington Heights and Inwood Oral History Project were a gold mine of anecdotes and information. (The book's epigraph comes from Schulman's interview with Denny Farrell.) I am also indebted to the *Police Off the Cuff* and *Love Thy Neighbor* podcasts.

The Wenlock Arms, a film by Ollie Verschoyle and Robert Makin, was an important early influence on my thinking about bars and community, as was Rosie Schaap's memoir, *Drinking with Men* (New York: Riverhead Books, 2013).

New York–Presbyterian Hospital did not respond to multiple interview requests for this book.

Notes

23 "not be the last time comfortable residents": Robert W. Snyder, *Crossing Broadway: Washington Heights and the Promise of New York City* (Ithaca, NY: Cornell University Press, 2015), 13.

26 "an absurd and lovely thing": Roger Angell, "Farewell My Giants," *Holiday*, May 1958, 159.

36 "But special doesn't come overnight": Earl Caldwell, ". . . And Those Who Are Gunned Down," *New York Daily News*, July 5, 1985, 34.

74 *"he'll get home to bang walls"*: Peter M. Walsh, ed., *12 Passports and a Stowaway* (New York: Branach Press, 1975), 24.

115 "aggressive, active, and good": James Dao, "Angered by Police Killing, a Neighborhood Erupts," *New York Times*, July 7, 1992, A1.

119 "The destruction and anger is understood": Eddie Borges, Henry E. Cauvin, et al., "Violence in the Streets," *New York Daily News*, July 7, 1992, 3.

121 "They shot him like a dog": James Dao, "Tension in Washington Heights; Amid Dinkins's Calls for Peace, Protesters Skirmish with Police," *New York Times*, July 8, 1992, A1.

121 "Rally with dignity, but no violence": Keith Moore and Don Singleton, "1,000 Cops in a Peace Mission," *New York Daily News*, July 8, 1992, 2.

125 "desperate and frightened": Snyder, *Crossing Broadway*, 183.

125 "The reason the morale": Laura Nahmias, "White Riot," *New York*, October 4, 2021.

126 "We have been saying for years": Nahmias, "White Riot."

155 "drunks and rowdies": George Orwell, "The Moon Under Water," *Evening Standard*, February 9, 1946.

155 "was a harbour for enjoying": Olivia Laing, "What Would Britain Be Without Drink?," *The Observer*, January 9, 2016.

162 "abandoned, orphaned, or removed": Stephen W. Nicholas and Elaine J. Abrams, "Boarder Babies with AIDS in Harlem: Lessons in Applied Public Health," *American Journal of Public Health*, February 2002, 163.

168 "I think it's entirely appropriate": Jessica Brockington, "A Big Welcome for Gerry Adams at Coogan's," *The Bridge Leader*, March 1996, 1.

183 "Social networks are more implied than real": Mindy Thompson Fullilove, Robert Fullilove, et al., "Towards a Comprehensive Understanding of Violence in Washington Heights," The Community Research Group of the New York State Psychiatric Institute and Columbia School of Public Health, July 1996.

191 "Five years after the rioting": Snyder, *Crossing Broadway*, 192.

206 "confidante and closest companion": Darren Ferguson, *How I Became an Angry Black Man*, unpublished manuscript shared with the author, 2011.

207 "I walked back and forth": Ferguson, *How I Became*.

208 "The bottom line is when": *Sing Sing Prison Documentary*, C-SPAN, June 1, 1997.

213 "In a section of New York City": Corey Kilgannon, "A Foot Race of Diversity and Harmony," *New York Times*, March 6, 2000, B4.

250 "care and consideration": Rob Walsh, "Coogan's Needs a Hospital's Care and Consideration," *Irish Echo*, January 11, 2018.

251 "another brick in the wall": Jeremiah Moss, "Save Coogan's," Jeremiah's Vanishing New York, January 11, 2018, http://vanishingnewyork.blogspot.com/2018/01/save-coogans.html.

251 "I think it's a huge mistake": Bill de Blasio, interviewed by Brian Lehrer, *The Brian Lehrer Show*, New York: WNYC, January 12, 2018.

262 "gentrification is not a neighborhood problem": author's notes from "Root Shock: Dr. Mindy T. Fullilove and Coach Dave Crenshaw in Conversation," New York, Word Up Community Bookshop/Librería Comunitaria, March 10, 2018.

264 "Coogan's got saved": author's notes from "Root Shock."

Index